There have been other books about Montgomery County, Maryland, but this book, Montgomery County: A Pictorial History, *is truly unique. It is an extremely well researched, beautifully illustrated and concisely written book that serves as a family album for every Montgomery County resident.*

The book is about people and places, their names and faces, that together, constitute the rich fabric of our beautiful community. In it, Montgomery County residents will find much to treasure; and newcomers and visitors will be able to share the heritage that has shaped who we are today.

Thoughtfully and skillfully captured in words and pictures, this pictorial history is dedicated to those County residents whose deeds and visions have made our community a great place to work and live.

It is with great pride that I introduce to you Montgomery County: A Pictorial History. *On behalf of all County residents, I thank the Donning Company, the author Margaret Coleman, and all the sponsors for producing this new and limited edition for Montgomery County, Maryland.*

Sincerely,

Sidney Kramer

Sidney Kramer
County Executive

The Donning Company/Publishers
Norfolk/Virginia Beach

Montgomery County
A PICTORIAL HISTORY

Text by Margaret Marshall Coleman
Photographic work by Anne Dennis Lewis

To the people of Montgomery County, Maryland,
who have made it and kept it
a nice place to live.

Margaret Marshall Coleman
Pleasant Springs Farm
Boyds, Maryland

Table of Contents

Preface

If time is counted by the number of words written about it, the decade just past is very long indeed. Unlike the 1880s, with its single newspaper, or the 1780s with none at all, the 1980s produced literally tons of newsprint concerning Montgomery County, not to mention courthouse records and government memorandums. With no intention of perusing it all, I chose the *Suburban Record* for careful reading, plus a smattering of other county and national newspapers. Three topics were repeatedly mentioned: the re-development of Silver Spring and Bethesda, the arrival of the high technology industry along the I-270 corridor, and the preservation of agriculture and open space in the upper county. The downside news was trash disposal. I focused on these matters, relating additional events with pictures and captions. There is much much more to tell—so many stories left untold of the fascinating people, families, and places within our county. The unknown heroes, the remarkable tale not found on film, the secrets, and the gossip remain for the next historian to describe.

Many of the photographs are informal, unposed, casual snapshots by and of real people, depicting life at home in Montgomery County during the 1980s. Some are treasured keepsakes. The eye of the professional photographer is represented, too, and here we see the true beauty of our county captured on film.

It would have been easy to write a very lengthy book about Montgomery in the 1980s. It was hard to write just one chapter.

Acknowledgments

Special thanks are due to Frederick Gutheim, author and professor, for his guidance along the way, and his helpful critique, and for reading of the manuscript. Thanks, too, to Edith Ray Saul for help and encouragement; to Dr. June Evans, associate director of the Potomac River Archaeology Survey, for assistance and for reading the paragraphs on Indians; and to R. E. McDaniel, staff archaeologist, Potomac River Archaeology Survey, for helpful material and discussions concerning the Indians and early local ecology.

In addition to Mr. Gutheim, readers were Lillian B. Brown, Nina H. Clarke, Mary Gordon Malloy, Eileen McGuckian, and Mark Wallston; their helpful suggestions and encouragement were greatly appreciated.

I thank Anne Bledsoe and Pat Burke of the Rockville Public Library for their patient assistance and the Montgomery County Historical Society personnel, including Marian Jacobs, Janet Manual, Jane Sween, and Genevieve Wimsatt, for help and for sharing their treasures.

Unless otherwise noted, all photography and copy work was accomplished by Anne Dennis Lewis, whose careful cropping of insignificant details and intricate enlarging transformed many faded, old snapshots into works of art.

Most of the research for this book comes from the old *Sentinel* newspapers filed at the Montgomery County Historical Society and also filed on microfilm at the Rockville Public Library.

The *Sentinel* is a primary source of material that gives the reader a sense of participation in the unfolding drama of history. The development of a county is made up of myriads of everyday happenings, local events that seem minor but which spread out to engulf and affect centuries and thousands of people.

The author has humbly tried to recreate moments in the years gone by in Montgomery County through the use of incidents and quotations found in the *Sentinel* newspapers 1885 to 1982.

The author also wishes to thank Neal Potter, the Montgomery County Council, and Margaret Cudney and Duc Hong Duong, the Office of Economic Development, for reading the chapter (Montgomery County in the 1980s) on the county's growth in the past decade.

Montgomery County
A PICTORIAL HISTORY

The place is, without question, the most healthful and pleasant place in all this country, and most convenient for habitation, the air temperate in summer and not violent in winter. It aboundeth with all manner of fish. The Indians in one night commonly will catch thirty sturgeons in a place where the river is not over twelve fathoms broad.... We have not rowed above three miles, but we might hear the falls to roar (Henry Fleet, a fur trader, 1624; quoted in *Founders of Maryland*, Edward D. Neill, Albany, 1876). Fleet explored the Potomac to Great Falls. The drawing is by G. Beck of Philadelphia and was published on January 1, 1802. Courtesy of Library of Congress

From 12,000 B.C. to A.D. 1300, Indians lived in the area known today as Montgomery County. The population grew dense in oval-shaped villages along the Potomac River, the area's thoroughfare at the time, and also its major mechanism for trading and communication (Dr. June Evans). One archaeologist, R. E. McDaniel, likens the Potomac of the past to Route 1 at Beltsville.

At one time, the islands in the Potomac were established trading centers. The word "potomac" is an Algonkin verbal noun meaning "trading place," and, indeed, the river drew trade from as far away as New York, North Carolina, and Ohio (F. Gutheim, *Potomac*).

Two of Montgomery's streams retain the names assigned to them by the Indians, the Patuxent River and Seneca Creek. An ancient route called Seneca Trail became part of the National Road, designated at various times the Georgetown-Frederick Road; Rockville Pike; Route 40; and, today, Route 355.

Fragments of the early cultures remain, representing Paleo, Archaic, and Woodland Indians. Artifacts have been dated by careful scientific analysis of remains such as pollen from the nasal cavities of the skulls of ancient creatures. In addition, some knowledge of the early tribes is gleaned from the broken pieces of pottery, weapons, and beads the settlers left behind them. In the ashes of ancient fires, archaeologists have discovered specimens of rhyolites and cherts, minerals which are not indigenous to this area, thus relating their owners' origins to other localities.

Today a cyclotron can date the relics to within five years. But the answers provided by technological data do not satisfy, but rather suggest a tantalizing mystery concerning the history of these people. Who were they? Where did they go?

Indians had disappeared almost competely by the time of European contact. New diseases and internal battles (both introduced by foreign fur traders) plus changing weather and loss of land are partial explanations. In some cases, however, Indians married the new immigrants, and their descendants remain in the county. For example, Mrs. Clara Talley of Boyds and Washington, D.C., remembers an ancestor who changed his name to Hebron from Black Lock. Scientific methods have not determined answers to questions about the first Mongtomery County residents. Perhaps the full story can never be told.

After Europeans began to settle the new land, Cecil Calvert, the second Lord Baltimore, established a precedent of land subdivision in the Montgomery County area. Baltimore found it profitable, indeed, to divide his holdings, and, at the same time, to remain at home in England counting his money.

Leonard Calvert, Cecil's younger brother, came across the sea to manage the family estate, which had been inherited from their father, Sir George Calvert. Sir George, a secretary of state and member of the House of Commons, had been granted title to the land on June 20, 1632. The grant included all of Maryland and the southern part of Pennsylvania, stretching east to the Delaware Bay. Sir George wanted to name the place Crescentia, but King Charles named it Maryland, in honor of his wife, Queen Henrietta Maria.

Instead of selling their land to settlers, the Calverts rented it for an annual tax called a "quitrent." Anyone who brought a prospective colonist to the colony was granted fifty acres of land; the newcomer received one hundred acres for himself, an additional one hundred for his wife, and fifty for each of his children and servants. The tenant could deed or will the property with the same quitrent to another, payable to Lord Baltimore.

Courthouse deeds record the land transactions, which were identified by their picturesque names. Perhaps the titles reveal some otherwise unremembered bit of historical significance or folklore; perhaps they recall memories; or maybe they are just whimsical words that happened to tickle a fancy. Names for early tracts include Indian Fields, Peach Tree Hill, Grandmother's Good Will, Friend in Need, Panther's Range,

In 1585 John White sketched a sixteenth-century ceremonial feast (at "C" and "D") in his *Indian Town of Secotan*. Although Secotan was near Roanoke Island, North Carolina, recent archaeological studies have revealed that similar villages were once common along the banks of the Potomac.

White's drawing also shows tobacco fields ("E"); a cornfield protected by a sheltered watchman ("F"); a garden of pumpkins and squash ("I"); a thatched house ("A"); a campfire ("B"); and cropland ("H"). Courtesy of Library of Congress

TB   20

17

Wolf's Cow, Maiden's Bower, Sarah Love, Molls Rattle, Brooke Grove, Pleasant Fields, Bears Neck, Bear Bacon, Brightwell's Hunting Quarter, Lay Hill, Conclusion, Dung Hill, Joseph's Park, Hermitage, Charley Forest, Cow Pasture, Girl's Portion, Leeke Forest, St. Winexburg, Carroll's Forest, Dan, Clean Drinking, Bradford's Rest, Higham, Discovery, Snowden's Manor, Clagett's Purchase, Huntington, Contention, Charles and Thomas, Archibald's Lot, Younger Brother, Dispute, Two Brothers, The Exchange, and Joseph and James.

Incoming Europeans taught the remaining Indians how to trap beaver and exchange the skins for goods. Trading posts included one run by John Clark, established in the mid-1700s at the town named for him, Clarksburg.

Tobacco was the money of the early settlers. The crop bought featherbeds and slaves, and it paid the rent. Lawyers charged their clients one to two hundred pounds of tobacco for their professional services, but one can only wonder how the collection plate looked on Sunday mornings.

Lord Baltimore encouraged enterprise among his tenants, and he did not mind making a capital investment to assist them. When he found that London buyers would pay premium prices for barrels of leaves from Virginia certified uniform in quality, Calvert instituted his own Tobacco Inspection Act. He built a warehouse at the mouth of Rock Creek, the Rock Creek Inspection House, which was the first of many government buildings in Georgetown (which was in Montgomery County until 1791). A government inspector certified the leaf size, quality, and uniformity of each outgoing barrel. The buyers liked it, and planters got more money for their product. Governor Thomas Johnson wrote in the 1700s that Georgetown was the best market for tobacco in Maryland. His words resulted in a flush of newcomers and land speculators.

After the settlers had a little extra money, they wanted a church. In 1693 the Anglican Church became Maryland's established church, and the residents of today's Montgomery County were in Prince George's Parish. By 1726 they were supposed to attend church in today's D.C., but it was difficult to attend services so far away; so in 1734 members petitioned for local "chapels of ease." Two chapels were built in 1738, one on the site of the present Rockville Cemetery and a second near Hawling's River. By 1747 the Monocacy Chapel was built near today's Beallsville. The Reverend Townshend Dade, a boyhood friend of George Washington, was

Tobacco was the major cash crop in Maryland for two hundred years. William Tatham sketched the marketing process in his book, *The Culture and Commerce of Tobacco,* published in 1800.

The huge fragrant leaves are shown drying, being packed into barrels ("hogsheads"), and being graded in a tobacco inspection house, perhaps the one at Georgetown. Courtesy of Library of Congress

Dr. Lionel DeMontigny, an American Indian living in Montgomery County today, is director of the American Indian Bank and a former assistant surgeon general of the United States. He is shown with possessions that once belonged to Montgomery County Indians and are now housed at the Smithsonian Institution in Washington, D.C. The mounted display further illustrates the lives of the Indians who once lived nearby. Photograph by Anne Dennis Lewis

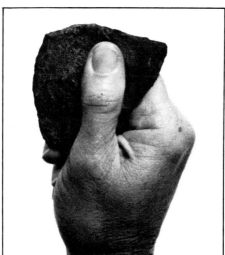

As the Ice Age glaciers disappeared, early mankind adopted the land now known as Montgomery County. About 3,000 B.C., a warming trend permitted the growth of desert plants such as the prickly pear cactus that grows today in isolated niches near the Potomac River.

The thickly populated Indian culture vanished by A.D. 1300, and the incoming European settlers found only the ruins of the long-establshed Indian culture. They saw no active native villages but sometimes observed transient parties crossing the piedmont to hunt or to raid. Today, however, several county residents testify to a genetic link with these first Americans.

Pictured are three relics found at Rupert Island, near Glen Echo: a spear point which is the only whole relic; a meat cutting tool, a sharp edge clutched in cutting position; and a broken scraper, which was perhaps used in tanning and softening the skins of large animals while held in the palm of the hand. Photograph by Anne Dennis Lewis

Beallsville's last pastor when Americans decided to discontinue support for a state church.

James and Deborah Brooke began the Sunday Spring Friends Meeting about 1745. Presbyterians were here early, too. They built a meetinghouse on Cabin John Creek in 1746 on land donated by Edward and Eleanor Offutt of Offutt's Crossroads (now Potomac). In 1772 Baptists organized the Seneca Baptist Church on land given by Ninian Beall of Ninian, and Methodists built a church about a year later in Laytonsville, near Goshen. At about the same time, Catholics began to hear regular mass from Jesuit John Carroll at Carrollton, his childhood home near Rock Creek (today's Forest Glen).

Education was private and not a thing of public record. But one school is listed for these precounty, prerevolution days. In 1732 an Anglican minister, the Reverend Mr. Booth, taught in a log cabin on upper Rock Creek.

Travelers of the time needed a place to stay overnight in the rough wilderness. They slept and dined at ordinaries, simple inns with plain fare and a fixed rate set by the government. One of these travelers was George Washington.

In April 1755 Major General Edward Braddock marched right past the trading post of John Clark and the ordinaries of Charles Hungerford and Michael Ashford-Dowden. Some sources say that he was accompanied by his young engineer-surveyor, George Washington. But, with or without George Washington, Braddock and his thousands of troops and supply wagons marched north on today's Route 355 and camped at Hungerford's Tavern (Rockville), Forest Oak (Gaithersburg), and Dowden's Ordinary (Clarksburg). All of Braddock's troops were prepared to fight for the king of England against the French and the Indians. That time the British lost, however, and Braddock was mortally wounded in a battle at Fort Duquesne (Pittsburgh). George Washington read the graveside service.

From the time of earliest settlement until 1700 local land grants were recorded as being located in Charles County; from 1700 to 1745, they were listed under Prince George's County. From 1745 to 1776, Montgomery County was included in Frederick County, whose boundaries encompassed all of western Maryland.

In 1776 Dr. Thomas Sprigg Wootton, delegated to the Maryland legislature from the lower district of Frederick County, proposed that the growing area in southern Frederick County be named Montgomery

The official flag of Montgomery County bears the coat of arms of Major General Richard Montgomery. The flag was endorsed by the Montgomery County Board of County Commissioners and the Maryland Assembly in 1937 and dedicated in 1944. Courtesy of the Montgomery County Historical Society

Montgomery County's settlers, innovative and somewhat desperate for shelter, used the materials they had at hand to construct their first homes. This building, shown here in its earliest known photo, was made of native fieldstone with a sod roof. Later the owner converted it to a stable for the livestock at Longwood, near Brookeville. It is no longer standing. Courtesy of Helen Thomas Nesbitt Farquhar

20

County in honor of General Richard Montgomery, the first general to die fighting for American independence. General Montgomery, who had died on December 31, 1775, became a hero throughout the emerging nation as soon as his death was known.

News traveled slowly in 1776. From Montreal, General Benedict Arnold dispatched an important message, but by the time the news was published in Maryland, Richard Montgomery had been dead almost two months. On February 22, 1776, Arnold's message finally reached *The Maryland Gazette*. Montgomery, Arnold said, "marched up in the face of their cannon and when he had nearly gained the pass received the fatal shot—or the town would have been ours." A surge of patriotism swept the country in response to this announcement. Colonists were now independent Americans. Earlier Maryland counties had been named to honor foreign majesties, such as Princess Anne, King Charles, and Prince George. Dr. Wootton, however, wanted to express his pride in the new nation and to honor the first fallen hero.

On September 6, 1776, Wootton introduced the following bill in Annapolis:

> Resolved, That after the first day of October next, such part of the said county of Frederick as is contained within the bounds and limits following, to wit: Beginning at the east side of the mouth of Rock Creek, on the Potomac river, and running thence with the said river to the mouth of Monocacy, then with a straight line to Parr's Spring, from thence with the lines of the county to the beginning, shall be, and is hereby erected into a new county called Montgomery County.

As so it was—and is, even though Richard Montgomery, a native of Ireland, a professional soldier who fought on the British side during the French and Indian War, and a resident of New York, never set foot in Maryland. However, neither did Princess Anne, King Charles, or Prince George.

By the time it was named Montgomery, the county already had a history that included established farms, towns, and homes, most of them with slaves. Some of the founders were the Reverend Townshend Dade; Ninian Beall; Richard Brightwell; Martin Charticr; Colonel William Joseph; John Addison; William Hutchison; Major John Bradford; Daniel Dulany; Richard Snowden; James Brooke; Nathaniel Wickham, Jr.; Samuel Pottinger; and Robert Peter. Descendants of

Major General Richard Montgomery, who died on December 31, 1775, was the first general to give his life for the new nation. The following September, Dr. Thomas Sprigg Wootton proposed to the Maryland legislature that a new county be named for the American hero. Courtesy of the Montgomery County Historical Society

these families remain, lending a continuity to our past.

With a 1782 population of 10,011 whites and 4,407 black slaves, and a growth by 1790 of more than three thousand each, the newly founded county approached the nineteenth century with a Farmers' Society and dreams of a river opened for passage through the county, connecting the Chesapeake Bay with the Ohio River.

George Washington was fascinated with the idea of a canal on the Potomac, and he set out to make it a reality. In 1785 Washington agreed to be president of the Patowmack Company, newly founded to open the river for navigation. Washington planned to clear rocks from the upper river; to improve the tributary streams of the Shenandoah, Monocacy, Antietam, and Conococheague; and to build a canal around Great Falls. No canal had been built on the continent before that time. So many curious onlookers came to watch and so many workers were needed that the Patowmack Company established a town at Great Falls. It thrived with a tavern, a gristmill, a sawmill, a forge, a market house, and numerous dwellings. As the years went by, people began to get tired of watching. After fifteen years the funds dwindled away, and financial backers lost their enthusiasm.

Mr. Washington, in the meantime, took another job. In 1789 he became president of the United States, and he looked around for a good site for its capital. Three years later he announced his choice, which included Georgetown in the new city of Washington. Montgomery lost her port but gained a unique position in the development of a nation.

The Patowmack Company, however, was destined to fail; the task was too hard and the money too scant. Still, six locks were completed by 1802. To the delight of the tourists, a riverboat traversed the flight of locks to rise seventy-five feet above the Potomac. Other boatmen waited in an ever-growing line, delighted at the proposed savings. By using the locks, shipping charges were less than half the cost of hauling freight by wagon. Business boomed, and the Patowmack Company paid its first dividend. (Alas, the dividend was also the last; the Patowmack Company declared bankruptcy in 1819.)

Along with new transportation, Montgomery's residents circa 1800 were seeking an alternative to tobacco as their major crop. The plant no longer flourished, and planters watched in distress as each year's mammoth leaves grew smaller than the year before. Their income dropped, and, in addition, their

This painting (circa 1776) of Elizabeth Wailes, the daughter of a Revolutionary War sea captain, bridges a generation gap by hanging in the home of her descendant, Elizabeth Hays Tolbert, the president of the Barnesville Town Council. Miss Wailes married Nathan Smith White; her dining room table is still used to serve the Tolbert family dinner.
Courtesy of Elizabeth Hays Tolbert

slaves, purchased to cultivate the tobacco, were out of work. The Patowmack Company came to the rescue. They hired the slaves to dig the ditch and cut and lay the stone that lines the canal, and they paid a sum of money to the planters for the services.

About this time two ingenious residents formed an organization that affected the future of agriculture, not only for the county, but for the entire nation as well. Thomas Moore and Isaac Briggs formed the Sandy Springs Farmers' Society. They experimented with various techniques, wrote laborious reports, and met to discuss their findings with other farmers who were searching for increased production. Their ideas fell on fertile soil; Thomas Jefferson, the nation's president, was himself an avid horticulturist. As a spinoff to the Farmers' Society, a national organization, the American Board of Agriculture, developed. James Madison was elected society president and Isaac Briggs the permanent secretary. ■

Leonard Hays (1759-1822), the son of Jeremiah Hays, founded the town of Barnesville along with William Barnes. Jeremiah Hays arrived in the area in 1774; 210 years later Barnesville is led by his great-great-granddaughter, Elizabeth Hays Tolbert, president of the Barnesville Town Council. Courtesy of Elizabeth Hays Tolbert

Pictured here is a typical home of the eighteenth-century Montgomery County settlers who worked hard to provide shelter and food for their families. The one-story log section (at left) was built circa 1768. Chestnut logs were cut from the surrounding forest, shingles split from native Virginia cedar, fieldstones gathered for the chimney, and wooden pegs cut and whittled. These local materials were collected and put together to create a house at little or no cost.

The frame part (at right) and the upper story are more elegant, and were built in 1804 with sawn pine siding. The porch and picket fence were added later, too. This photograph was taken in 1912 with the owners, Rhoda, Willey, and Edith Austin, in the foreground.

Water came from the spring, and electricity was never installed. The family grew its own potatoes, eggs, and apples for cider and vinegar; also, it raised its own turkeys and hogs. The cash crop was first

tobacco, and then wheat, which was carted to Darby's Mill in Bucklodge. Despite the intensive labor required to keep body and soul together, Rhoda Austin found time to grow flowers. The house is currently owned by the author and still has no plumbing or electricity. Courtesy of Malcolm Walters

The Austins stored milk, butter, and other perishables in this simple frame house, which was built over a spring, the family's sole source of water. Courtesy of Malcolm Walters

23

Francis Cassatt Clopper built this mill on Clopper Road in 1834. Using power created by water falling on a wooden wheel's slats, the millstones ground wheat into flour and corn into meal for local residents. Similar mills were located on streams throughout the county and were a very important facility for the area's residents.

In addition to this gristmill, there was a woolen mill on the property, which manufactured blankets for Civil War soldiers. Courtesy of Idella Leaman

The wide majority of voters in Montgomery County had united at the polls in 1800, afraid that Thomas Jefferson, if elected, would free their slaves. Opponents of Jefferson won with ease locally, 931-327. Despite Montgomery County's vote, Jefferson was elected president twice, but slavery did not end.

The Montgomery countryside grew no calmer as war with England approached. British soldiers invaded Washington, and, as the Capitol, the White House, and the Navy Yard burned, President Madison and his cabinet fled to Brookeville, there attending to the affairs of state and to the young country's gold.

The president and his cabinet found roads in Montgomery County quite primitive. About the same time as their flight to Brookeville, Benjamin Hallowell wrote that, to get to Sandy Spring from Baltimore, he had to take a stage to Laurel and rent a horse to ride through uncleared brush for thirty miles. Also, from Baltimore, Hallowell asked directions to Montgomery County.

"Why, there is *no* way; it is the most out of the way place in the world," he was told.

Eventually, roads began to progress. The Washington Turnpike Company formed in 1805 to improve the Georgetown-Frederick Road from the boundary of the District of Columbia to Clarksburg. By 1828 the new road, Rockville Pike, was open. Tollkeepers collected amounts ranging from twelve and one-half cents for twenty sheep to twenty-five cents for twenty cows or a stagecoach with more than one horse.

However, there was no money for maintenance. Within two decades, the Rockville Pike was deeply rutted and almost completely washed away. By the mid-nineteenth century, however, Montgomerians did have a comfortable mode of travel, the Chesapeake and Ohio Canal. The C & O Canal Company took over the project from the bankrupt Patowmack Company. And, with great ceremony, President John Quincy Adams turned the first shovelful of earth to begin new construction at Little Falls on July 4, 1828. (At the same time, a few miles away in Baltimore, Charles Carroll flipped the ceremonial spade to begin the Baltimore and Ohio Railroad.)

Irish indentured immigrants supplied canal labor, and the Irish were troublesome. For one thing, they tended to marry the boss's daughter. Or a green-eyed, black-haired Irish daughter married the boss himself. And the boss could not expect his father-in-law to sling a pick! Then, too, the Irish workers split into two factions, the Cordonians and the Longfords. Strikes and feuds broke out, and the state militia was called in to restore order. A cholera epidemic brought the infighting to a tragic end. So many Irish canal workers died that mass burials were held at nearby Catholic churches, such as Saint Mary's in Barnesville. Many Irishmen were interred in unmarked graves where they fell alongside the canal.

Obtaining financial support for the canal was not easy and never certain. The merchants of Baltimore agreed to lend funds if the company built a branch canal to connect their city with the canal. Baltimore would thus become the largest city on the Potomac River! But when an engineering survey showed this scheme to be impossible, Baltimore withdrew the offer. About this time, in 1842, a chance event of far-reaching proportions occurred. It all happened because a lady fell off her horse.

Francis Preston Blair, editor of the Washington *Globe* newspaper and a member of President Andrew Jackson's Kitchen Cabinet, went for a ride in the country one fine day with his daughter, Elizabeth. Elizabeth was an expert horsewoman; but she was distracted by a letter she was reading from navy Lieutenant Samuel Phillips Lee. When Selim, her mount, stumbled on a rock, Elizabeth went right over his head.

Selim ran off. Blair and Elizabeth followed, and they found Selim drinking from a beautiful spring. Sunlight sparkled on the mica enclosing the bubbly font, making the mica glitter like gems on a velvet scarf. Blair and Elizabeth were enchanted. Without further delay, the property was purchased and named Silver Spring. Blair built a roomy, two-story house and set an acorn-shaped summer pavilion near the spring. Elizabeth married the lieutenant, and her father moved from his Washington home, Blair House, but retained the residence. Blair was a strong influence through four presidential administrations: those of Jackson, Van Buren, Buchanan, and Lincoln.

From Francis Blair's home in Silver Spring was to come a long line of influential people: Postmaster General Montgomery Blair and his brother, General Frank Blair; U.S. Senator Francis Preston Blair Lee; "Mr. Montgomery," Colonel E. Brooke Lee; Acting Governor Blair Lee III; Montgomery County Council President Elizabeth Lee Scull; and, in 1982, council member David Scull. And a street in Silver Spring was named Selim. ■

Hungerford's Tavern was the subject of Benjamin Henry Latrobe's sketch dated October 9, 1811, *Out of Robb's window Montgomery Courthouse*. Charles Hungerford's tavern was designated the new county's courthouse in 1776. Not only was it considered the most central site, but it was located at the strategic crossroads of the Georgetown-Frederick Road and the road from Bladensburg to the mouth of the Monocacy River.

Two years earlier a patriotic crowd had gathered at Hungerford's. Led by Captain Henry R. Griffith and Dr. Thomas Sprigg Wootton, the group had adopted the Hungerford Resolves, which was a vow to break off commerce with Great Britain until the Intolerable Acts were repealed.

After the subsequent battles were over, Dr. Wootton was asked to represent the residents of lower Frederick County at a convention in Annapolis. He did so and sponsored an act to create a new county between the Patuxent, Potomac, and Monocacy rivers and Parr's Spring, to be named for a hero of the new nation, Richard Montgomery.

After the creation of Montgomery County, Hungerford's Tavern and its neighborhood got a new name, Montgomery Courthouse. It was renamed Williamsburgh in 1786 and Rock-ville in 1803.

From 1803 to 1812 and again from 1814 to 1817, Benjamin Latrobe, the famous architect, worked in Washington and frequented Montgomery County, sketching and painting scenes of interest. He was appointed by Thomas Jefferson as surveyor of public buildings in the District of Columbia, and he designed the south wing of the Capitol and modified the White House and the Patent Office. After the British burned the Capitol in 1814, Latrobe rebuilt certain portions. Courtesy of The Papers of Benjamin Henry Latrobe, Maryland Historical Society

27

Benjamin Henry Latrobe sketched
an elephant in Clarksburg! Dowden's
Ordinary is at the left, welcoming
guests with its tall sign near the
Georgetown-Frederick Road. Cour-
tesy of The Papers of Benjamin
Henry Latrobe, Maryland Historical
Society

Benjamin Henry Latrobe sketched
Clarksburg on August 2, 1810 in his
Sketchbook XI-II; the drawing is
entitled *Pencil Sketch of Clarksburg
and Sugarloaf Mountain.* The work
was probably done when Latrobe
was a guest at Dowden's Ordinary,
for this view of Sugarloaf Mountain
can be seen from a hillside a few
hundred feet from the site of the razed
hotel. The colonial village stretches
north below the viewer; several of the
houses date from the early 1800s. The
road pictured was once called Seneca
Trail. Just beyond the area shown in
Latrobe's sketch the trail intersected
a second Indian route which connected the mouth of the Monocacy
River with Parr's Spring, today the
spot where Howard, Carroll, Frederick, and Montgomery counties
meet.

Known as the Georgetown-Frederick Road, Seneca Trail became a
part of the National Road, later
known as Route 40 and then as
Route 240. Today it is Route 355 and
is also called, along its path, Wisconsin Avenue, Rockville Pike, and
Frederick Road. Courtesy of The
Papers of Benjamin Henry Latrobe,
Maryland Historical Society

This watercolor, [*illegible*] *on the Sugarloaf Mountain Nov. 3rd, 1816*, depicts an early scene of life on Sugarloaf Mountain. Benjamin Henry Latrobe deserves a place of honor in the annals of Montgomery County. By way of his pencil sketches and watercolors, he left a record of everyday life and ordinary scenes. Courtesy of The Papers of Benjamin Henry Latrobe, Maryland Historical Society

Isaac Briggs of Sandy Spring and Triadelphia demonstrated the important consequences of living next door to the nation's capital through his contributions to the development of his country.

Briggs moved to the area in 1793 to survey the proposed Federal City. He was elected a fellow of the Society for Useful Knowledge in 1794 and a fellow of the American Philosophical Society in 1796. In 1797 he taught school at Sandy Spring. Briggs went west as surveyor general of the Mississippi Territory in 1799. His friend Thomas Jefferson wrote, "Isaac Briggs, in point of science, in astronomy, geometry, and mathematics, stands second to no man in the United States."

With Thomas Moore and Caleb Bentley, Briggs built the town of Triadelphia at the turn of the nineteenth century. The three had married three daughters of Robert Brooke of Brooke Grove.

Briggs and Moore founded the Sandy Springs Farmers' Society, and Briggs was elected the first president. Briggs was also a bank president. He was the chief engineer of numerous projects from New Orleans to the Erie Canal and, in 1823, accepted the job of investigating a canal route to link Baltimore with the Potomac River.

Briggs died at his log house, Sharon, near Sandy Spring, leaving a legacy of national recognition.
Courtesy of Helen Thomas Nesbitt Farquhar

Hannah Brooke Briggs, the wife of Isaac, wore her modest Quaker bonnet August 24 through 26, 1813, when President Madison's cabinet stayed at her home in Sandy Spring, a safe twenty miles from the burning capital which had been invaded by the British. The cabinet brought with them the young nation's gold which was to be kept by Isaac Briggs, the president of the Bank of Columbia.
Courtesy of Helen Thomas Nesbitt Farquhar

Roger Brooke, a member of the innovative Quaker community in Sandy Spring, was active in Sandy Springs Farmers' Society and was president of the Montgomery County Agricultural Society during its first fair, held at Rockville on September 12 and 13, 1822.

A few years later Brooke, along with other local farmers, became interested in establishing a silk industry, and the Montgomery County Silk Company was chartered in 1836. Farmers imported mulberry trees and silkworms and earnestly tended their expensive new enterprise. But three years later the industry ended, leaving mulberry trees galore to delight generations of Montgomery County mockingbirds. Courtesy of Helen Thomas Nesbitt Farquhar

This is Francis Preston Blair of Silver Spring and the Blair House in Washington, D.C. Courtesy of Blair Lee III

Elizabeth Blair, whose fall off a horse founded Silver Spring, is shown. Courtesy of Blair Lee III

Although Samuel Phillips Lee was a Lee of Virginia, he fought for the Union during the Civil War and was promoted to the rank of admiral. He came home to Silver Spring and his wife, Elizabeth Blair Lee. Courtesy of Blair Lee III

Martha Purdy Butler was "sold as a babe in arms along with her mother," according to Wilson Wims (Mrs. Butler's descendant and a resident of Clarksburg).

Mrs. Butler did not publish her memories of slavery, but Josiah Henson, another Montgomery County slave, did so, and described a scene which may have been similar to the one experienced by Martha Butler: "My brothers and sisters were bid off one by one, while my mother, holding my hand, looked on in an agony of grief...then she was separated from me, and put up in her turn. She was bought by a man named Isaac Riley, of Montgomery County, and then I was offered to the assembled purchasers. My mother, half distracted with the parting forever from all her children, pushed through the crowd, while the bidding for me was going on, to the spot where Riley was standing." Henson's mother begged Riley to buy her baby. He responded with kicks and blows, and six-year-old Josiah was sold to a Rockville tavern owner. Later, however, the child was purchased by Riley and grew up at the Riley farmhouse on Old Georgetown Road in Rockville.

Harriet Beecher Stowe read Henson's book, and she wrote a novel, set in Montgomery County, that moved a nation—*Uncle Tom's Cabin.* Courtesy of Mrs. Altia Wims and Wilson Wims

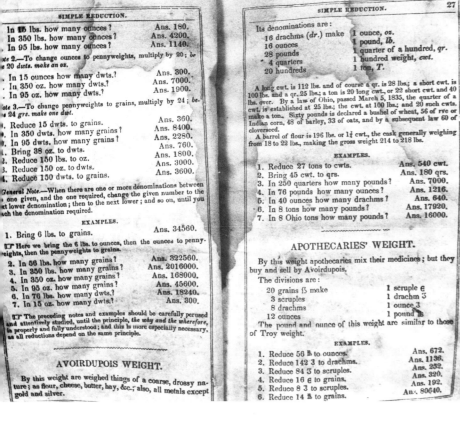

In 15 lbs. how many ounces?   Ans. 180.
In 350 lbs. how many ounces?   Ans. 4200.
In 95 lbs. how many ounces?   Ans. 1140.

ote 2.—To change ounces to pennyweights, multiply by 20; *be*
20 dwts. make an oz.

. In 15 ounces how many dwts.?   Ans. 300.
. In 350 oz. how many dwts.?   Ans. 7000.
. In 95 oz. how many dwts.?   Ans. 1900.

ote 3.—To change pennyweights to grains, multiply by 24; *be-*
24 grs. make one dwt.

. Reduce 15 dwts. to grains.   Ans. 360.
. In 350 dwts. how many grains?   Ans. 8400.
. In 95 dwts. how many grains?   Ans. 2280.
. Bring 38 oz. to dwts.   Ans. 760.
. Reduce 150 lbs. to oz.   Ans. 1800.
. Reduce 150 oz. to dwts.   Ans. 3000.
. Reduce 150 dwts. to grains.   Ans. 3600.

General Note.—When there are one or more denominations between
one given, and the one required, change the given number to the
xt lower denomination; then to the next lower; and so on, until you
ch the denomination required.

EXAMPLES.

1. Bring 6 lbs. to grains.   Ans. 34560.
☞ Here we bring the 6 lbs. to ounces, then the ounces to penny-
eights, then the pennyweights to grains.

2. In 56 lbs. how many grains?   Ans. 322560.
3. In 350 lbs. how many grains?   Ans. 2016000.
4. In 350 oz. how many grains?   Ans. 168000.
5. In 95 oz. how many grains?   Ans. 45600.
6. In 76 lbs. how many dwts.?   Ans. 18240.
7. In 15 oz. how many dwts.?   Ans. 300.

☞ The preceding notes and examples should be carefully perused
and attentively studied, until the principle, *the why and the wherefore*, is
properly and fully understood; and this is more especially necessary,
as all reductions depend on the same principle.

AVOIRDUPOIS WEIGHT.

By this weight are weighed things of a coarse, drossy nature; as flour, cheese, butter, hay, &c.; also, all metals except
gold and silver.

Its denominations are:

16 drachms (*dr.*) make	1 ounce, *oz.*
16 ounces	1 pound, *lb.*
28 pounds	1 quarter of a hundred, *qr.*
4 quarters	1 hundred weight, *cwt.*
20 hundreds	1 ton, *T.*

A long cwt. is 112 lbs. and of course a qr. is 28 lbs.; a short cwt. is
100 lbs. and a qr. 25 lbs.; a ton is 20 long cwt., or 22 short cwt. and 40
lbs. over. By a law of Ohio, passed March 5, 1835, the quarter of a
cwt. is established at 25 lbs.; the cwt. at 100 lbs.; and 20 such cwts.
make a ton. Sixty pounds is declared a bushel of wheat, 56 of rye or
Indian corn, 48 of barley, 33 of oats, and by a subsequent law 60 of
cloverseed.

A barrel of flour is 196 lbs. or 1¾ cwt., the cask generally weighing
from 18 to 22 lbs., making the gross weight 214 to 218 lbs.

EXAMPLES.

1. Reduce 27 tons to cwts.   Ans. 540 cwt.
2. Bring 45 cwt. to qrs.   Ans. 180 qrs.
3. In 250 quarters how many pounds?   Ans. 7000.
4. In 76 pounds how many ounces?   Ans. 1216.
5. In 40 ounces how many drachms?   Ans. 640.
6. In 8 tons how many pounds?   Ans. 17920.
7. In 8 Ohio tons how many pounds?   Ans. 16000.

APOTHECARIES' WEIGHT.

By this weight apothecaries mix their medicines; but they
buy and sell by Avoirdupois.

The divisions are:

20 grains ℈ make	1 scruple ℈
3 scruples	1 drachm ʒ
8 drachms	1 ounce ℥
12 ounces	1 pound ℔

The pound and ounce of this weight are similar to those
of Troy weight.

EXAMPLES.

1. Reduce 56 ℔ to ounces.   Ans. 672.
2. Reduce 142 ℥ to drachms.   Ans. 1136.
3. Reduce 84 ℥ to scruples.   Ans. 252.
4. Reduce 16 ℈ to grains.   Ans. 320.
5. Reduce 8 ℥ to scruples.   Ans. 192.
6. Reduce 14 ℔ to grains.   Ans. 80640.

Lock 13 in Bethesda, along with its lock house, is shown. The structures are part of the Chesapeake and Ohio canal system. Courtesy of National Park Service

An 1849 edition of *Parke's Practical Arithmetic* found in the 1768 house belonging to the author serves as evidence of schooling long before public education was made a Maryland policy. The textbook, written by Uriah Parke, was designed "for the Use of Schools and Men of Business," according to the cover.

Inside the book was found a problem of daily life that had been worked out by the student, James H. Austin. "Three men bought a grind stone 30 inches in diameter. Each man paid an equal share and they wished to grind off their several shares successively. Required the thickness of each share no allowance being made for the eye."

In 1857 scaffolding was in place for the Union Arch across Cabin John Creek, part of the conduit bringing water to Washington from the Potomac. The name "Cabin John" is thought to stem from that of Captain John Smith, who described the Potomac in 1608 and traveled close to the creek that bears his name.

Sandstone from the quarries at Seneca was brought by canal and laid in place; then the timbers were removed. The bridge was a genuine triumph for American engineers. It was the largest single-span stone arch in the world, and it witnessed many changes. According to local legend, slaves hid in a secret passageway, making the arch part of the underground railroad. Jefferson Davis was secretary of war when this photograph was taken, and his name was engraved on the brass marker. His name was removed when he became president of the Confederate States of America; it was restored by President Theodore Roosevelt in 1909. A small hotel was built in the sylvan setting underneath the bridge, which flourished at first, but was later abandoned. Conduit Road was renamed MacArthur Boulevard to honor the World War II hero. Courtesy of Library of Congress

Chapter 3
1850-1872

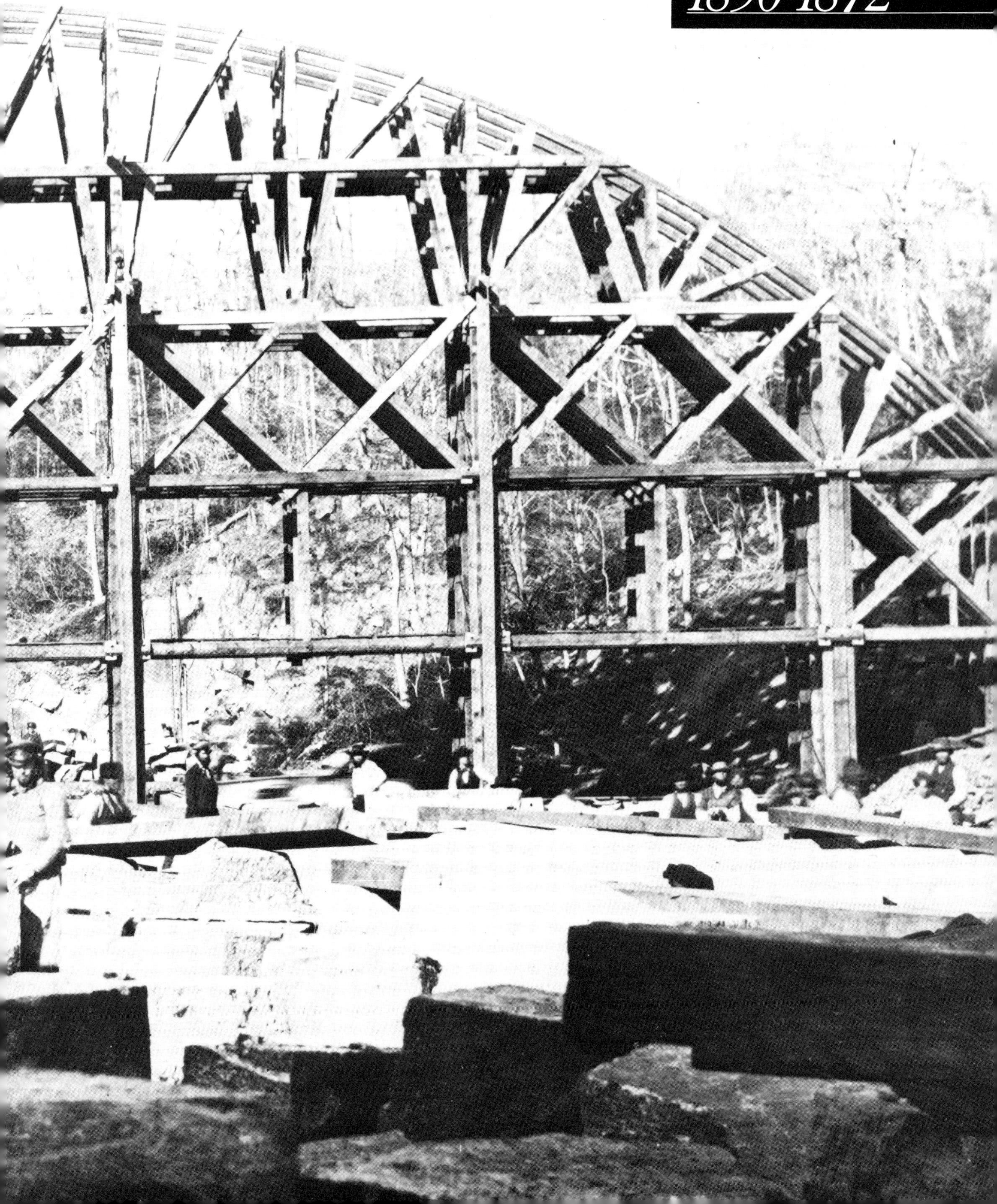

The soil continued to become more exhausted, and Montgomery County farmers found it necessary to move on or scratch hard to survive. Population had decreased between 1830 and 1840 as planters abandoned their fields and headed west in search of new land. Entire towns, such as Barnesville, picked up and moved—in this case, to Barnesville, Ohio.

In 1855 Matthew Fields founded a newspaper in Rockville and established an ongoing record of everyday life in Montgomery County—a time capsule. Within the yellowed, brittle pages are passions and prejudices, the prices of bread and shoes yesterday and a hundred years ago, and the progress and development of a county.

Fields named his paper *The Sentinel on the Watchtower of Democracy*. He took firm editorial stands on issues of the day, and he sharply criticized opposing viewpoints. Fields made no attempt to hide his Southern sympathies, possibly reflecting the opinion of the county's majority. For example, he hinted at local slave rebellion in January 1857. "The excitement and anxiety consequent upon the rumors of negro insurrection have generally subsided," he wrote. "There were some poor negroes so deluded as to suppose that if Mr. Buchanan were elected they would be freed from slavery." As a result of quick action, he noted, the Montgomery County status quo continued, with its quiet villages and the respectful "and servant-like manner of the negro."

Fields even printed ads for slaves. "For Sale—a very likely negro boy, seven years old on the first day of July, 1856...well grown and is to serve until he is thirty years of age."

He did the same for runaways. Ann Maria Weems, fifteen years old, was described as "a bright mulatto; some small freckles on her face...slender, sandy hair. Parents both free, live in Washington city. Went away with someone in a carriage. $500 reward."

West of Rockville, work on the canal progressed despite the odds against it. By 1833 the entire Montgomery portion of the canal had been completed. And in 1850 the 184.5 miles of the C & O opened, linking Cumberland with Georgetown. The canal revitalized local agriculture. Farmers gained access to wider markets; they could load their crops onto barges tied at a nearby lock and then send the goods to the Port of Georgetown and from there to Baltimore and an ocean-going vessel. Crops could also be stored in Georgetown

Amos Farquhar gazes at Mathew Brady's camera. Amos was the first of a long line of Montgomery County Farquhars. He and his wife, Mary Elgar, moved to Mechanicsville (Olney) in 1825. Amos taught at Fair Hill School and served as the postmaster of Mechanicsville for eleven years. Courtesy of Helen Thomas Nesbitt Farquhar

warehouses until prices were better. The canal brought guano, lime, and plaster to fertilize and condition the soil; thus, corn and wheat began to be grown.

The C & O brought added prosperity to the county by selling water to the Georgetown millers. Water falling from a height of seventy-five feet created breathtaking amounts of energy, and it was not wasted. Water wheels spun, grinding the grain into cornmeal and flour.

Canal boatmen made up a legendary and colorful chapter in Montgomery history. They intermarried and socialzed within their group. Their children sometimes caught a few weeks of school during the winter when

This dashing gentleman is William Norris Harris (1789-1873), from the foothills of Sugarloaf Mountain. Today, the Harris farm on West Harris Road in Barnesville is owned by former Postmaster General J. Edward Day and his wife. Courtesy of Charles Harris Jamison

Sarah Piles Harris (1800-1873), wife of William Norris Harris, marks her place in the Bible as she watches the artist through her delicate, horn-rimmed glasses. Courtesy of Charles Harris Jamison

the canal froze, but for the most part every hand was needed on board the family barge, to make sure the baby did not fall overboard, to prod the mules, to patch leaks, and to buy dinner along the pathway.

Lock keepers sometimes sold produce to barge families from the garden patches kept beside their white-washed stone cottages, thus augmenting their incomes. Sometimes, chicken and "roastin' ears" of sweet corn could be purchased from "Montgomery County merchants," the term given enterprising slaves from nearby farms who had poultry and vegetables to sell.

The planters prospered, too. They paid off their mortgages, in part, with sales of hay and feed for the

boatmen's mules. But most of their financial upswing came from the increased soil fertility and the access to world markets for their grain that the canal provided.

There were no railroads in Montgomery at this time. The turnpikes were rough but well-traveled from Washington to Brookeville or Rockville; farther north, overland travel was considered dangerous. The best-advised stayed at home or took the canal, floating down the quiet stream, nibbling on a chicken leg fried by a Montgomery County merchant.

Slavery continued; Montgomery County had not seen her last war. The Potomac River, not the Mason-Dixon line, may have been the true frontier of the Civil War. From 1861 to 1865, Montgomery County's river was the watery line that separated the United States from the Confederate States of America.

Montgomery County was sprinkled with the blood of both Yankees and Rebels. From Fort Stevens (Saint John's Academy), to the Seventh Street Turnpike (Georgia Avenue), to Clopper, to Great Falls and the river, soldiers fought and died. No major battles occurred in Montgomery County, but numerous skirmishes were just as deadly to the soldiers involved.

Residents of Montgomery County divided their loyalties. Neighbor armed against neighbor, brother against brother. Families split, never to reunite. Strong feelings for the gray or the blue disrupted the ties of blood and culture as the Potomac River became the war front, dividing the "North" (Montgomery County, Maryland) from her nearby neighbors in the "South" (Loudon County, Virginia).

Quakers in Sandy Spring believed that slavery was morally wrong and had already freed their slaves. But their neighbors in nearby Unity, Ridgely Brown and Thomas Griffith, organized mounted volunteers for the C.S.A., and George R. Gaither led a contingent of Montgomerians across the river to enlist in the Virginia cavalry. In 1861 the flag of the Confederate States of America flew briefly from the Rockville courthouse mast.

Montgomery's Union officers included E. H. Brooke, M. P. Engle, Joseph S. Lewis, and the son and son-in-law of Francis Preston Blair, General Frank Blair and the promoted lieutenant, Admiral Samuel Phillips Lee.

Confederate sympathizers sent secret messages across the Potomac, and Edward Stabler, the postmaster of Sandy Spring, organized a network of Union spies. Sentinels were stationed in the woods near the river, on rickety stands in tall trees reached by hastily constructed ladders. In addition, the Union army strung two military telegraphs from the Capitol to Poolesville and to Frederick.

Montgomery citizens of Confederate sympathy looked toward Poolesville where they rallied around Colonel Elijah Veirs White. Born just east of town, White married a neighbor and moved to Loudon County, Virginia in 1856. The young couple retained their close family relationships, fording the river frequently with easy familiarity.

On the morning of September 6, 1862, the gray-clad Army of Northern Virginia crossed the Potomac at

The Clarksburg Band stops by the wooden sidewalk (circa 1860) in front of a house that still exists. The Tallyho wagon with the trumpet painted on its side has, unfortunately, vanished. Courtesy of the Clarksburg Civic Association

39

White's Ford. The band went first and, once ashore in Montgomery County, they dried off their cornets and French horns and set up an impromptu concert, piping the soldiers across the river. Local citizens heard the music and came to enjoy the entertainment. Meanwhile, someone raided a barge on the C & O Canal and came away with watermelons for everyone, as Matthew Fields watched, notebook in hand.

For three days the lines of troops came, as more than thirty thousand men crossed the river into Maryland. By the nightfall of September 8, the last of the barefoot infantrymen sloshed onto the miry bank and lowered his rifle and bedroll from over his head.

Two of the officers, Colonel White and his commander, General Stonewall Jackson, went to Dickerson for dinner, followed by their men. White's mother-in-law, Mary Elizabeth Trundle Gott, collected her friends and prepared ham, fried chicken, potatoes, corn, squash, and blackberry pie for the sudden but welcome guests.

Montgomery County was full of troops in September 1862, from Poolesville to Clopper, from the district line swarming north and west out Georgia Avenue through Olney, from Rockville Pike through Clarksburg and Hyattstown, from River Road to

Sketches of Civil War activity in Montgomery County appeared in *Harper's New Monthly Magazine* in September and October 1866. Courtesy of Library of Congress

SIGNAL-STATION, MONTGOMERY COUNTY.

VIEW FROM HEAD-QUARTERS, DARNESTOWN.

40

Offutt's Crossroads and Seneca, and from Falls Road to Rockville, where Union General George G. McClellan headquartered. The following June, Confederate General J. E. B. Stuart captured Judge J. Bowie and approximately 250 Union soldiers coming north on the pike into Rockville. Along with the troops, Stuart confiscated their long train of army supply wagons and the team of six mules that pulled each one. Again, in July 1864, troops crossed the county, this time rebels under General Jubal Early; they plundered and gleaned from Veirs Mill Road to Georgia Avenue and to Rabbit's Post Office.

To add to the confusion of loyalties, Colonel White commanded a contingent of old neighbors and childhood friends in addition to his Virginia troops. Called the Montgomery County Confederates, the cavalry harrassed Union forces all during the war with well-maneuvered sneak attacks, crossing and recrossing the river they knew so well.

In the *Sentinel,* Matthew Fields covered as many local battles as he could. He reported that so many Union soldiers fell into the Potomac during the Battle of Ball's Bluff that the flavor of fish was affected; Fields reported that the fish tasted terrible, like

ENCAMPMENT OF SIGNAL PARTY, DARNESTOWN, MARYLAND.

TOPOGRAPHICAL HEAD-QUARTERS, NEAR HYATTSTOWN, MARYLAND.

TOPOGRAPHICAL ENCAMPMENT, MAGRUDER'S.

"dead Yankees."

Fields upheld the Confederate cause in flaming editorials. Twice his presses were broken by Union troops, and twice he was locked up in the Old Capitol Prison, to be defended by his friend and a member of Lincoln's cabinet, Montgomery Blair. Montgomerians were frightened for their lives, and they were overwhelmed with despair at the terrible war so close at hand.

On January 3, 1865, the *Sentinel* published the following on the front page:

"This Cruel War"
by Callie Swantson

Is there a friend? is there a home
That this cruel war has left alone?
Is there a mother who has not wept?
Is there a father who has not kept
An eager eye o'er the news, to hear
From sons who march at trumpet's call,
Until they fall by the cannon ball?
Is there a widow who is bereft
Of her staff and solace, and none are left
But a lonely boy to cheer her pain.
Who will not weep when the youth is slain?
Is there a sister whose tearful eyes
Are dry when she hears her brother dies?
Oh! God, be with us, and give us peace,
And grant that this cruel war may cease.

The Mongtomery County courthouse was pressed into service as a hospital for the Union wounded. At last the curtain began descending on the Civil War, but not before a final tragedy, the assassination of President Lincoln on Good Friday, April 14, 1865. The murder was the result of a plot conceived by John Wilkes Booth, and was part of a conspiracy to kill Secretary of State William Seward and Vice-President Andrew Johnson as well.

Booth's accomplice, George Andrew Atzerodt, was assigned to murder Andrew Johnson. As Booth was aiming his pistol at the back of the president's head, Atzerodt was standing in the Kirkwood Hotel just a few feet from Johnson, his intended victim, a large Bowie knife sharpened and ready to strike a murderous blow. But Atzerodt could not commit murder. He turned and fled the site and the city, returning to the home of his cousin, Hartman Richter, in Old Germantown, Montgomery County. There, he was captured on April 20, to hang along with Mary Surratt, Lewis Paine, and

Although the Civil War is often romanticized, those involved were filled with sadness and compassion for the cause and for the many lives lost. Southerners, committed to a belief they felt was right, were emotionally shattered at the news of Lee's surrender. In addition, they were frightened for their future at the mercy of their conquerors.

In his weary and stoic expression Colonel Elijah Veirs White, of the Confederate States of America, seems to reflect the futility felt by the Southerners. White was a native of Montgomery County and the leader of the Montgomery County Confederates. Courtesy of the Montgomery County Historical Society

Tabler, wearing his wartime uniform, stood in front of the Davis House on the wooden sidewalks of Hyattstown to have his picture taken. The telegraph poles and tree-lined dirt roads disappeared long ago, but the Davis House and the two-storied, white frame house on the opposite side of "Main Street" (Rt. 355) remain. Courtesy of Friends of Historic Hyattstown

MAIN, ST. HYATTSTOWN, M. D.

Davy Herold—all convicted of conspiracy in Lincoln's assassination.

The last war fought in Montgomery County left a lot of cleaning up to do. Invading troops had used school desks and church pews for firewood; soldiers from both sides had stolen horses and chickens and generally terrorized the countryside.

Lincoln's Emancipation Proclamation decreed freedom for the slaves in the Confederacy, although the slave status of those in Montgomery County was not legally affected by Lincoln's address, since Maryland was not officially in rebellion against the Union.

But slavery was abolished by constitutional amendment in December 1865. Blacks could, then, elect to stay with their former masters or to go out into an unfriendly world, jobless and unprepared for independence. Farmers who had fed, clothed, and protected their slaves as property, whose capital was tied up in them, suffered financial loss. They could neither afford to pay for their

services nor reach a mutually acceptable agreement with their former workers to exchange labor for a roof and bread.

Wandering blacks and returning soldiers mingled on dusty roads, looking for answers, looking for homes. Many blacks stayed in Montgomery County on land near their former homes. As time passed, agreements were reached; property owners deeded to the blacks the marginal land, the rocky soil, the marshy areas. In exchange, blacks worked to pay a specified sum until the land belonged to them and the title, they were assured, was recorded in Rockville.

Nearly half of Montgomery's population was black between 1830 and 1860. However, many of these blacks were free people. In Sandy Spring were Montomery's first free black community and the first black school.

Other blacks left the county and went to the cities of Washington and Baltimore, where there were more opportunities for employment. Those who stayed

43

formed close-knit villages, helping and encouraging one another, staying apart from the houses of white Montgomerians. Each cluster built a church, usually Methodist, the largest and most rapidly growing denomination in the county at the time.

Black public schools were established in 1872 by state law, twelve years after the Maryland legislature voted to fund public schools for white children. State funds for blacks were augmented by part of each tax dollar from black property owners. The Montgomery County Board of School Commissioners paid teachers a salary, but the amount differed between white and black educators. In the 1870s a black teacher received twenty-five dollars and white teachers seventy-five dollars for one term. Thus established, segregated schools would continue in Montgomery County for more than eight decades.

Blacks felt the sting of segregated housing and schools, and their white counterparts knew the desperation of severe property loss and economic upheaval. In addition, political harmony was difficult at the county level as a large number of Southerners were faced with the knowledge of Union victory and Confederate defeat. Montgomery County's war wounds were bitter and deep; more residents wept at Lee's surrender than cheered for Union victory. ∎

Union soldiers guard Silver Spring, the home of Francis Preston Blair. Falklands, the home of Montgomery Blair, had already been burned to the ground by Confederates. Courtesy of Library of Congress

Hard times were common just before the Civil War. The Montgomery County soil was worn out, and, unless one lived near the C & O Canal, there was no easy way to get guano and lime to replace lost nutrients. Farmer Alfred Ray (1824-1895) of The Highlands in eastern Montgomery County found he could no longer grow sufficient crops to feed his large family and needed to find a new job. He went to work for the Baltimore and Ohio Railroad, building bridges and culverts from Washington to Point of Rocks.

During the Civil War, confusion reigned, and innocent men were often mistakenly jailed, as was Alfred Ray. Although presidents Franklin Pierce and James Buchanan had appointed Ray justice of the peace,

he was arrested and taken to the Old Capitol Prison on June 25, 1864. He was charged with having Confederate sympathies.

But even more trouble was in store for Ray and his family. Taking advantage of the owner's absence, General Jubal Early invaded The Highlands. His Confederate troops spread their tents on the lawn and hungrily raided Ray's gardens and crops.

Fortunately Ray's friend and neighbor in Silver Spring, Francis Preston Blair, intervened with President Lincoln, and Ray was soon released.

From Alfred Ray and his wife, Eleanor Merryman Gatch Ray, were to come a long line of valued Montgomery County citizens. Courtesy of Edith Ray Saul

The Alfred Ray family (circa 1870) stands on the porch of their house, The Highlands. The house was built by William Carroll, the grandson of Daniel Carroll, on part of Joseph's Park, an early land grant.

Later, The Highlands was sold to Clarence Moore, the huntmaster of the Chevy Chase Club, who planned to move the club to the property. But in 1912 he took a voyage on a brand new ship, the *Titanic,* and he went

down with it. Years later, The Highlands was sold as the site for the Church of Jesus Christ of Latter-day Saints' Washington Temple in Kensington. Courtesy of Edith Ray Saul

Postmaster General Montgomery Blair was a member of President Abraham Lincoln's cabinet. He was involved in Montgomery County affairs and spoke at rallies in Rockville. He also helped get his friends and neighbors out of jail, including *Sentinel* editor Matthew Fields, who had been accused of making treasonable statements in his newspapers, and William H. Offutt, for his attempt to recover a fugitive slave.

But Montgomery Blair's client of most lasting fame and significance was Dred Scott. Blair must have been puzzled at the landmark civil rights decision of Chief Justice Roger B. Taney that Scott, as a black man, was not and could not be a citizen of the United States and had no right to come before the courts. Blair had defended Scott at his trial, referred to historically as the Dred Scott case. Courtesy of Library of Congress

Union General Frank Blair, seated in the center, is surrounded by his staff. Courtesy of Library of Congress

Montgomery citizens did not forget their Southern bonds. Years after the end of the war, local citizens built a memorial to the Confederate soldiers who had died July 12, 1864, in a skirmish near Silver Spring. Photograph by Dr. Leonard Tuchin

Sandy Spring's Fair Hill School was held in the building pictured. Before and after the school's use of the building, it was a dwelling. Richard Brooke, a Quaker who fought in the Revolutionary War against the pacifistic principles of his religion, constructed the building. Later Whitson Canby, a member of another well-known Quaker family, purchased the house for eight Irish families. The commune manufactured pots and sold their wares at the markets of Mechanicsville (now Olney).

The Baltimore Yearly Meeting, in association with Sandy Spring Friends Meeting, purchased the building in 1815 and later opened Fair Hill School, where Benjamin Hallowell taught. It remained a school under various names from 1819 until 1865, when Civil War activity closed it.

During the Civil War, troops from both sides crossed the schoolyard, including those of generals Johnson, Burnside, and Hooker. Confederate General J. E. B. Stuart reportedly brought to the girls' school thousands of his troops who stole horses, bivouacked in the fields, burned the fence rails, and dug up four acres of potatoes! Understandably, the girls were terrified. Teacher Mary Coffin hid valuables under the hearth in a box the same size as the bricks. As a result of the invasion, parents withdrew their daughters, and Fair Hill School closed.

A series of private owners lived at Fair Hill until it burned down in the 1970s. This photograph was taken about 1900. Fair Hill's lot is now the site of the Village Mall Shopping Center in Olney. Courtesy of Roger Lamborne

As part of the Lincoln assassination conspiracy, George Adzerodt was assigned to kill Vice-President Andrew Johnson. But Adzerodt could not bring himself to do the deed. Instead, he fled to the home of his cousin in Old Germantown in Montgomery County, where he was captured. He was tried, convicted, and hanged for conspiracy in the Lincoln case. Courtesy of Library of Congress

Hartman Richter, Adzerodt's cousin, was also taken into custody, but he was completely exonerated and released. He returned to his home in Old Germantown. Courtesy of Library of Congress

John H. Surratt conspired with John Wilkes Booth, a fellow boarder at the rooming house of his mother, Mary Surratt. John Surratt was in Canada on April 14, 1865, the day Lincoln was shot. He escaped the hangman's noose, but his mother was executed.

Surratt eventually returned to the United States and lived in Rockville, teaching school and earning additional money by delivering an occasional lecture at the courthouse. Courtesy of Library of Congress

Soldiers walk west on Fisher Avenue in Poolesville during the Civil War. From the collection of Charles Elgin; courtesy of Library of Congress

This photograph of the Rice farmhouse on Germantown Road near Darnestown was taken about 1877. Millard Lee Rice, fourth from the left, wears a mustache. The only other person identified is Eva Vinson Wyand, second from the left. Courtesy of William Fawsett Rice

Enoch George Howard (shown here circa 1870) was born a slave near Unity. He became a prosperous landowner and the founder of a prominent family of educators, journalists, and magistrates. Howard was the slave and field foreman of Beal Gaither. It was his job to sell the farm's produce at the market in Baltimore. In addition, he had a small plot of land for his own use, and he sold its produce as well. Over the years he saved three thousand dollars. In 1857, 47-year-old Enoch George bought freedom for himself, his wife Henrietta, and his five children, Greenbury, John, Mary Alice, Marian, and Martha, with his savings. Also, he purchased Locust Villa, the tract of land and eighteenth-century stone house where they lived.

Howard prospered, and he purchased a total of six hundred acres of land. He hired teachers for his children and built them a school in the 1860s. His daughter Martha married John H. Murphy and moved to Baltimore to found the *Afro-American* newspaper. Their son, George Murphy, became a public school principal and the father of Judge William Murphy. William Murphy, Jr., is currently the judge of the Circuit Court of Baltimore. Courtesy of Mabel Howard Lawson

51

Henrietta Howard was the wife of Enoch George Howard. She is pictured here circa 1870. Courtesy of Mabel Howard Lawson

Although he had been born a slave, Gary Green (1832-1900) became a prominent member of the Quince Orchard community and a skillful carpenter and builder in Darnestown and Germantown.

He married Matilda Mason; they had twelve children, all of whom he struggled successfully to educate. In March 1874 Green requested funds from the Montgomery County Board of School Commissioners to hire a teacher for the Quince Orchard Colored School. The board agreed, provided that the schoolhouse and lot were deeded to the county. On April 14, 1874, Gary Green and his associates, James Ricks and Carlton Moss, conveyed the property to the county. The Green descendants remained in Montgomery County, valuable and respected residents of Fellowship Lane in Quince Orchard. Courtesy of Carroll Greene, Jr.

Mules pull freight over the Union Arch, circa 1865. Courtesy of Library of Congress

John Clark founded this store on the Frederick-Georgetown Road. One of the Civil War-period telegraph poles lining the road was used as a hitching post for shoppers' horses. William

Willson, Clark's son-in-law, followed Clark in the merchandising business. Courtesy of Boyds/Clarksburg/Germantown Historical Society

Louise Hall, the granddaughter of Roger Brooke Farquhar, poses circa 1870. Her calling card is also shown. Before the telephone was invented, ladies visited carrying a calling card to leave with servants if their friends were not at home. Courtesy of Helen Thomas Nesbitt Farquhar

A little boy stands in one of Brookeville's dirt streets, looking toward the general store and thinking, perhaps, of the penny licorice sticks within. Courtesy of Helen Thomas Nesbitt Farquhar

This Montgomery County general store (circa 1870) sold everything from millstones and shepherds' crooks to bedsprings and wagon wheels. In those days it was quite unheard of for women to wait on customers, although they often did the bookkeeping. The hired help usually lived upstairs while the owner lived across the street in a fine, large house.

Although the sign reads "B. H. Dudrow," this store was commonly referred to as the Dudrow/Darby Store. It is located in Hyattstown just north of the fire station. The building was featured years later in a 1951 Department of Agriculture study of general stores in rural America. Courtesy of Friends of Historic Hyattstown

E. Francis Baldwin, the chief architect for the Baltimore and Ohio Railroad, designed this elegant brick station with a slate fish-scale roof and an iron roof crest for the prosperous railroad town of Boyd's Station. In 1928 a new generation of engineers widened the track and attempted to move the station to the other side, causing the structure to fall apart. From the collection of Nell Staley; courtesy of the Boyds/Clarksburg/Germantown Historical Society

On May 24, 1873, the first train steamed across Montgomery County on the Metropolitan Branch of the Baltimore and Ohio Railroad, a distance of forty-two and three-quarter miles, connecting points west with the nation's capital. The railroad provided the cutting edge of economic transformation; it meant prosperity for poor, rural Montgomery County, suffering from war wounds, worn-out soil, and labor problems without solutions.

Wherever the train came, transportation patterns, agriculture, and urban development were swept up in a hurricane of change—fields touched by the miracle of nitrogen, a booming housing industry, and incredibly swift travel. Cultural ties strained irrevocably as the adventurous, the young, and the unemployed boarded the train and left their homes.

Previously near-worthless land along the tracks rocketed in price. Speculators wanted the land for housing. Farmers wanted it for the easy access to new fertilizers, and as a means to ship crops to market quickly and inexpensively. Also, a prosperous dairy industry developed because milk could be shipped and sold before it soured.

Community leaders and landowners had struggled to influence the proposed path of Montgomery's railroad. And, when the tracks were in place, the population moved to be near the train. New towns sprung up, and their residents grew richer. They added gracious Queen Anne-style porches just as close to the tracks as the B & O officials would allow. On summer evenings the enchanted owners could sit on the porches and watch the trains go by.

Agricultural changes occurred when lime and guano were delivered inexpensively by train. Farmers turned unproductive pine woods into lush cropland. With soil improvement, an acre of land gave thirty bushels of golden wheat where it had previously yielded eighteen. Most farms already had a family cow. Before, farmers had sold cream for needed cash and fed the "skimmed milk" to the hogs. But the new generation of farmers bought more cows, built huge dairy barns, and shipped whole milk to the Washington market by train. They also added bay windows and turrets to the family house.

The railroad brought plentiful steam power, making possible new tools and inventions. The new jigsaw, for example, could easily fashion a bracket of gingerbread trim for the corners of a porch. The train opened

In 1873 the Metropolitan Branch of the Baltimore and Ohio Railroad began service from Point of Rocks to Washington city and changed the economy and sociology all along the tracks. The Seneca Bridge in Boyds, pictured, was the longest railroad trestle yet engineered at that time. A railroad employee checked the bridge continuously for sparks that might cause a fire, by walking across and back after each train passed.

The high trestle was abandoned in 1928, but the stone pillars and a few of the long wooden timbers remain below, in Little Seneca Creek. From the collection of Leroy Morgan; courtesy of the Boyds/Clarksburg/Germantown Historical Society

James Alexander Boyd came to this country in 1844 from Ayrshire, Scotland. He went to work on the railroad as a stonecutter. He worked and studied and became a highly respected civil engineer in such cities as Philadelphia, Parkersburg, Cincinnati, Memphis, and Baltimore. In 1861 he and his wife, Sarah Rinehart Boyd, sailed to Brazil to build railroads for Dom Pedro, the emperor.

In 1866 Boyd came back to Baltimore and obtained the contract for several difficult sections of the Metropolitan Branch of the Baltimore and Ohio Railroad. To house his crew, he bought land in the wilderness near the convergence of the Little Seneca and Ten Mile creeks. He soon owned more than 1,100 acres of the abandoned land, which was considered worthless for agriculture.

In 1873 the Metropolitan Branch opened for rail traffic. Boyd brought in Peruvian guano and lime and transformed the broom-sedge and scrubby pines to lush pastures and productive fields of grain, bordered with orchards and ponds. He installed miles of whitewashed board fences and built a mansion, a dairy, barns, windmills, and tenant houses. A model dairy farm appeared. James W. Garrett, president of the B & O Railroad, was so grateful for the fine industry along the tracks that he built a fancy brick station at Mr. Boyd's rail stop and on it lettered "Boyd's Station." A town grew up around the station, which for a time was a very prosperous village. It became the center of the dairy shipping business in Montgomery County.

When Boyd died on Christmas Eve, 1896, all the trains on the Metropolitan Branch stopped at Boyd's Station for the funeral services.

Today the village built around James Boyd's railroad station has been nominated to the National Register of Historic Sites and Places and to the Masterplan for Historic Preservation in Montgomery County. Courtesy of the late Eleanor Maughlin Young

up possibilities for horseless and barefoot upcountians. No longer did the jobless poor have to hunker down in an old log cabin and scratch out a meager existence.

Black women, highly trained in household skills, took the train to Washington and worked all day, returning late in the afternoon to tend their own homes and children. Many blacks left rural Montgomery County. The exodus occurred when jobs became abundant in the towns downcounty and in the city of Washington. At the same time farmers needed less help due to steam-powered mechanization, which the railroad introduced.

However, no bells rang in Rockville for the nation's centennial. Instead, Montgomerians celebrated with enthusiasm on September 6, 1876, Montgomery County's one hundredth anniversary. Thousands poured into the Rockville Fairgrounds to hear the speeches and poetry written for the occasion and to view the six glass cases of memorabilia including, according to the exposition case's description, a piece of wood from George Washington's casket and a lock of his hair!

Again, more new towns sprang up alongside the railroad tracks. By 1890 thirteen crowded passenger trains passed through western Montgomery every day except Sunday, stopping at Dickerson, Barnesville, Buck Lodge, Boyd, Little Seneca, Darby, Germantown, Waring, Clopper, Ward, Gaithersburg, Washington Grove, Derwood, Rockville, Halpine, Randolph, Windham, Garrett Park, Knowles, Capitol View Park, Forest Glen, Linden, Fenwick, Silver Spring, Takoma, Lamond, Stott, Terra Cotta, University, and, finally, Union Station. Everywhere the trains stopped, the villages grew and prospered.

Praise the Lord for the railroad and the new prosperity. Pretty, white frame churches became the central attraction of most new railroad towns. Later, the churches got steeples and bells to ring on Sunday mornings.

Commuters formed social groups, holding holiday parties that rolled from Dickerson to Union Station and chipping in to buy Christmas presents for the conductors.

A few miles west of the tracks, the C & O Canal was more than holding its own. In 1869 the company had achieved unprecedented gain from a happy combination. Governor Oden Bowie appointed top managerial talent to lead the company, and canal barges were filled with coal in West Virginia and floated down the canal to

With the Metropolitan Branch of the B & O Railroad came prosperity—and the steam-powered jigsaw. Curved wood and various trim patterns display the creativity of the artisan who built this Kensington house for William M. and Georgia Knowles Mannakee in 1890. From the collection of Edith Ray Saul; courtesy of the Kensington Historical Society

Washington. As a result of the enterprise, the canal showed a profit for several years.

During this period a long-lasting pattern of political affiliation was formed. In general, white men became Democrats and black men, who voted for the first time in 1870, were Republicans. Women could not vote, but not everyone believed the status quo should remain. Francis and Caroline Hallowell Miller led the movements for woman's suffrage, black civil rights, and prison reform. Unlike most white Montgomerians, the Millers were not Democrats. They, along with most of their neighbors in Sandy Spring and Damascus, voted the Republican ticket.

The Civil Service Act of 1883 meant that government workers could count on their jobs despite changing administrations. Hence, they could and did buy homes in Montgomery County.

As a result of the act, developers bought the farms close to the district line and the railroad tracks. Trolley lines were added to link the B & O with the new Chevy Chase Village and Chevy Chase Lake, plus two amusement parks, Glen Echo Park and Bethesda Park at Tennallytown. ■

The railroad gave birth to a new county industry, the milk business. Milk could be quickly cooled by means of groundwater heat exchangers in springhouses. Courtesy of Neal and Marion Potter

Conveniently located alongside the tracks of the Metropolitan Branch of the B & O Railroad, the Forest Oak Hotel in Gaithersburg got a lot of business. Courtesy of Idella Leaman

Presbyterian Chapel
Germantown Md.

In 1873 the Metropolitan Branch of the B & O Railroad began to run trains halfway between the old log Presbyterian chapel at Pleasant Hills in Darnestown and the Neelsville Presbyterian Church. The people of Germantown moved a mile to the east to be near the tracks, and a new town grew up with two churches, one Methodist and this one, the Germantown Presbyterian Church. Courtesy of Idella Leaman

The Bowman brothers of Germantown and members of their family pose before their lovely new home, which attests to the potential for prosperity among mill owners. The Bowmans owned and operated the Bowman Brothers Mill in Germantown, alongside the tracks of the Metropolitan Branch of the B & O Railroad. Courtesy of Jean King Phillips

In 1849 a road was constructed in Montgomery County connecting two Presbyterian congregations, one at Nealsville (later Neelsville) and one at Darnestown. Later, the stained-glass windows and expensive architectural details were added to the Neelsville Presbyterian Church, reflecting the prosperity of the railroad era. Courtesy of Idella Leaman

ealsville Church.

Two-thirds of the new congregations organized in Montgomery County from 1870 to 1910 were Methodist. Pictured here is St. Paul's Methodist Church, built in 1886 in the blossoming railroad suburb of Kensington. On hot Sundays, the church usher handed each worshipper a fan. To increase their comfort further, Kensington Methodists installed striped awnings to cool the interior of their church.

In 1899 Kensington mayor George Peter purchased the building for Christ Episcopal Church, and the Methodists built a larger sanctuary on Armory Avenue. From the collection of Edith Ray Saul; courtesy of the Kensington Historical Society

The Bowman Brothers Mill (at the left) shipped their products under the trade name Silver Leaf Flour. Mail was collected at the store on the right, which was run by Perry Waters, Richard Waters, Mr. Brandenburg, Mr. Dickerson, Ray Smith, William Clements, and Herbert King. A second store provided competition.

History, it is often said, repeats itself. Old Germantown crumbled when the Metropolitan Branch of the B & O Railroad opened about a mile to the east. Then, when Interstate 270 came through east of the railroad, the town shifted again. The Germantown shopping facilities pictured here were replaced by the Germantown Commons. Courtesy of Idella Leaman

Judging by the appearance of Veirs Mill Road (circa 1885) not too much attention was lavished on roads at this time. Courtesy of Dorothy Troth Muir

Three generations of an important and lasting Montgomery County family gathered at the Ashton cross-roads home in Tanglewood. The men, from left to right, were Albin Gilpin Thomas, George F. Nesbitt (senior), and Richard Thomas. The women, from left to right, were Mary Thomas Jackson; Helen Thomas Hallowell; Louisa Thomas Brooke; Emily Thomas Massey; Susannah, wife of Albin G. Thomas; Lydia Gilpin Thomas; Ellen Jackson (the little girl on the grass); and Anna Thomas Nesbitt, who is holding her baby, Helen Thomas Nesbitt, born in 1897. On either side of bicyclist Richard Thomas are his wife, Harriet, and their daughter, Lillie. Courtesy of Helen Thomas Nesbitt Farquhar

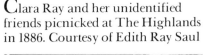

Clara Ray and her unidentified friends picnicked at The Highlands in 1886. Courtesy of Edith Ray Saul

Friends Celia Bowie (right) and future Montgomery County Councilman George F. Nesbitt (left) exchange a confidence at Tanglewood, near the historical Quaker village in Sandy Spring, circa 1900. Courtesy of Helen Thomas Nesbitt Farquhar

The hair wreath shown here belonged to the Joseph Collins White family. Victorian wedding and funeral guests would leave the hostess locks of hair which were then fashioned into intricate designs and shaped into wreaths. Courtesy of Kay Moore

The building materials most often used in nineteenth-century Montgomery County were those that were closest to the site. Thomas Sullivan of Great Falls easily obtained Seneca sandstone, and he built his house with the same material that was used to build the original Smithsonian castle in Washington. In this picture, dated August 28, 1895, are, from left to right: Edgar R. Perry; Bertha L. Perry; the couple's one-month-old son, Ralph L. Perry; Cora Perry (Ball); Thomas Sullivan; Marian Hester Perry Sullivan, Thomas's wife; Susan Ball; and Lizzie Sullivan. Courtesy of Barbara Dangler

The local sandstone was also used to build Seneca School on River Road. In addition to the neighborhood youngsters, the sons and daughters of the C & O Canal employees attended school at Seneca. Lock keepers and barge operators needed their children's help most of the year. But winter's ice closed canal operations and freed the children to attend school.

In 1981, through the efforts of Mary Anne Kephart and other members of Historic Medley District, the crumbling schoolhouse was rescued from abandonment and restored as a school museum. Courtesy of Helen Riley Bodmer and Ray Riley

Two girls from The Highlands visited the black family that was living in the Henry Clay cabin on the Ray family estate, circa 1880. Water was collected in the rain barrel in the foreground, and a mattress aired from the second-story window of the log house. Courtesy of Edith Ray Saul

Sandstone, cut at a Seneca quarry by stonecutters, was loaded onto canal barges and sent to Washington for structures such as the original Smithsonian building, called the "castle." The material was also used for less grand but equally permanent local construction projects, such as the Seneca schoolhouse.

Jack Clipper, pictured second from the right, was once a slave. Born in Virginia, he was freed by Union troops after a battle in Hanover County. He remained with the soldiers and helped the quartermaster locate and supply food. After the war, he boarded a Yankee ship in Port Royal, Virginia, and sailed to Baltimore, looking for a job. With his powerful physique he had little difficulty earning a living cutting cordwood and then sandstone.

Jack Clipper built a house upstream from the quarry near the canal, and he married Martha Johnson from Big Pines, a settlement near Potomac. Ten children were born in the house: Bosey, George, Sy, Cleveland, William, Isaac, Barbara, Julia, Martha, and Harry. Three of the sons built homes on Clipper Lane in Bethesda.

Jack Clipper died in 1903. He was never sure of his birthdate, but he was thought to have been fifty-five years old. Courtesy of Bernice Clipper

Three young cousins relax after a family reunion at the home built by Benjamin Fawcett near Colesville. They are, from left to right, Raymond Clagett, Margaret Baker, and Stella Clagett. Courtesy of Eveleen Hobbs Carter

A symbol of progress, this brick house was built by William Waters, Jr., in 1817. The photograph was taken circa 1860. The house was constructed of bricks either brought from England as ship ballast, or made from clay taken from the property, or with some of each; sources of information disagree.

The Waters family, of English descent, prospered. They owned many slaves, and they constructed outbuildings until the estate resembled a small village. Members of the family built several large homes along Waters Road. William's grandson, Horace Waters II, opened a general store in Germantown and invested in a dairy barn and cows. Horace's son, Julian, owned the farm from 1904.

In September 1933, the Farm Women's Market opened in Bethesda. Mrs. Eleanor Cissell Waters, Julian's wife, became president of the organization and drove her automobile to market each week, loaded with her farm's produce.

In 1962 the land was sold to a developer; it stood empty until 1981 when it was burned to make way for town houses, thus completing the march of progress. Courtesy of Ella Virginia Waters Gochenour

In July 1895 Lycurgus Cashell supervised the haymaking operation at Montmorency (also called Llewellyn Fields) on the southwest corner of the Norwood-Layhill crossroads. Montmorency, a prosperous farm, was owned by Hazel B. Cashell, Lycurgus's father. Rebecca Cashell, in her long, black dress with the leg o'mutton sleeves and white apron, gathered eggs. Nearly everyone in the photograph wore a hat, either a coolie-style or a straight-brim straw hat; a white muslin cap; or a wide-brimmed straw sunbonnet. Courtesy of Mary Groomes Hobbs

George Jefferson Belt is shown leaving Montgomery County to fight for his country in the Spanish-American War, circa 1898. Belt is seated on his ship's deck, second from the right in the front row. Courtesy of Eveleen Hobbs Carter

Presbyterian Scotch-Irish settled in Darnestown. They marched with General Edward Braddock to fight the French and Indians in 1755. They fought in the Revolutionary War twenty years later, and put down the Whiskey Rebellion in 1794. Back home in Darnestown, they worshipped in a log chapel at Pleasant Hills and built a church in 1855, which enlarged over the years. Germantown Road stretched from Pleasant Hills to the Neelsville Presbyterian Church.

In 1867 Andrew Small, a leading church member, willed thirty-five thousand dollars to the Neelsville and Darnestown Presbyterian churches for a private academy at Darnestown. Classes began in the church basement, and the substantial, three-story school building was completed in 1872. The Andrew Small Academy is shown here circa 1890.

In 1907 the Montgomery County Board of School Commissioners obtained use of the building for a public high school, and they purchased the land in 1927. In 1954 an elementary school was constructed on the site. Courtesy of William Rice

These students at Andrew Small Academy, circa 1890, are, left to right in the first row: Mary Rice, Mattie Howard, Natalie Allnutt, and Lucille Rice; in the second row are: George Saverwein, Tootie Herter, Edward Athey, Reid Hammond, unknown, Worthington Tschiffley, and Tommy Stern. Courtesy of William Fawsett Rice

At Colesville (or Notley) School on Notley Road on December 5, 1899 thirty students, from ages five or six to the teens, gather around their sober teacher to have their picture taken. The little girl in the white pinafore in the front row is Effie Ray (later Hobbs). Courtesy of Eleanor Hobbs Bailey

Dr. William A. Warfield, pictured here circa 1899, worked in the anatomy, bacteriology, and obstetrics departments at Freedmen's Hospital in Washington, D.C. Dr. Warfield was born in Hyattstown in 1866 and grew up at Dowden's Ordinary in Clarksburg; he more than likely attended Clarksburg Negro School. He graduated from Howard University Medical College in 1894. In addition to his position as physician and surgeon on the Freedmen's Hospital staff, Dr. Warfield taught anatomy and bacteriology in the medical department at Howard University. Courtesy of Moorland-Spingarn Research Center, Howard University

This is the Mutual Fire Insurance Company of Montgomery County building in Sandy Spring after the 1878 addition. Two of the directors stand on the porch of the original 1857 building.

The company was formed in 1848 by Thomas McCormick, A. Bowie Davis, C. Farquhar, E. J. Hall, Samuel Ellicott, Joshua Pierce, Edward Lea, Joseph Bond, W. H. Farquhar, Benjamin Hallowell, Thomas P. Stabler, Mahlon Kirk, William P. Palmer, Caleb Stabler, Robert Moore, Richard Brooke, George Brooke, and Jonathan D. Barnsley. From the collection of the Sandy Spring Museum; courtesy of Roger Lamborne

The family reunion—what a charming way to spend a summer day! Here the King/Watkins family surrounds Mr. and Mrs. Alonzo Watkins (the elderly couple, center, in the fancy chairs) in Cedar Grove, 1890. Courtesy of Harrison and Gladys King

Edward Farquhar (1843-1904) of The Cedars in Sandy Spring was photographed circa 1880. Farquhar was considered one of the brilliant men of his time. Known as a philosopher, poet, scientist, preacher, and literary authority, he was a professor of English literature at Columbian University, now George Washington University.

He helped organize and frequently lectured to the Washington Society of Philosophical Enquiry, and he spoke in Sandy Spring Friends meetings on religion and ethics, quoting freely in Greek and Latin as well as in English. Courtesy of Helen Thomas Nesbitt Farquhar

Francis and Caroline Hallowell Miller, pictured circa 1890, were firmly rooted members of Quaker society and the community of intellectuals and educators. They were also Republicans in a Democratic county, striving for civil rights and woman's suffrage at a time when neither subject was popular.

Following their marriage in September 1852, Caroline's father, Benjamin Hallowell, gave the couple thirty acres of his Sandy Spring farm, Rockland. There, the Millers built Stanmore, their home; around 1860 they opened a boys' boarding school, also named Stanmore. From 1867 to 1871 Stanmore operated as a girls' school.

In 1867 Caroline took over the school, freeing her husband for his law practice. In 1878 the school was moved back to Rockland, and Caroline joined Frances E. Willard and Susan B. Anthony in the struggle for woman's suffrage.

The Millers were staunch Republicans and were often faced with determined opposition, as is illustrated by the following incident: just before the Civil War, Francis Miller organized a Republican rally in Rockville. When he arrived at the meeting hall, the door was padlocked. Undaunted, he found a crowbar, pried off the lock, and proceeded with the rally. Courtesy of the Montgomery County Historical Society

Turn-of-the-century little boys in Montgomery County wore white sailor middies, and little girls wore big satin bows in their hair and lacy, ruffled dresses. The children pictured are Helen Thomas Nesbitt and George F. Nesbitt, Jr., who grew up to serve on the Montgomery County Council in 1950. Courtesy of Helen Thomas Nesbitt Farquhar

As the nation's centennial approached, President Ulysses S. Grant issued a request for local histories. He hoped that by so doing, Americans both north and south would be drawn together with a sense of community pride after the end of the bitter Civil War. In response to the presidential request, T. H. Stockton Boyd wrote a book called *The History of Montgomery County, Maryland from its Earliest Settlement in 1650 to 1879* and published it three years later in Clarksburg. He is pictured here in the home of his parents, the Reverend and Mrs. Reuben Boyd. From the collection of Clarence Day; courtesy of the Boyds/Clarksburg/Germantown Historical Society

This pretty whitewashed cottage, part log and part frame, belonged to the rural postmaster, Charles T. Johnson, in the village of Germantown. Postmaster Johnson is shown with his wife and family in 1895. Courtesy of Idella Leaman

Three adventurous people appear to be marooned in the Potomac near Great Falls. Courtesy of Idella Leaman

The Alban Gilpin Thomas family of Tanglewood in Sandy Spring (circa 1898) pose together.

Leg o' mutton sleeves and long skirts did not prevent these young Quaker ladies from riding bicycles and climbing trees at Tanglewood, the Thomas family home. Alban Thomas is standing fifth from the right, and his wife, Susannah, is fifth from the left. Their son, Frederic L. Thomas, gallantly holds the bicycle handlebars for one young lady.

Mr. Thomas owned a store in Ashton, organized and directed the Citizens National Bank of Laurel, was president of the Savings Institution of Sandy Spring, and established the First National Bank of Sandy Spring.

Alban and Susannah's granddaughter, Helen Thomas Nesbitt, was born at Tanglewood and moved just one mile away to The Cedars when she married Arthur Farquhar in 1919. Courtesy of Helen Thomas Nesbitt Farquhar

Hallowell Maus Spencer, born in 1864, was fascinated with the new science of photography. He took pictures between the years 1885 and 1899, including himself in most of his photographs. The cord to the camera extends from his left hand in this picture. From the collection of Laurence Halstead; courtesy of the Montgomery County Historical Society

No gingerbread trim adorned this unpainted farmhouse in Quince Orchard. Hanson and Martha Anne Carlisle Ricketts knew what it was like to work hard; Martha Anne was just one generation removed from Ireland's potato famine. Although

their funds were limited, their kindness knew no bounds: when their own children grew up, the Ricketts raised a homeless child, Bessie Hommiller, the child shown. Courtesy of Mamie Berry Curlis

Jacob Corbett comes a-courtin' Miss Alice Leaman, circa 1896. Corbett drove his sulky all the way from Hagerstown to Old Germantown just to see Miss Alice, a distance of fifty-two miles. Courtesy of Idella Leaman

George and Annie Earp pose at the photographer's studio on their wedding day, their hairstyles and clothing impeccably correct. Courtesy of Eleanor Hobbs Bailey

The automobile comes to Wheaton, and H. C. Hickerson adds four new gasoline pumps to his long line of merchandise. Courtesy of Malcolm Walters

H.C. HICKERSON

BETHOLINE

H.C. HICKERSON
GENERAL MERCHANDISE

Job guarantees for government workers were bringing them to Washington on a permanent basis, and Montgomery's landowners responded with a tentative move toward a housing industry. These early ripples would result in a tidal wave of building which, by the 1980s, would sweep the county from the Patuxent to the Potomac and from the district line to Parr's Spring.

Despite the incoming white-collar workers, farming remained the foremost occupation in Montgomery County. Dairying was the leading industry with twelve thousand dairy cattle grazing the green pastures beside the still waters of the Seneca, Rock Creek, and their tributaries and branches. Tobacco still grew on 134 county acres. The Washington markets sold poultry and eggs from Wheaton and Colesville, potatoes from Colesville, Wheaton, and Olney, corn and wheat from all the rural areas of Montgomery, and milk and vegetables from along the B & O Railroad and communities close to the district.

It fell to the hard-working huckster to distribute the agricultural products. He made a colorful sight with his horse and wagon and, later on, his pickup truck piled with fresh brown eggs and country sausage, cornmeal from local mills, potatoes, onions, collard greens, and whatever else was growing in his or his partner's truck patch garden. He might go to the markets to sell his produce. Or he might travel a select route where he was well known and always welcome, for, in addition to delivering food, the huckster served the very useful function of communication, relaying messages and news along his route.

In 1912 about 85 percent of the country was farmland, and 90 percent of the residents earned their living by agriculture. During the next twenty years, twenty-three thousand acres of farmland were converted into housing lots.

For the most part, the persons purchasing the new homes worked for the federal government. No longer dependent on the political party currently in power, Washington-based bureaucrats could look around for permanent homes and bring the wife and kids from Kansas, Queens, or elsewhere.

As a spinoff of the Civil Service Act of 1883, the housing industry in Montgomery County expanded briskly and created jobs. Montgomery lumber mills sawed and planed Montgomery trees, and local carpenters hammered and nailed the new houses. House

In Kensington's first automobile, Dr. Anthony M. Ray drives on the grounds of The Highlands in 1904. If Dr. Ray could look into the future, he would see the Capital Beltway and, to his left, the multiple spires of the Mormon temple.

"The automobile comes to Kensington," someone wrote on the back of the snapshot. Courtesy of Edith Ray Saul

servants streamed into the growing communities at Silver Spring, Chevy Chase, Bethesda, Wheaton, Capitol View, Somerset, Takoma Park, Cabin John, and Great Falls.

Since the heads of the households worked in Washington, the newcomers oriented toward the capital city. They shopped on Seventh Street and rode the trolley and railroad to plays and concerts in town. Public transportation connected residents from along the Metropolitan Branch with Washington, D.C., Kensington, Great Falls, Bethesda, and Chevy Chase. Their children attended public schools in the District of Columbia, tuition-free as long as their fathers or mothers worked for the federal government. District officials put a stop to this practice within a few years. In 1914 the Washington, D.C., Board of Education voted to exclude Maryland students. Montgomerians responded by supporting a bond issue to build public elementary

Highway construction on Clarksburg Road began in 1907. Walter Breau, far right, was the boss; next to him is Lee Day. Lee's little brother, Madison, far left, carried spring water to quench the thirst of the unidentified Irish and black men who were building a road between

the colonial town of Clarksburg and the Victorian railroad village, Boyds.

To make the road, rock was shipped by train to Boyds and carted by draft horses like Sam and Jerry, pictured. Workers lived in a two-story log house adjacent to the Day home in Burdette; the road company fur-

nished their food and lodging.

One of the Day brothers, Clarence, later traveled the road every day for forty years as the Clarksburg postmaster. From the collection of Clarence Day; courtesy of the Boyds/Clarksburg/Germantown Historical Society

and high schools.

Political party rosters shifted from a Democratic majority. Many suburbanites moved to Maryland from Northern and Midwestern states, and they continued to register as Republicans in their new towns.

Jim Crow legislation, begun in the late nineteenth century, increased during the early 1900s. Separate facilities for whites and blacks included theaters, railroads, and restaurants, as well as schools. Regulations were posted which forbade social integration, such as blacks and whites entering the courthouse by the same door.

In the growing urban areas, people became more and more concerned about their drinking water and sewage disposal. A typhoid fever epidemic in 1913 resulted in a new sewage system for Rockville. The twelve hundred residents obtained drinking and household water from two community wells. There were

twenty flush toilets in Rockville; the remaining homes had privies. The town scavenger cleaned the privies regularly, dumping the residue into the village stream, Monkey Run, carefully emptying his containers below the wells.

This method worked well until two concurrent circumstances occurred—the unusually wet winter of 1913 coupled with a visitor in town who was ill with typhoid fever. This person's waste was added to the effluent in Monkey Run. Heavy rains interfered with the normal drainage pattern and forced the infected waste back up the pipes serving the wells. As a result, the water of 90 percent of Rockville's population became contaminated. Twenty-one people contracted typhoid fever, and three of them died.

This was enough to frighten the other Montgomery towns, and the citizens appealed to their state legislators. In response, the Maryland State General Assembly created the Washington Suburban Sanitary Commission, to be responsible for sewer and water facilities in Prince George and Montgomery counties.

The WSSC began to build reservoirs at Burnt Mills (completed in the 1930s), Triadelphia (1940s), and Burtonsville (1950s). Privately-owned filtration plants were absorbed into the WSSC, and a new one was built on the Potomac in the 1960s to supplement a regional facility at Blue Plains which had been built in the 1950s.

The year after Rockville's typhoid fever epidemic, a more widespread dread engulfed Montgomerians. America was drawn into its first world war. The nation's capital had brought prosperity to its neighbor, but now the people realized the danger in case of enemy attack on the District of Columbia.

Montgomery's citizens did whatever they could to help win the war. Miss L. T. Stonestreet recruited women volunteers to substitute for drafted men to help with the crops. As the chairman of the Mongtomery County Unit of the Woman's Land Army of America, she interviewed recruits and farmers, too, at Autrey Park, the farm of Joseph H. Bradley.

Mrs. John H. Gassaway of Rockville invited local ladies to her kitchen to make jelly for the boys at Camp Meade, and they produced 106 glasses from this collective effort.

The "Over There Exhibit" in Baltimore demonstrated bombs made from nitroglycerine salvaged from fats normally thrown away or fed to the hogs. Montgomery farmers were told to fatten hogs without feeding them these extra fats. "Let Uncle Sam's cannons feed that to the foe," urged the local press.

Montgomery schoolchildren helped by collecting pits and nuts and by participating in National Tag Day. The fruit seeds were made into gas masks to protect American soldiers from the "Hun's gas that stings, blinds and kills." Each respirator required seven pounds of pits. On National Tag Day, January 30, 1918, schoolchildren went from door to door, tagging coal shovels to remind homeowners to use less fuel.

Children raised money too. Public school teachers accepted donations and chalked in gauges as visual reminders of the class quotas for war money contributions. Schoolteacher V. E. Woodward wrote a memorial to a small pupil who died in June 1918. All the school loved little Charles, she wrote, "with his merry eyes and winsome ways, and our hearts are heavy with grief. Never again will Charles come to school, never again to say, 'Here's my $1, Miss Bessie, will it take us Over the

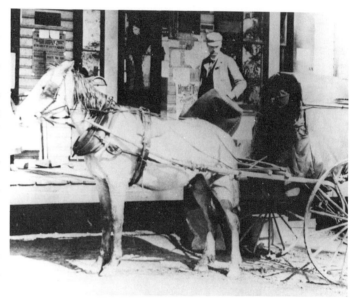

Mail arrives at Sandy Spring, circa 1905. Copy by Roger Lamborne; courtesy of the Sandy Spring Museum

Top?'"

Everyone was expected to work on the war effort. Idlers were fined under the Compulsory Work Laws of March 10, 1918. A Lytonsville man paid fifty dollars when he missed his assigned job at the Kensington farm of Robert Curran.

Forty-four servicemen did not return to their Montgomery County homeland after the war. Those who died fighting in World War I were William E. Atwood, Francis F. Barber, Junius I. Boyle, Walter M. Briggs, Colin J. Broadhurst, Albert O. Burgdorf, Edwin H. Chinn, Edward C. Cissell, Andrew J. Dailey, Jr., Lindsay Edmonds, Ernest W. Emery, Frank T. Hagan, Abraham Foster, Adolphus M. Graham, Basil R. Graham, Leo Heffner, Frederick N. Henderson, Charles H. Hood, Paul L. Hull, Norman H. Iglehart, George B. Johnson, Henry K. Lenhart, John Howard Lindsay, Charles F. Linthicum, William T. Lusby, Davis H. Mackay, John W. Nicholson, Benjamin Perry, Jr., George Plummer, Jr., Clifford H. Poole, Norman Boyer Price, Davis Neeper Richards, John William Saxon, Leroy Small, Theron Eaton Smith, Edward Smith, William G. Toone, John Douglass Wade, John Walter, Charles F. Wedderburn, Victor M. Whitside, George Arnold Wilburn, Allaire Emery Woodson, and Robert J. Worthington. ■

In 1902 Mr. and Mrs. James Boyd Maughlin set out for Boyd Presbyterian, the church named for Maughlin's uncle, James Alexander Boyd. The top of Eleanor Ray Maughlin's Sunday hat can be seen over the back of the perfectly matched pair of bay mares. Boyd's fine house, Bonnie Brae, faces the railroad tracks. The dirt lane is bordered with a well-trimmed hedge, lined with whitewashed fence, and set with fruit trees. Today this site is covered by a lake. Courtesy of the late Eleanor Maughlin Young

The Brainard H. Warner family posed in 1901 for this picture. In the early 1890s Brainard Warner bought the property south of the small railroad village of Knowles Station, and he developed it into a planned suburb with large, elegant homes and tree-lined streets. The wide front lawns and trimmed hedges reminded Warner of English gardens, so he named his town Kensington.

From left to right, in the top row, are Brainard Warner, Jr.; Rebecca; Southern; and Parker. In the middle row are Anna; Brainard, Sr.; and Mrs. Warner, who is holding Hamilton. In the front row are Phillips, Mary, and Margaret. From the collection of Edith Ray Saul; courtesy of Kensington Historical Society

Montgomerians of the mid to late nineteenth century vacationed at the Cabin John Hotel, shown above (circa 1905). Here, they could enjoy dancing in the spacious ballroom, strolling the elaborate gardens to the banks of the Potomac, listening to a giant music box in its own cylindrical house, or climbing the many turrets to view their surroundings.

About the time of the Civil War, Joseph and Rosa Bokinger designed and built this exact reproduction of an ornate Alsacian tavern and located it just west of the Cabin John Bridge.

At the turn of the century the resort could be reached by trolley car, and it grew in popularity. The man in the left foreground may be President William Howard Taft, but he is not positively identified.

Reflecting the added prosperity from the new transportation system, the Bokingers added an amusement park. However, the venture grew less and less successful, and Bokinger heirs sold the property to the American Land Company for development in 1912.

During the Great Depression

unemployed people inhabited the rambling, abandoned resort. On a chilly April night in 1931, the hotel was completely demolished by a fire allegedly started by the uninvited guests. From the collection of Charles J. Burner; courtesy of Montgomery County Historical Society

Properly Victorian, Rosa Mary Harper Beall stands beside her seated bridegroom, James Allen Beall, at the photographer's studio, shortly after their marriage in 1901.

From the *Sentinel,* on November 22, 1901, is a description of the wedding: "Married at St. John's, Forest Glen, November 20 at nine o'clock A.M. by Rev. Father C. O. Rosensteel, were James Beall and Rosie Harper. After the ceremony a nuptial mass was held by which the couple received special blessings. The altar was decorated with a profusion of chrysanthemums and burning candles." Photo by Paul Tralles, Washington, D.C.; courtesy of Ione Beall Sorensen and James Sorensen

Pictured at White Oak (circa 1917) from left to right are Rosa Mary Harper Beall; Lucretia Ione Beall; Eugene Anthony Beall; Lillian Marlowe with her baby, Bernice; William Leroy Harper; and Lucy Agnes Beall.

Perhaps it was because of Father Rosensteel's special blessings in the old church founded by John Carroll that the marriage of James and Rosa Beall was an exceptionally happy one.

Daughter Ione recounts a memory from a few years later:

"Father pushed his wheelbarrow through the deep woods to get pure white sand from a special stream bank. He trundled it back for us, dumped it under the maple tree, and then took our picture playing in it.

"The tree, too, was a giant toy for our amusement. We climbed into the branches, and it became for us our ship! Or a house! We had lots of fun with the sand and the maple tree." Courtesy of Ione Beall Sorensen and James Sorensen

Three little girls cool off in Rock Creek, wading in the pretty stream between their grandfather's house, The Highlands, and Forest Glen Seminary in 1904. The girls are Ray Wilson (later, Waters), aged eleven; Virginia Wilson (Townsend), aged nine; and Anne Wilson (Bullard), aged four.

Today, the site is Route 495 between the Mormon temple and Walter Reed Annex. Rock Creek was rerouted for construction of the beltway. Courtesy of Edith Ray Saul

This is the younger class of the two-room White Oak School (circa 1917) at the southeast corner of Route 29 and Stewart Lane. The youngsters loved to play at Burnt Mills, the property of a Mr. Wimsatt. Mr. Wimsatt let them run across his dam, use his boats, swim, or ice skate, depending on the season. One rule, however, was strictly enforced—no child was to set foot on his fine, velvety golf course lawn.

From left to right in the bottom row are: unknown, Leroy Harper, George Clark, unknown, unknown, and unknown. In the middle row are Myrtle Lusby, Blanche Talbott, Mildred Miller, Margaret Clark, unknown, Louise Boetler, unknown, and Kenneth Clark. In the back row are William Lusby, Chester Hardesty, Edward Clark, unknown, Augusta McCeney, John Clark, and Lucy Beall.

The road behind the children leads to Pine Hill, a black community, which had a school for black children. Courtesy of Ione Beall Sorensen and James Sorensen

Across from White Oak School stood the interesting house of George Harper (1841-1920) who was also the owner of Mrs. Harper's Woolen Factory on the Point Branch. Apparently, different parts of the home were built at different time periods, since the front facade was constructed of half vertical and half horizontal siding boards.

Harper spun exciting tales of his youth. He tried to join the Montgomery County Confederates, but was captured on his way to enlist and jailed in the Old Capitol Prison as a prisoner of war. He found that Belle Boyd, the famous spy, was a prisoner there as well. She had been caught carrying messages from the Confederacy back and forth across the Potomac. She entertained her fellow prisoners with her sweet, sad songs and her lovely voice, and young Harper remembered her forever.

Soon released and undaunted, Harper transported Confederate spies in his buggy for the remainder of the Civil War. Whenever he was halted by Union soldiers, he wove them a story, saying that his companion was his father.

Pictured in the buggy (circa 1912) are Harper and Frank Molina. Frank came to White Oak from the Sisters of Mercy orphanage in Baltimore as a part of their program for homeless youths. The Harpers hired Frank to work and live on their farm. The Sisters required that the orphans attend school a certain number of days each year and be treated fairly; a supervisor came around regularly to check on the conditions of the boys. Following the orphan court policy, Frank's wages were deposited in the bank, and when he reached the age of eighteen, the sum was given to him. Referred to as "Home School Boys," Frank Molina and other Maryland homeless youths of the time were thus able to start adult life with a tidy nest egg. Courtesy of Ione Beall Sorensen and James Sorensen

Students at Olney School prepared for fingernail inspection by their teacher, circa 1900. Kerosene lamps brightened the classroom on cloudy days and illumined the picture of George Washington and the framed phrase which appears to read, "Montgomery County the Shining Star." Olney School was located on the present site of St. John's Episcopal Church. Courtesy of Roger Lamborne

Students at the Andrew Small Academy gather on the school's steps (circa 1908). The girl at front in the center is Bennie M. Rice. At the right, Guy Allnutt holds his straw hat. Courtesy of William Fawsett Rice

Miss Blanche E. Braddock began teaching in Montgomery County in 1878. For years she boarded with Mrs. Lydia Etchison Moore over the Etchison general store and walked to the one-room schoolhouse across from Mount Tabor Methodist Church. Here, she poses with her students at Oaklawn School in May 1909. Courtesy of Mrs. Gladys King

This is a portrait of Blair Lee, the grandson of Francis Preston Blair; the son of Elizabeth Blair Lee, who helped name Silver Spring; the father of E. Brooke Lee; and the grandfather of Acting Governor Blair Lee and former Montgomery County Council president, the late Elizabeth Scull.

Blair Lee himself was a very powerful man for about two decades until 1915. Lee began his political career in 1896, running for Congress and campaigning for the presidential candidate William Jennings Bryan, a reformer. Under Lee's guidance, the silver-tongued orator spoke in Montgomery County on several occasions.

Politics aside, Lee was an attorney with a great enthusiasm for innova-tive ideas. He spoke with ease to good-government leagues and to political scientists. He was elected to the state senate in 1905 and to the United States Senate in 1913. He resigned from office in 1915 to run for governor of Maryland but was defeated, thus ending his political career. Courtesy of Blair Lee III

President William Howard Taft played golf at the Chevy Chase Club on June 28, 1909. Courtesy of Library of Congress

Before gasoline engines were adopted by American farmers, President Theodore Roosevelt sought to help farmers by breeding a strong, fast, and hardy farm animal. Roosevelt turned to the Department of Agriculture and the Smithsonian Institution, who built an experimental breeding facility in Bethesda. The parents of this "zebhorse" foal, shown in 1909, were a male zebra, donated to Roosevelt by King Menelik of Abyssinia, and a native mare.

European breeders had already produced an animal they called a "zebula" by crossing zebras and donkeys, but Roosevelt's zebhorse was strictly an American innovation, and the project was carried over into the presidency of Roosevelt's successor, William H. Taft, who was president from 1909 to 1913. Courtesy of National Archives

The Ezra Troth family poses on the boulders at Burnt Mills, the spot enjoyed so much by President Theodore Roosevelt. "Mother and I had a most lovely ride the other day, way up beyond Sligo Creek to what is called North-West Branch, at Burnt Mills, where is a beautiful gorge, deep and narrow, with great boulders and even cliffs. Excepting Great Falls it is the most beautiful place around here" (Letter to Ted; White House, June 21, 1904." In *Theodore Roosevelt's Letters to His Children*). Photograph courtesy of Dorothy Troth Muir

For just one nickel, visitors could walk across the river on this wooden footbridge and see Great Falls. From the Thompson collection; courtesy of the National Park Service

Corby's Mother's Bread delivers across the Northwest Branch in Colesville while a barefoot boy and his friends stand on a bridge. From left to right are Grace Parkhurst (later Hyatt); Dorothy Troth (Muir); Lydia Alderton (West); Ruth Troth (Gribbon); and Ezra Thomas Alderton. Courtesy of Dorothy Troth Muir

The side of a barn is a fine place for advertising, as shown here at Ezra Troth's Burnt Mills, circa 1908. Courtesy of Dorothy Troth Muir

Hand-cut logs topped with some type of thatching forms the Troth barn at Burnt Mills, circa 1908. The rider has his horses ready, not for show, but for work; he wears his multipurpose neckerchief and smokes, perhaps, Owl Brand tobacco in his hand-rolled cigarette. Courtesy of Dorothy Troth Muir

On the roof of the spring house at Burnt Mills was built a gazebo, a charming, rose-covered spot to sit and visit. Ezra Troth stands in the doorway of the stone spring house, and his wife, Lydia, holds their baby, circa 1908. Courtesy of Dorothy Troth Muir

From 1890 until the canal closed in 1924, John Riley kept the Seneca lock. From the canal company management, he received a house; adjoining land for raising vegetables, pigs, cattle, chickens, and horses; and a salary of thirty-five dollars a month from April through October, and ten dollars a month when the boats did not run but the lock needed repair.

He married Roberta Jane Ricketts on October 22, 1890, and their seven babies were born in the two-bedroom house built of native sandstone. They named the children Cleveland, Upton, Raymond, Ernest, Katherine, Mervin, and Helen.

When the children were little, Bertie Riley was always very fussy about keeping the gate to the tiny yard in front of the house closed. She realized that the canal was a hazard for toddlers, but the canal could not be fenced in because the space was needed for people and produce. The day this photograph was taken, the gate was left open. This would happen again, with tragic consequences. On September 23, 1905, three-year-old Katherine Riley fell into the six-foot-deep canal and drowned.

Bertie was uncomfortable living on the canal after this accident, and she persuaded her husband to buy a house on River Road. She collected her other daughter and five sons and walked up the road, but John remained behind and tended his lock.

John Riley continued to work his lock until the canal closed in 1924. From a tintype belonging to Riley's daughter, Helen Riley Bodmer

John Riley's wife, Roberta Ricketts Riley, bundled up her remaining children and left the stone lockhouse after her baby fell into the canal and drowned. She found a little house for her family on River Road, and there today, hanging on the wall, is a picture of the little girl, Katherine. Courtesy of Helen Riley Bodmer

Courtesy of E. B. Thompson, historic negative collection; original negative in Thomas Hahn collection, from *Chesapeake and Ohio Canal, Old Picture Album,* by Thomas F. Hahn; National Park Service photograph

Clara Jane Crawford Bowman was an ardent Methodist. In 1903, she and her husband, Charles, gave land to build Trinity Methodist Church in Germantown. She was superintendent of the Sunday school for many years. For her continuous service to the church, she was awarded a lifetime membership in the Methodist Women's Society; she wore the pin for the rest of her life and was buried with the single adornment on her black dress. Courtesy of Jean King Phillips

ME Church South
Germantown MD.

Germantown Methodists first worshipped together in a log chapel on the east side of Clopper Road at Route 118. But the membership divided in 1902, and some of them built Trinity Methodist Church, a mile farther east, near the railroad tracks. Others built Methodist Episcopal Church South in Old Germantown, pictured here. Like the log chapel, it was built on Route 118 near Clopper Road.

This church and the Germantown Presbyterian churches were later converted into dwellings and yet again rehabilitated as office spaces. The Methodist log chapel's adjoining graveyard still remains. Courtesy of Idella Leaman

The 1905 Poolesville baseball team had a pinch hitter from St. Johns the day their picture was taken. Numbered by the photograph's original owner, they are: 1, Luther Cruit; 2, Dawson Trundle; 3, Bridge Spates in the bowler; 4, Charles Sellman; 5, Ernest Beall; 6, Jess Mossburg; 7, Maynard Sellman; 8, Hartley Wootton; 9, Grover Pyles; 10, Harry Talbott; and 11, Randolph Luhn. Courtesy of Charles & Dorothy Elgin

Pretty Virgie Staley holds an armful of wild flowers that she has picked from the banks of Ten Mile Creek near the "Beauty Spot" created by her father, Fleet Staley, for his summer guests at the Fleet Staley Hotel.

People fled Washington in the summertime and came out to the country on the Metropolitan Branch of the B & O Railroad. Fleet Staley built his resort to give them a place to stay, and developed the private park he called his Beauty Spot. Today the flowers are gone, and the site is under the waters of the lake at Boyds. Courtesy of Nell Staley

Judge P. Hicks Ray sits at his carved and polished wood desk at the old county courthouse, his important papers weighted with a brick to keep them from being blown away. The window is open to catch any summer breeze, and the interior shutter can easily be closed in drafty wintertime. The iron pipe behind Perry Waters, the judge's clerk, may be a mail chute. Courtesy of Eleanor Hobbs Bailey

In the early 1900s, nearly everyone in rural Montgomery County raised turkeys, and Jessie Elgin Ritchey (right) and Emma Douglas Hodgson were no exception. Courtesy of Charles and Dorothy Elgin

This is the family of John Howard. John Howard donated the land for the schoolhouse on Howard Chapel Road, and he contributed generously to the church across the road from the school. From left to right are Christeen Howard Vonce, Leon Vonce, Hattie S. Howard, and Hallie Howard Denby. Leanna Howard is seated. Courtesy of Mabel Howard Lawson

A steam tractor demonstrates its ability by pulling a log at the Rockville Fair. Courtesy of Eveleen Hobbs Carter

Mrs. Harriett Thomson rides side-saddle on her horse, The Pink Admiral, by Columbian out of a standardbred mare, at the Chevy Chase Hunt in 1911. Courtesy of Edith Ray Saul

Marian Love, an orphan, came to Montgomery County in the early 1900s. She married Herbert Howard, the grandson of Enoch George Howard, and she had one child. She worked very hard and died of tuberculosis at the age of twenty. Courtesy of Mabel Howard Lawson

Reuben T. Baker worked hard as a tenant farmer in Redland and Darnestown. By 1902, however, he and his wife, Mary Belt Baker, had saved enough money to buy a substantial farm of their own in Colesville. In 1909 the prosperous Mr. Baker took his two grown children, Henry F. Baker and Margaret K. Baker (Hobbs), to Washington to have their picture taken. Photograph by C. E. Kerfoot, Washington, D.C.; courtesy of Eveleen Hobbs Carter

This circa 1910 photograph shows two policemen: Ruby Downs, on the left, and his unidentified companion. Courtesy of Mamie Berry Curlis

William and Maria Elizabeth Lorraine Waters of Pleasant Fields, Germantown, enjoy an afternoon on a pier, circa 1910.

When the Waters family brought their first parcel of land in the area encompassed by today's Germantown masterplan, the deed was recorded at the Frederick County Courthouse. Richard Montgomery and George Washington, too, were unknown young men in 1755, the date a previous William Waters purchased the first part of his 816-acre estate, Conclusion.

This William Waters, however, lived in Prince George County. His son, Basil Waters, inherited Conclusion. Basil married Anne Pottinger Magruder, daughter of Colonel Zadok Magruder, a Revolutionary War officer. Basil built his bride a brick house and gave Conclusion a new name, Pleasant Fields. Two daughters, Susannah and Mary, and four sons, Zachariah, William, Robert, and Zadok Magruder Waters, were born there. Mary died in infancy. Tragedy struck harder in April 1824. Anne, aged forty-five, Susannah, aged eighteen, and nine-year-old Robert died and were buried in a quickly established family graveyard on the farm. The cause of death was listed as black measles.

Basil's son, Zachariah, inherited Pleasant Fields when his father died in 1844 at age eighty-three. Included in Basil's will were the family slaves. To Zachariah were left twelve slaves: George, Richard, Thomas, Mary, Clair, Charlotte, Jack, Carolina, Mariah, Horace, Nelson, and Harriet. William received three slaves: Gubo, Prifo, and Ellen; and Zadok Magruder got the slaves Otho, Mary Ann, Eliza, Kitty, Louisa, and Bill, according to Basil Water's will,

recorded in the Montgomery County Courthouse, Liber Y, Folio 338.

Zachariah sold Pleasant Fields to his cousin, William Alexander Waters, a physician. Dr. Waters deeded the farm to his son, Charles Clark Waters. Each successive owner farmed the land in the crop of the day, from tobacco, to wheat, to corn.

Charles Clark Waters completed the final addition to the house and included improvements such as the

ice pond shown in the photograph. Ice was cut from the pond in wintertime and layered with straw in the icehouse, providing for iced tea and ice cream in August. But in the spring and fall, the pond was a fine spot for his children, William and Maria, to fish.

The Waters family lost Pleasant Fields during the Great Depression. But the grand house still stands and the land, although surrounded with

housing, is carefully farmed. From wilderness, to plantation, to farmland, to meticulously zoned and controlled development, the Waters family farm is a microcosm of Montgomery County history. Courtesy of Marian Waters Jacobs and the Montgomery County Historical Society

By the early 1900s, several trolley lines were carrying passengers in Montgomery County. The lines included the Rock Creek Railway, the Glen Echo Railway, the Washington and Glen Echo Railway, the Connecticut Avenue Line, the Washington and Great Falls Railway, the Georgetown and Tenallytown Railway Company of the District of Columbia, the Tenallytown and Rockville Railway Company and the Washington and Rockville Electric Railway Company. But public transportation in Montgomery County did not last long. By 1914, when this picture was taken, many of the tracks were already abandoned. The ones shown may have been part of the line to Bethesda Park on Wisconsin Avenue, an amusement park with a ferris wheel and a dance pavilion which was destroyed by a hurricane in 1896 and never rebuilt.

This trestle is near Sycamore Island and provided a challenging Sunday afternoon hike in 1914 for Harriette H. Esch (center) and Larry (left) and Ethel Prior, all of Kirke Street in Chevy Chase. Courtesy of Harriette H. Esch and Marion Esch Potter

Harriette H. Esch, Ruth Sieker, and an unidentified friend enjoyed an unusually mild New Year's Day in 1914. They are shown seated on a lock of the C & O Canal. Courtesy of Harriette H. Esch and Marion Esch Potter

110

One of these children grew up to buy this one-room schoolhouse— little Mamie Berry (in the center, toward the right), who wears a white pinafore and a ribbon holding up her long curls. She converted Seneca School (also called Berryville) on Berryville Road into a comfortable and attractive home.

The students (circa 1910) are, from left to right in the front row, Doyle Lowery; James Wilson; Raymond Mossburg; unknown; Raymond Davis, holding the slate; Upton Riley, Huston Downs, unknown; Roy Davis; and Harry Curtis. In the second row are: unknown, Clarine Miles, Mary Mossburg, Charlie Lowery, Ernest Riley, Mamie Berry, Leon Lowery, Virginia Miles, Will Pollard, and Tom Downs. In the back row are: Reeves; Elsie Peter; Raymond Riley; Helen Downs; Elsie Miles; the teacher, Mrs. Rhodes; Blanche Downs; Margarete Peter; Gladys Miles; and Walter Collier.

The Laytonsville School, built in 1912, was replaced by a new school building on the same site in 1951. From the collection of Roger Lamborne

111

Ida May Moore, pictured here, married Walter Thomas Allnutt on November 20, 1912. A few years earlier Ida May's schoolteacher, Blanche Braddock Cramer, and her school superintendent, Earle B. Wood, had sent the young lady to special classes because she was exceptionally bright.
Courtesy of Gladys King

No longer educated in a one-room schoolhouse, Kensington youngsters of 1919 gathered in front of their consolidated school in a day when bare feet seemed to be a popular style for little boys.
Courtesy of Edith Ray Saul

Augusta Ward, the daughter of Harrison Ward, married Charles Dow King on November 29, 1911. Customs of the day called for a dark, wool traveling suit and a wide-brimmed hat trimmed with silk flowers for the bride.

The groom dressed in high style, too, and wore a dark, three-piece suit and high button shoes. The pleasant expression on Mr. King's face can be seen today on the faces of the many King descendants. Courtesy of Harrison and Gladys King

The park Glen Echo began when Edmund and Edwin Baltzley, twin brothers from Philadelphia, planned an exclusive resort surrounded by mansions such as the stone castles they built for themselves.

Three street railways served the resort, the Glen Echo Railway, the Connecticut Avenue Line, and the Washington and Great Falls Railway.

Taking advantage of the excellent public transportation, the Baltzleys appealed to property buyers, advertising Glen Echo as "The Rhine country of Washington" overlooking "the river, picturesque, wild and romantic."

They added the Glen Echo Chautauqua Association in 1891. The chautauqua was destined to have one grand and glorious year when the immense stone amphitheatre was filled to its capacity of ten thousand people. But the following year typhoid fever struck in epidemic proportions, and the chautauqua was forced to close.

It remained for the urban transportation company, Capital Traction, to consolidate the railways and open Glen Echo as a successful amusement park, which is pictured here in 1914. Courtesy of Eveleen Hobbs Carter

Martha Farquhar and Rebecca Miller, photographed here in 1915, were members of the Women's Christian Temperance Union of Montgomery County, which received a certificate of incorporation in 1915, although the organization had been active since 1874. Chapters throughout the county included a W.C.T.U. branch in Sandy Spring, Oakdale, Laytonsville, Kensington, Gaithersburg, Rockville, Colesville, Spencerville, and Fairland. Courtesy of Mrs. Eva Watkins

The Women's Christian Temperance Union organized in 1874. Frances Willards led the movement, and her Heavenly Birthday, February 17, is still celebrated with luncheons, programs, and flowers.

The Colesville W.C.T.U. Hall is pictured here in 1898, the same year it was built, but the first Montgomery County W.C.T.U. had met in Spencerville in the year of national organization; Mary Jane Duvall was president, and Lillie B. Stabler was vice president.

The Spencerville W.C.T.U. remains active with close to a hundred members in 1982. Courtesy of Ruth Hobbs Minnick

This is the Colesville School in 1915. In the front row from left to right are Joe Bean, Ida Johnson, Richard Bean, Catherine Johnson, Ignata Lechlider, Edith Hobbs, Lester Johnson, Donald Hobbs, and Amelia Lechlider. In the second row are James Anderson, Edward Lechlider, Estelle Thompson, Irving Davis, Betty Ray, Alvin Wall, Melvin Woodard, and Dalton Johnson. In the third row are William Thompson, Dorothy Cissel, Mary Tucker, Edith Veitch, Clarence Lechlider, Gladys Baker, Louise Hutchinson, and Mary Hutchinson. In the fourth row are Mae Hobbs, Ethel Christopher, Helen Lechlider, Forest Thompson, and Harry Woodard. In the rop row are Catherine Hutchinson; Mildred Ray; Sophia Davis; the teacher, Luther M. Watkins; Helen Thompson; Lulu Richardons; and Maurice Nicholson. Courtesy of Mary Hobbs Beorum

On the Fourth of July at the baseball park in Kensington, circa 1915, each youngster wears white and carries an American flag. Courtesy of Judge Alfred Noyes

Montgomerians called it "The Electric," and they loved the trolley, shown here coming into Kensington. Courtesy of Malcolm Walters

One passenger boards at the rear of the electric railway, traveling to Chevy Chase, circa 1915, and a second buys a newspaper from a paper boy. From the collection of LeRoy O. King; courtesy of the Montgomery County Historical Society

In 1913 Senator Newland's original Kirke Street in Chevy Chase looked quite different from its present appearance. Courtesy of Harriette H. Esch and Marion Esch Potter

Women marched for suffrage in front of the Capitol in 1915. Many Montgomery County women joined the march, among them Ethel Rose Reid of Burdette. It was relatively easy for her to go to Washington, although she lived on a farm in rural Montgomery County. She boarded the Metropolitan Branch of the B & O railroad at Boyd's Station and got off at Kensington, where she caught "The Electric" streetcar on Connecticut Avenue and rode to the march's starting point. Tracks in the foreground indicate that Ethel could have ridden very close to this spot.

Later, she married the boy next door, Charles G. Linthicum, to help with farm chores and raise a family. But never would she neglect to vote. From the Library of Congress; courtesy of the *Courier*

Looking like a typical suburban homeowner of the 1900-1920 period, Fred Esch left his new house in Chevy Chase each morning, carrying a briefcase and wearing a neatly blocked hat and a celluloid collar. He walked the few blocks to the Connecticut Avenue trolley station, where he took the trolley to his government office in Washington, D.C. Courtesy of Henriette H. Esch and Marion Esch Potter

The Laurel stage leaves Sandy Spring Store in 1917 for its final trip. The old gray mare and her bay mate with their well-trimmed hooves and carefully brushed manes are about to be replaced with gasoline power. From the collection of the Sandy Spring Museum; courtesy of Roger Lamborne

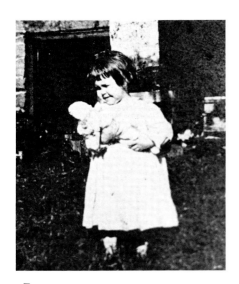

Louise Gott cuddles a rag doll in front of Buck Lodge, the house near Dawsonville that belonged to her grandfather, Benjamin Collinson Gott.

The doorway behind the doll's head leads to the cellar where Mariel Rebecca Gott, Benjamin Gott's wife, kept her mare during the Civil War. Troops from both sides roamed the fields and roads looking for food and mounts. All of the Gotts' horses were stolen except for one, Mariel Rebecca Gott's riding mare, which was saved by a very determined owner. When she heard soldiers approaching, Mrs. Gott led her favorite mare down the steps into the dirt-floored basement beneath the house. There it stayed until Mrs. Gott was certain that all the troops were gone. Then came the hard part. Although the animal had gone graciously down the stairs, she flatly refused to come up them. The reluctant horse eventually came out of the basement, but not without considerable coaxing.

Benjamin Gott's home was built in 1812 by his father, Richard Gott. It was part fieldstone and part frame, with a front porch reached by a series of steep steps; it contained a schoolroom. The kitchen was separate, connected by a covered passageway. A stone stable housed the horses. Additional outbuildings included three red-painted frame buildings, an icehouse, a cooling house, a spring house, a cow barn, and a family graveyard. All are gone now. Courtesy of Louise Warfield Gott Bowman

Mariel Rebecca Gott, who hid her horse in the cellar during the Civil War, is shown. Photo by Bacrach and Brothers, Washington, D.C.; courtesy of Louise Warfield Gott Bowman and Jean King Phillips

This photograph was taken during the fiftieth wedding anniversary of John T. Warfield and Rebecca Virginia Dorsey Warfield in 1917; they are surrounded by their descendants.

From left to right in the front row are Kenneth Higgins, Seth Henry Warfield, Eugenia Warfield, John T. Warfield, Eugene Higgins, Mary Cornelia Warfield, Vernon Griffith; Jessie T. Higgins, and Louise Warfield Gott (later, Bowman).

In the second row are Edwin Higgins, Lucile Higgins (Clark), Mariel Virginia Gott (Howard), Daisy Higgins (Richards), Cornelia Warfield (Griffith), and Warfield Higgins.

In the third row are Stantion Pilcher; Jennie Warfield; Hannah Warfield (Pilcher); William Warfield, Lillian Griffith (Warfield); John T. Warfield, the patriarch; Rebecca

Virginia Dorsey Warfield, the matriarch; Molly Warfield (Higgins); and Greenberry Gaither Griffith.

In the back row are Seth Warfield, Reuben Warfield, Annie Warfield (Gott), Nathan Elwood Gott, Lee Clagett Warfield, and Charles Higgins. Courtesy of Louise Warfield Gott Bowman and Jean King Phillips

Built in 1857, the sandstone-constructed Union Arch looks like a rainbow in the sky over the small hotel. Guests apparently arrived by descending the steep steps from Conduit Road (MacArthur Boulevard), strolling the rustic path, and crossing the picturesque low bridge.

Today the small hotel is gone, but the bridge remains. Courtesy of Library of Congress

At the Montgomery Lane-Wisconsin Avenue intersection near Edgemoor in Bethesda, W. J. O'Donnell once sat beside his blacksmith shop, patting the head of his old hound dog.

Shown here, Mr. O'Donnell's new wagon wheel replacements contrast sharply with the trolley tracks in the foreground. The smith had enough customers, but he augmented his income by renting advertising wall space to the Corby's Mother's Bread and Laxtos companies. Courtesy of Brooks Photographers

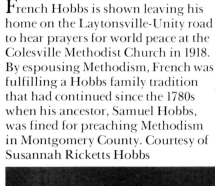

French Hobbs is shown leaving his home on the Laytonsville-Unity road to hear prayers for world peace at the Colesville Methodist Church in 1918. By espousing Methodism, French was fulfilling a Hobbs family tradition that had continued since the 1780s when his ancestor, Samuel Hobbs, was fined for preaching Methodism in Montgomery County. Courtesy of Susannah Ricketts Hobbs

In 1918 an epidemic called Spanish influenza spread over the county. Meetings were cancelled; churches were closed and members urged to pray. Death resulted from complications which followed the flu; the most common complications were pneumonia, meningitis, and ear infections.

Doctors were especially vulnerable, and three local physicians died within two weeks: C. N. DeVilbiss, Carlton N. Etchison, and John D. Holland. At that time the only hospital in the county was the privately owned Seventh-Day Adventist Hospital in Takoma Park. Concerned about the complete lack of such a facility for most of the

county. Dr. Jacob W. Bird opened Wrenwood Hospital in a two-story dwelling on New Hampshire Avenue in Ashton, near Olney.

This was quickly outgrown, so he purchased twelve acres from the widow of Dr. William E. Magruder and built a modern, one-floor, H-shaped hospital. His emphasis was on excellent nursing care and a well-equipped operating room.

Dr. Bird opened his hospital, the Montgomery County General Hospital, in 1921 to enthusiastic community acclaim. This photograph shows the dedication ceremonies of the hospital. From the collection of Montgomery General Hospital; courtesy of Roger Lamborne

World War I was a stern reality and the Kensington Women's Club expressed its patriotism with a wartime pageant in 1917, "Spirit of America." The United States was created by people of all nations, and women's club members expressed their appreciation by dressing in the costume of foreign lands, native Americans, and two timely heroes, Uncle Sam and Charles Lindbergh.

From left to right in the first row are Mrs. Jean Dunkin Noyes, Mrs. Ronsaville, Mrs. Graves, Mrs. Farrell, unknown, Mrs. Hay, Mrs. William Ashworth, unknown, Marian Ronsaville, Elizabeth Williams, and unknown. In the second row are unknown, unknown, Virginia Ronsaville, Edith Wright, Mrs. Wakefield, Mrs. Milburn, Mrs. John Williams, and unknown. In the back row are unknown, Mrs. James Adams, unknown, Mrs. William Lewis, unknown, and Mrs. Grace Ryan. Identifications by Judge Alfred Noyes, courtesy of Malcolm Walters

The children of the Kensington Women's Club echoed their mothers' patriotism with a pageant of their own. Courtesy of Judge Alfred Noyes

Five patriotic ladies of White Oak seriously support the war effort. Miss Julit Harper is seated in the center of the front row. On weekdays, Miss Harper worked at the Bureau of Printing and Engraving, taking advantage of her county's proximity to Washington, D.C. Courtesy of Ione Beall Sorensen

These ladies in Boyds supported the American Red Cross by knitting socks for the boys over there, circa 1917. Courtesy of the late Eleanor Maughlin Young

Patriotic Montgomerians helped get in the crops during World War I. Here, Edith Ray Saul works with an unidentified soldier to shuck corn near Kensington. Courtesy of Edith Ray Saul

In 1917 cadets marched out to greet the day at Briarley Hall in Poolesville. Reflecting the patriotism of World War I, a military academy took over the girls' school of the same name, which had been established in 1899. Courtesy of Charles and Dorothy Elgin

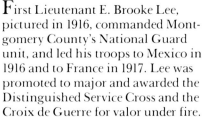

First Lieutenant E. Brooke Lee, pictured in 1916, commanded Montgomery County's National Guard unit, and led his troops to Mexico in 1916 and to France in 1917. Lee was promoted to major and awarded the Distinguished Service Cross and the Croix de Guerre for valor under fire.

After World War I he shifted to different activities, but he remained a member of the National Guard and earned a promotion to the rank of colonel in World War II. Courtesy of Blair Lee III

Airplanes were open, quite primitive, and without parachutes, but this fearless Quaker from Sandy Spring, Lieutenant Arthur Douglas Farquhar, piloted the flimsy craft over the Austrian Alps during World War I. He was knighted for bravery by the Italian government, and he is shown here with his sash; he also received the Distinguished Service Cross and the Croix de Guerre.

Returning home to The Cedars, Farquhar helped found the Sandy Spring Volunteer Fire Department and the Sandy Spring Lion's Club, and he served as director of the Mutual Fire Insurance Company. Courtesy of Helen Thomas Nesbitt Farquhar

Clayton Ricketts, who was from Quince Orchard, had his picture taken when he was overseas with Lieutenant E. Brooke Lee in Bordeaux, France. When he came marching home again, he married the prettiest girl in Seneca, Helen Peters. Courtesy of Mamie Berry Curlis

In 1919 gas stations were as few and far between as the tin lizzie's tank was small. Carl Esch fills 'er up in Chevy Chase. Courtesy of Neal and Marion Esch Potter

One month after she married her soldier, Clayton Ricketts, Helen Peters Ricketts died from a fall off her horse. Courtesy of Mamie Berry Curlis

Rock Creek Park had playground equipment as early as 1919. Fred H. Esch teaches the art of the seesaw to his daughters, Marion (left) and Jane. As Mr. Esch worked for the federal government and had only one day off each week, the trip to the park probably took place on a Sunday. Courtesy of Neal and Marion Esch Potter

A Montgomery County volunteer fire department assumed a patriotic pose just before the big parade on the Fourth of July, 1927. Kensington people celebrated the holiday with baseball games and another pageant, which always included Chester Dixon's reading of the Declaration of Independence. Courtesy of Malcolm Walters

In the Montgomery County countryside, the sunniest skies portend the worst summer storms. Thus, the pleasant decade before the Great Depression shed an aura of peace and plenty from the newly mechanized farms to the blossoming suburban towns that lined the roads near Washington, D.C.

It was a good time, a time of enthusiastic citizen organizations and the men's quartet from Darnestown Presbyterian Church at the three o'clock worship service; a time of bustling grain mills and belching tractors; Hupmobiles and cement roads; a time of ice cream for two thousand Methodists at the Washington Grove campground; a time of running water, electric lights, telephones, and radios; a time of W.C.T.U., whiskey stills, and professional police; a time of the Maryland-National Capitol Park and Planning Commission; and a time of E. Brooke Lee, the county boss.

Wages were $1 an hour, movies a quarter, or fifteen cents for kids. And a seven-room house in Rockville cost $1,150 with easy terms. A Nash touring car was $935, and a new Ford cost $295 F.O.B. Detroit.

Through their local paper, Montgomerians discovered the moving picture shows playing in Rockville at the Seco, a "place of mirth and joy." They learned a new vocabulary from Prince Albert roll-your-own tobacco advertisements, words such as "joyhandout" and "smokehappiness." They were invited to a live performance at the Seco to hear the Marine Kings of Jazz-bo; to see snappy, scrappy boxers; to have some complimentary good smokes; and to hear close-up harmony and dragout syncopation by the band. Men only, please: "It's a stag affair," said the *Sentinel*.

It was, for the most part, a gentle time. The new technology boomed, but the changes could be understood and explained. Electricity seemed like magic, but it was predictable. A man could work out his problems, determine his own destiny, work hard and get ahead, save pennies and buy a house.

Families stayed close. One son took over the farm, and the other boys went to work at the local stores and built houses on corners of the homestead—the parcel of land near the road. The girls got married, and they learned to cook and can the modern way from Miss Blanche E. Corwin, the county's home demonstration agent from 1922 to 1932.

Growth continued to be a significant aspect of Montgomery County life, as population bounded ahead by 41 percent during the twenties, centered in Bethesda and Wheaton. The new suburban Montgomerians demanded a good education for their children, and graded, multiroomed facilities were built. Schools began to consolidate, and the number of schoolhouses began to drop from 108 in 1917 to 66 in 1949.

School buses were purchased to transport white children to the big new schools. However, schools for blacks were not so conveniently reached. Students had to walk miles or grow up without schooling. Black educators received books and equipment discarded from white schools, and they were paid far less than their white counterparts. In 1922 black teachers could earn a maximum of $520, while, at the same time, white teachers could reach a top salary of $2,100.

Prohibition was the law, and the professional police department, needed to enforce this law, was formed in 1922. Two years later the police found "the largest still ever captured in the county," according to the *Sentinel*; it was seized by Police Chief William L. Aud.

During this decade, E. Brooke Lee assumed the role of a strong leader, and he became a benign but very powerful county boss. In 1927 Lee put together an agency of professional planners, the Maryland-National Capital Park and Planning Commission, to serve Prince George and Montgomery counties.

In combination with the Washington Suburban Sanitary Commission, M-NCPPC provided a professional approach that resulted in orderly development. The two bicounty agencies had the authority to issue bonds and make decisions beyond the limits applied to county agencies. They planned for and regulated new school buildings, parks, new shops, and sewer lines, all related to suburban growth.

And Montgomery County changed from a rural to a suburban county. ■

During the building boom of the 1920s the Silver Spring Building Supply Company, located next to the railroad tracks, couldn't hire enough men to drive their trucks or load the rail cars parked on the siding. Courtesy of Malcolm Walters

Sawing, planing, ripping, cutting—the Eisenger Mill in Bethesda was caught up in the thriving Montgomery County housing industry of the 1920s. Courtesy of Malcolm Walters

Alden A. and Charlotte Waugh Potter bought this thirty-five-acre farm in the rural Montgomery County countryside in 1920 and took a picture of their new home. Many changes later took place. Since the farm was near Georgetown, where canal boats docked and unloaded, Mr. Potter was able to buy lime and fertilizer handily and improve the soil. He was also close to several local water-powered mills, and hauled grain to be ground into livestock feed. He built a dairy route and delivered milk to customers in nearby Washington. He added plumbing to the house and removed the privy shown in the photograph. Adding to the family income, Charlotte Potter was one of the first to rent a stall at the Farm Women's Market in Bethesda where she sold produce from her garden, tarts and cookies from her kitchen, and firewood from her woodland.

The Potters improved the entrance lane and planted flowers to grace the premises. But, bowing to progress, the property was forcibly sold to make way for updated transportation, and today the house site is the interchange of the Capital Beltway (Route 495) and the George Washington Parkway. Courtesy of Neal and Marion Esch Potter

Neal Potter takes the reins, prophetically, in 1922. In spite of an exceptionally heavy snowfall the previous night, Neal's father, Alden A. Potter (standing), was determined to deliver his milk. When the drifts proved too deep for his truck, he built a sled, hitched up the horse, and got the milk to his customers. Neal's brother, Lloyd A. Potter, sits in the sled, tending the tall containers of milk. Years later, Neal Potter served on the first Montgomery County council, a position he continues to fill in 1984. Courtesy of Neal and Marion Esch Potter

Louise Gott (Bowman), a beauty from an old Montgomery County family, smiles for her photographer in the 1920s. Photograph by Cline-dinst, Washington, D.C.; courtesy of Jean King Phillips

135

Many Montgomerians switched from trains and trolleys to cars during the 1920s. On Sunday afternoons they enjoyed driving on the National Highway from Georgetown to Frederick and farther west. The Weems Inn in Middlebrook was built to serve these hungry tourists, and it was known far and wide for its delicious chicken dinners, fixed country style in china serving bowls. After dark, guests could find their cars by the light of the kerosene lantern near the roof. Courtesy of the Boyds/Clarksburg/Germantown Historical Society

Standard equipment in the new Montgomery suburbs was the hand-operated lawnmower, shown here in the hands of little Jane Esch, circa 1920. Courtesy of Neal and Marion Esch Potter

Baseball was the "in" thing in the 1920s. Every town had its team and, with a star like Walter Johnson just around the bend in Germantown, it is no wonder that the village of Boyds won the Montgomery County baseball championship in 1922. In the front row, left to right, are _____ Lemerick, second baseman; DeLaney Best, shortstop and third baseman; Pat Roche, second baseman; and Findlay Pollock, catcher. In the middle row are James "Put" Gill, catcher, a wounded veteran from World War I; Laurence Burdette, the superb pitcher; _____ Terflinger, manager; Bob Williams, outfielder; and Tuck Waters, standby pitcher. In the back row are Sonny Anderson, John Emory "Army" Pollock, and _____ Babyton. Courtesy of J. Harrington and Beulah M. Austin

A 1920s brochure promoting Montgomery County was published by Greater Montgomery County, Incorporated in Rockville, Maryland. It was printed by Judd and Detweiler of Washington, D.C.

According to the pamphlet, "Glorious glimpses of America's most soul-satisfying landscapes are rolled into a single panorama here. Nowhere else in America can residents enjoy the unusual advantages made possible to dwellers in Montgomery County," with its pleasing climate. Also emphasized were the zoning regulations that prohibited the establishment of objectionable manufacturing plants: "Industry cannot encroach from the city to mar the countryside." In addition, the glamorous city of Washington was vaunted as "the threshold of Montgomery County," and residents could "share its stirring social life." Montgomery County was called "the actual realization of an ideal unachievable elsewhere." Not only was the county beautiful, but it was also safe, because "a competent police force of salaried and uniformed officers has kept the county free from the disorderly conditions of organized commercial vice." Courtesy of Eveleen Hobbs Carter

Maybe it's her trousers and helmet, but this old gray mare just ain't what she used to be. Members of the Kensington Volunteer Fire Department brought the mare in from pasture to appear in the Fourth of July parade with a banner reading "Kens. Vol. Fire Dept., 1909 to 1920." Courtesy of Malcolm Walters

A Confederate soldier overlooks the county seat, Rockville, facing south. The statue, erected in 1913, carries the message: "To our heroes of Montgomery County, Maryland. That we through life may not forget to love the thin gray line." Vinson's Drugstore is behind him, with its soda fountain and its nickel pay phone. Courtesy of Malcolm Walters

In 1923 Harriette Esch clipped this aerial view of Chevy Chase from the rotogravure section of the *Evening Star*. In the foreground is the Chevy Chase Club, where President Taft played golf in 1908. Connecticut Avenue connects one side of the picture to the other. Raymond Street runs diagonally across the right corner with Bradley Boulevard paralleling about a block south of Raymond but hidden by the trees.

Chevy Chase was one of Montgomery County's first planned subdivisions. Senator Francis G. Newlands, one of the county's first real estate developers, founded the Chevy Chase Land Company in 1887, just a few years after the Civil Service Act of 1883 made it possible for government workers in Washington to keep their jobs despite changes in administrations and thus be able to buy a house. Newlands developed a suburb of lasting beauty. He bought more than 1,700 acres and built large houses with community zoning, architectural controls, schools, churches, water, and sewers. He added the Chevy Chase Lake for charm and a trolley for the convenience of the government workers who would buy his houses.

And buy them they did! Government worker Fred H. Esch bought a house on Kirke Street in Chevy Chase in 1913. A later Esch home on Brookville Road is at the center top. Mr. Esch worked six days a week at the Interstate Commerce Commission. Mrs. Esch's mother, Georgina Fish, lived with the young couple and worked at the Veteran's Administration. Both rode the trolley downtown to the District of Columbia to work every day but Sunday.

In 1918 the family decided to move a little farther out in the country to Martin's Addition to Chevy Chase. They sold the Kirke Street house in two days, at a time when the Montgomery County housing market was booming.

In 1925 Mr. Esch and Mrs. Fish, together with other federal workers, had their work week reduced to five and one-half days, and the family rejoiced at this step into a life of leisure. Courtesy of Harriette H. Esch and Marion Esch Potter

Members of the Chevy Chase Fire Department look clean and impressive, as does their fire engine. Senator Francis G. Newlands's planned development, Chevy Chase, needed a fire department; these men filled the bill with their gasoline-powered fire engine, one of the first ones built. Courtesy of Malcolm Walters

Prominent Montgomery County businessmen and federal bureaucrats prepare for a swim at Chevy Chase Lake. Courtesy of Malcolm Walters

Trucks line up early at the train station and shovel in coal for home delivery in Bethesda. Courtesy of Malcolm Walters

The Chevy Chase Land Company installs a swimming pool. In the background is the Chevy Chase Lake trolley station, now located just over the Frederick County line above Hyattstown. It was moved and restored by Edward Knowles. Courtesy of Malcolm Walters

During a pleasant outing on Chevy Chase Lake, a young lady might lean back on the cushions and read poetry as her young man paddled the canoe.

In 1887 United States Senator Francis G. Newlands started the Chevy Chase Land Company, including the Rock Creek Railway that invited development up Connecticut Avenue to the district. Newlands also offered large building lots and Chevy Chase Lake as inducements to new construction. At the lake he built a powerhouse to run the streetcars, light the streets, and furnish electricity. The land company purchased more than 1,700 acres of land for a planned village with strict zoning and architectural controls. Courtesy of Malcolm Walters

The Maryland mine, one of several in Montgomery County, yielded small amounts of gold between 1900 and 1940. Located near Great Falls, it was already abandoned when this picture was taken.

Identified on the photograph by small letters, "a" was the trestle for ore cars; "b" was the primary crusher on "c," the concrete foundation, where the ore was crushed into three-inch pieces, lifted by a bucket elevator, and crushed again at "d." The ore then passed through "e," a ten-stamp mill and "f," a ball mill. At that stage, the ore passed through an impact amalgamator where it was combined with mercury and passed over concentrating tables where gold-bearing sulfide minerals were recovered. Courtesy of the U.S. Geological Survey

This is an abandoned gold mine near Great Falls. Not only gold but also mica was once mined in Montgomery County, but none of the ventures met with lasting success. However, the Clarke, Maryland, Ford, Watson, Montgomery, Eagle, Harrison, Irma, Kirke, and Bethesda mines produced about five thousand ounces of gold between 1866 and the late 1940s.

Gilmore's mica mine near Springbrook bustled in the 1880s, and it continued its success through the 1920s. The transparent sheets of mica were used for automobile windows and in the front doors of stoves. Courtesy of Edith Ray Saul, from "Living in Montgomery County, Maryland," Picture Portfolio Series

Mamie Berry was an Irish girl from her green eyes and playful smile to her high-top laced shoes with the stylish pointed toes. Mamie is shown before her marriage to John Curlis. Courtesy of Mamie Berry Curlis

In September in Montgomery County long ago, children of all ages and sizes, but not all colors, went to school together in one-room schoolhouses.

Shown here are six of the students who attended Boyds Negro School, circa 1920. From left to right in the front row are Mary Hebron, Clara Luckett and Bessie Hebron. In the top row are Della Hawkins, Mae Doy, and Mary Turner.

Their teacher, Mrs. Laura Halestock, taught the three R's and other subjects, too. She taught the youngsters to make mats from cornstalks; to sing tunes she played on the piano; to cook delicious, thick soup for their noonday meal; and to love one another and share what they had with those less fortunate. Courtesy of Clara Luckett Talley

"The 'Square' from the West," Square Corner in Olney (circa 1920), was the intersection of Routes 108 and 97. R. P. Soper stands at the left, ready to deliver both groceries and mail. Letters were slipped into the wooden box on his front porch should Mr. Soper's store happen to be closed. Courtesy of Roger Lamborne

The first school bus in Montgomery County and, reportedly, in Maryland, picked up children in rural Poolesville, brought them to Poolesville School, and delivered them home in the late afternoon. Courtesy of Charles and Dorothy Elgin

143

Two of the children who attended Boyds School in 1921 were wards of the orphan's court in Baltimore. Both Lola Benzinger and Walter Melvin lived with local farm families and helped with the chores. From left to right, seated, are J. Harrington Austin and Walter Melvin; standing are Thomas Nicholson; Laura Smith; Lola Benzinger; the teacher, Sarah Soper, with a hand on Lola's shoulder; James Boyd "Buddy" Maughlin; David Maughlin; and Charles Israel. Courtesy of Mr. and Mrs. J. Harrington Austin and Walter Melvin

Just off the school bus parked in front of Sherwood High School, two young boys in knickers wait before crossing the dirt road, circa 1920. Courtesy of Roger Lamborne

At White's Ferry, a cabled raft called the *General Jubal Early* carried the Fred Esch family and their brand-new, 1923 Mitchell automobile to Maryland from the Virginia shore of the Potomac.

In early autumn this part of the river is not very deep, a fact known by natives of nearby Poolesville such as Elijah White. In September 1862, Colonel White and his commanding officer, General Stonewall Jackson, led thirty thousand Confederate troops across the Potomac at this spot. While the band played "Dixie" on the Montgomery County shore, the infantrymen waded across, holding their rifles above their heads. Courtesy of Harriette H. Esch and Marion Esch Potter

In 1920 two little girls took their dollies for a walk in Chevy Chase on a dirt Brookeville Road near Bradley Lane. Jane (left) and Marion Esch (right) didn't worry about the wobbly vehicles in the background. Courtesy of Marion Esch Potter

Montgomerians have always loved to go to the beach in the summertime, and as soon as he bought his first automobile, Fred H. Esch of Chevy Chase took the family to Chesapeake Beach. But it rained, turning the dirt roads quickly to miry mud, and the Ford had to be rescued by a team of transportation experts from another century. Courtesy of Harriette H. Esch and Marion Esch Potter

This trolley station had already been abandoned when Harriette H. Esch was photographed visiting the site, circa 1920. Courtesy of Harriette H. Esch and Marion Esch Potter

Dirt roads were fine for horses but bad for cars; this Kensington road was covered with macadam soon after this photograph was taken. Here, an unidentified man holds his summertime straw boater beside his new Ford, circa 1924. Courtesy of Malcolm Walters

Isaac and Cassandra Swailes Bell, photographed here circa 1920, lived in many Montgomery County villages during the late nineteenth and early twentieth centuries. From Popular Grove to Tobytown, from Berryville to Sugarland, and from Emory Grove to Sandy Spring, the growing family with five boys and three girls farmed and kept a store. On Sundays they drove their horse and buggy to the nearest African Methodist Episcopal church; every summer they traveled to the Emory Grove Campground for the annual meeting.

The Bell family was firm in its political convictions; Isaac lent his talents to the Republican party and spoke at rallies throughout the area.

When the children graduated from elementary school, the Bell family moved to Washington. Jobs were easier to find in town, and the children could get more education there. Isaac went to work as a

doorman at Kann's Department Store, and Cassie made hats and dresses for Washingtonians. She was quite skillful and creative and also made all her own clothes, including the fashionable outfit she wears for the photographer. Courtesy of John Henson Bell

The Montgomery County police force had this photograph made by Malcolm Walters in 1927. The men were standing just outside their basement headquarters at the red brick courthouse, Rockville. Daily life for lawkeepers was different then; these policemen were especially adept at chasing bootleggers on their motorcycles, raiding illegal whiskey stills, and catching cattle rustlers. Should an emergency arise, they could always blow their whistles. Left to right they are Roy Snyder, Roy Bodmer, Guy Jones, Lawrence Claggett, Chief Alvie A. Moxley (seated), Harry Merson, Robert Darby, Joe Oldfield, and Earl Burdine. Courtesy of Malcolm Walters

An unidentified man stands on the wooden sidewalks of Poolesville with a pig under each arm. The gas streetlight at his left shoulder was one of several which were lit each night and snuffed out at dawn by Charlie Kohlhoss. Courtesy of Charles and Dorothy Elgin

Leatha Summerville and six unidentified children pose in front of her home on West Willard Road in Poolesville about 1919. Inside the house, with its broken windows and cedar shake roof, laundry hangs up to dry. Outside, the grass in the yard has almost disappeared under the shuffle of so many little bare feet. A bucket hanging from a nail on the tree indicates that the source of water was not within the house. The two benches in the yard appear to have come from a public building.
Courtesy of Charles and Dorothy Elgin

Montgomery County communities built their own churches and fire stations. One local group, the Modern Woodmen of America, had a band which played at many events throughout the country to raise money for worthy purposes, such as the fire station in Laytonsville. They are shown here at the Rockville Fair in 1924. Standing, from left to right, are Jerry Williams; Mr. Kimble; Francis Plummer; Professor Watkins, the leader, wearing a white shirt and tie; Howard Bosley; Guy Howers; Russell Moore; Will Gaither; William Hawkins; Charlie Fraley; Garner Duvall (the young boy); Ernest Hawkins; Ralph Sinyard; Koly Barber; and Clarence Green. Seated, from left to right, are Grover Armstrong, Dorsey Plummer, Chester Hawkins, Bill Williams, Luther Howard, and Leslie Duvall.
Courtesy of Harrison and Gladys King

149

Arthur G. "Doc" Elgin (right) and his brother, Charles W. Elgin (left), founded Elgin Brothers' Drug Store in 1910. Courtesy of Charles and Dorothy Elgin

The soda fountain at Elgin Brothers' Drug Store was the pride and joy of Poolesville. During Prohibition there was nowhere in Montgomery County where one could sit up to a bar and order a beer legally. At Elgin Brothers', however, Montgomerians could find a high stool like the ones pictured, plop their elbows on a spotless marble counter, and order a tangy lemon phosphate for a nickel or a creamy chocolate soda for ten cents. Each treat featured a squirt of syrup mixed by the pharmacists from a family recipe that is still carefully tended by a descendant. Courtesy of Charles and Dorothy Elgin

Spurrier's Store in Poolesville carried all sorts of dry goods as shown by owner Mr. Howard Spurrier, center, and Claude Reddick, on the left, with two unidentified clerks. Courtesy of Charles and Dorothy Elgin

This is Liberty Milling Company in Germantown, circa 1924. In 1888 the five Bowman brothers built a mill along the Metropolitan Branch of the B & O Railroad. Its capacity for rail shipment made the enterprise prosperous. It grew, and local wooden water-powered mills shut down.

Through World War I and World War II, this mill shipped flour overseas, providing for American soldiers as well as foreign troops. The original building burned about 1916 and was rebuilt in 1924. A. R. Selby purchased it and produced flour until the mill burned in the late 1960s. Courtesy of Jean King Phillips

Before television, pageants were a popular form of community entertainment. Fortunately, Montgomery County had a resident with an inventive, inquisitive mind who bought one of those funny-looking black boxes with fragile glass plates and took pictures of his friends and neighbors. His name was Malcolm Walters.

Malcolm Walters lives in the Kensington home where he was born in 1894. He remembers when horse-drawn sleighs and buggies stopped for repairs at the blacksmith shop on Georgia Avenue, and he recalls the election days when voters marked their choices on long paper ballots at a table set up in Hickerson's Grocery.

Mr. Walters took this photograph near the armory in Kensington. The continental soldier was his friend, the future judge Alfred Noyes. Paul Revere was played by Osmer Hartshorne and Benjamin Franklin by Jack Schrivener, but the woman who played Mrs. Revere is unidentified. To the right of Jack are Mrs. Kaiser, Marian Ronsaville, and William Armstrong. Courtesy of Malcolm Walters

On April 27, 1928, the Federation of Women's Clubs of Montgomery County presented a pageant at the Rockville Fairgrounds. Three hundred Montgomerians participated in the event, called a "Historical Spectacle" and containing "Twenty Episodes of County Progress." Governor Albert Ritchie was the guest of honor.

The federation, a very progressive group, invited a professional photographer, Malcolm Walters. Thus, Montgomerians of today have a visual record of Montgomery County's earliest days as portrayed by residents of 1928.

This scene shows "The Golden Age of Colonial Maryland," by the Dawsonville and Darnestown Inquiry Club. Courtesy of Malcolm Walters

On April 27, 1928, the federation's Gaithersburg branch presented "The Coming of the White Man," which depicted Leonard Calvert visiting Archiku, the chief of the Piscataways. Basil Waters played Calvert; William Griffith, the cavalier; John Caulfield, the Jesuit priest; Margaret Griffith, the Indian maid; Rich Caulfield and Elgie Riggs, Jr., the two Indians; Henry Riggs, the sailor; and Otho Trundle played Archiku. Courtesy of Malcolm Walters

On April 27, 1928, the Rockville and Cabin John branches of the federation presented a pageant depicting the first county court meeting at Hungerford's Tavern, called in 1777 to swear in the first sheriff of the county. Included in the presentation were Charles Jones, Richard Thompson, Samuel Magruder, James Offutt, Elisha Williams, Edward Burgess, William Deakins, and Brooks Beall, only seven of whom are shown. Courtesy of Malcolm Walters

Girls proudly participated in athletic events at the Rockville Fairgrounds on Educational Day, circa 1927. Educational Day began in 1914, with thousands of public school students traveling by train to Rockville. The organizers hoped to promote enthusiasm and support for public schools at a time of rising educational costs and considerable complaint among taxpayers.

The 1914 festivities began with a speech contest at the courthouse, which was won by E. S. Prescott, Guy Neel, Jonathan J. Baker, Wightman Smith, Paul Twomby, and Edgar Harbaugh Logan. Next, the thousands of students assembled and marched through town to the fairgrounds, led by the Rockville Band. Bursting into spontaneous yells and songs, the marchers, according to the local press, were received "amid exclamations of wonder and praise from onlookers."

At the fairgrounds the girls danced and drilled, and the boys competed in athletic contests such as broad jumps and relays. By 1915, girls were per-mitted to enter athletic events, a challenge which they readily accepted. The following year, officials eliminated the oratory and dance to devote the day to sports.

Left to right (front row), they are Helen Riggs (Hill), Alice Walker (Gloyd), Annie Walker, and unknown; (back row), Ethel Green, Mary Lee Griffith, Janet Walker, and Alverda White (back row).

Educational Day began in 1914 and continued annually until 1941.
Courtesy of Malcolm Walters

Competitors pose during Educational Day at Rockville in 1926. From the collection of Edith Ray Saul; courtesy of Malcolm Walters

Students from Kensington Elementary School assemble for Educational Day on May 8, 1926. The Rockville Fairgrounds grandstand is behind them. From the collection of Edith Ray Saul; courtesy of Malcolm Walters

By the mid-1920s, girls were permitted to participate in sports at Germantown High School. Courtesy of Ella Virginia Waters Gochenour

Sweet young ladies from Kensington prepare to play ball, their long stockings nattily held by garters at knee-length for the event. Courtesy of Malcolm Walters

155

In this photo G. W. Bell had just hung out the freshly killed Christmas geese and turkeys, enticing customers to his A & P store. Pillars were festooned with red crepe paper, countertop trees wrapped with tinsel, and the tub of fresh fish conveniently displayed. The bowl of fruit in the foreground could be purchased as a gift to the hostess of a party or gathering.

Mr. Bell always wiped his hands neatly on his large, white apron before waiting on customers, and he carefully removed his thumb from the sausage before reading his immaculate scales. His floors were kept clean and sweet-smelling because he swept them each evening with fresh sawdust.

This print was made from one of Malcolm Walters's many glass negatives. It is interesting to note the sharp image he captured, from the thirty-five cent frankfurters in the showcase at the front right; to the

three hams set on top of the side showcase; to the letters on the back wall, "Bake a Pie!" and "A & P, established 1859, where economy rules." Courtesy of Malcolm Walters

The Piggly Wiggly store in Rockville displays an appetizing array of fresh produce in its storefront. Courtesy of Malcolm Walters

With no hydrants available, Montgomery firefighters filled their tanks from a stream near a narrow dirt road lined with log houses. Courtesy of Malcolm Walters

In 1911 the Daughters of the American Revolution renamed the National Road the National Memorial Highway and commissioned a statue, the *Madonna of the Trails*, by sculptor Jo Davidson. Twelve copies were cast in concrete and placed along the pioneer road to the west. This madonna stood near the intersection of Wisconsin Avenue and Old Georgetown Road in Bethesda.

Copies were also placed in Washington, Pennsylvania; Wheeling, West Virginia; Springfield, Ohio; Richmond, Indiana; Vandalia, Illinois; Lexington, Missouri; Council Grove, Kansas; Lamar, Colorado; Albuquerque, New Mexico; Springerville, Arizona; and Upland, California.

In March 1982 the Montgomery statue was moved and carefully stored to prevent harm during the construction of the Bethesda subway station. The monument will be restored to Bethesda following the completion of the Metro station and set down in the public plaza planned for the area on top of the station. Courtesy of Malcolm Walters

In this group are the Montgomery County Board of School Commissioners with teachers and administrators of Kensington Elementary School. The hatless gentleman in the center of the front row is Edwin Broome, the county school superintendent; second from the left in the front row is Miss Hawk, a teacher. The first person on the left in the second row is Mrs. Grace Ryan, the principal of Kensington Elementary School. Courtesy of Malcolm Walters

Selected to illustrate the benefits of good nutrition, Neal Potter was presented to the photographer by an unidentified woman about 1924. With his clear bright eyes and his impish grin, he is the picture of good health. No wonder, as Neal's father, Alden Potter, owned the dairy with the cleanest milk in the county, measured by federal standards. His mother, Charlotte W. Potter, raised nearly all the family food in her organic garden. Courtesy of Neal and Marion Potter

Customers of the Al-in-One Radio Corporation could arrive by car or by train at the pleasant Halpine Station. Courtesy of Malcolm Walters

Judge Robert Peter and an unidentified lady admire a picture of General Richard Montgomery. Courtesy of Malcolm Walters

In this very modern (circa 1927) Montgomery County picture, electrical refrigeration makes ice cream a reality, and a gasoline-powered vehicle can be summoned to one's door by ringing Kensington 91. On the other hand, customers may be seated at the "up-to-date soda fountain" inside. Courtesy of Malcolm Walters

The Kensington Volunteer Fire Department Rescue Squad looks for survivors in a very wrecked car, but the jaunty striped ticking tacked to the door appears to be the only thing intact. Maynard Hawkins is the driver. Hezekiah Magruder sits beside him, and Boots Stubbs, who would have to cling to the pole if the car were in motion, stands and relaxes in the back. Courtesy of Malcolm Walters

A group of people keep a date for Saturday afternoon at McKeever's in Kensington. From the collection of Edith Ray Saul; courtesy of the Kensington Historical Society

Mother, may I go out to swim?
Yes, my darling daughter.
Hang your clothes on a hickory limb,
But don't go near the water.

Behind the questioning young girl, Montgomerians splash in the ol' swimmin' hole on the Northwest Branch, near the intersection of Kemp Mill and Randolph roads. Courtesy of Eveleen Hobbs Carter

Sweets to the sweet! A young man treats two pretty girls to a freshly baked pastry at the Community Bakery and Pastry Shop in Kensington. Courtesy of Malcolm Walters

James Anderson winks broadly, one arm around Woodward Adams and the other tapping the shoulder of his teacher, Miss Lillian Shuman. The remaining students, however, appear serious as they graduate from Fairland School's high school in January 1924. Courtesy of Emma Snyder Wootten

Watching the trains go by on the Metropolitan Branch of the Baltimore and Ohio Railroad are, from left to right, "Black Sammy" (at the far left), Eleanor Ray Maughlin, Eleanor Maughlin, Sarah Ellen Maughlin, and Dr. Anthony M. Ray. James Alexander Boyd built this house in Boyds and named it Bonnie Brae. Courtesy of the late Eleanor Maughlin Young

Parked near White Oak (now Hillandale Shopping Center) is Arthur Ayres, the driver. Lucy Beall and Ellsworth Wallich giggle in the rumble seat, and Ernest Cooney and Ione Beall pose on the running board. Courtesy of Ione Beall Sorensen

A 1927 bathing beauty rests at Indian Rock in Rock Creek. Courtesy of Malcolm Walters

The brand-new Little Tavern No. 6 sparkles in the sunshine, circa 1927. According to the plate beside the door, ladies are invited to share the bargain of hamburgers for a nickel. Courtesy of Malcolm Walters

Every day of the nine years that she taught at Boyds Negro School, Miss Lillian Giles played the piano and led the students in singing the Negro national anthem by James Weldon Johnson, "Lift Every Voice and Sing." Attempting to instill in the pupils hope for a brighter future, Miss Giles insisted they learn all three verses of the powerful song.

The 1928 class was more fortunate than earlier black children, in that they could go to high school in Montgomery County. Rockville High School was completing its second year as the first secondary school for blacks in Montgomery County. Before 1927 black youngsters continued school outside the county boundaries only.

Henrietta Thomas (Randolph) was one of the students; she is fourth from the left in the top row. Her grandfather, Harry Thomas, was a substantial landowner and farmer in Boyds. Courtesy of Boyds/Clarksburg/Germantown Historical Society

"Lift Every Voice and Sing"

Lift every voice and sing, Till earth and heaven ring,
    Ring with the harmonies of Liberty; Let our rejoicing rise
High as the list-ning skies, Let it resound loud as the rolling sea.
    Sing a song full of the faith that the dark past has taught us
Sing a song full of the hope that the present has brought us;
    Facing the rising sun of a new day begun,
Let us march on till victory is won.

Stony the road we trod, Bitter the chastening rod,
    Felt in the days when hope unborn had died;
Yet with a steady beat, Have not our weary feet
    Come to the place for which our fathers signed?
We have come over a way that with tears has been watered.
    We have come, treading our path thro' the blood of the slaughtered;
Out from the gloomy past, Till now we stand at last
    Where the white gleam of our bright star is cast.

God of our weary years, God of our silent tears,
    Thou who hast brought us thus far on the way;
Thou who hast by Thy might, Led us into the light,
    Keep us forever in the path, we pray
Lest our feet stray from the places, our God, where we met Thee,
    Lest our hearts, drunk with the wine of the world, we forget Thee;
Shadowed beneath Thy hand, May we forever stand
    True to our God, True to our native land

—James Weldon Johnson

Harrison Gilmore Ward and Ara Thrift Ward are shown on the occasion of their fiftieth wedding anniversary in 1929. The lives of Mr. and Mrs. Ward made a statement about Montgomery County people, a visual paragraph of words like "gentle," "kind," "sweet," and "temperate." Their lives illustrated continuity through six generations of one Montgomery County family. The Wards were people of the earth, and they were earthy, tending the soil as they cared for their marriage and bringing forth the best in both cases.

Harrison and Ara were married in 1879 at the home of the bride's father, Samuel Thrift, near Gaithersburg. They settled a few miles to the west on a lane with a whimsical name, Turkey Foot Road in Travilah. There they lived, tilling the Montgomery County soil, supporting the Darnes-

town Presbyterian Church, and raising a family, until their lifespans ran out.

With stability and kindness they lived together, and seven of their children were back home for the Ward's golden wedding anniversary in 1929: Alburtes Ward King, Mamie Ward Miles, Nettie Ward Boyer, Lula Ward Cissel, Garnet Ward, Spencer Ward, and William H. Ward.

Their grandchildren and great-grandchildren are providing stable leadership in Montgomery County communities today. Also present for their grandparents' celebration in 1929 were Harrison King; Dorothy, Betty Lou, Helen, and William Miles; Clark, Dawn, and Douglas Boyer; Albert and Howard Cissel; and Wards named Frances, Margaret, Jane, Hope, Ira, Paul, Alfred, Maurice, Charles, Herbert, and Wilbur. Today these grandchildren have children and grandchildren in Montgomery County. Courtesy of Malcolm Walters; identifications by Gladys King

This is the Rockville High School basketball team and its coach in 1928. Courtesy of Malcolm Walters

Girls with bobbed hair, white dresses, pearls, and mary janes wear the latest style for this 1920s event. Courtesy of Malcolm Walters

At the intersection of Clopper and Germantown roads, Horace Waters's general store served busy Germantown. The door is flanked by two examples of the Germantown bay window, designed with the builder's distinct architectural trademark. The Germantown window varied slightly in the two-story Germantown homes of Herbert King (now demolished) and John Upton Leaman, among others.

Preserved on film is an ordinary day at the Horace Waters store. Germantown men sat on the front porch and gossiped. An occasional farmer came by to purchase hemp for his single-tree harness; the hemp was measured and cut from the big bales outside.

From left to right, the men are Horace Waters, unknown, unknown, Fred Marth, Upton Leaman, John Leaman, and Wash Earp.

Mr. Horace Waters always wore a tie and white shirt to work, and this day is no exception. He made it a practice to write all purchases in his day book with meticulous care. And no one paid cash. Consequently, there was little reward for the robber who shot and killed Horace Waters shortly after this picture was taken. Courtesy of Idella Leaman

This unidentified gentleman stands by his brand-new car on the grounds of old Saint Mary's Church in Rockville. Courtesy of Malcolm Walters

During the 1930s, schools in Montgomery County began to switch from the all-ages, all-sizes variety. Students in this consolidated Montgomery County class are all about the same size and age. Courtesy of Malcolm Walters

The 1930s was a time of opposites, of foreclosures and progressive schools, evangelism and alphabet soup. Illustrated ads with visual appeal appeared in the local press for the first time, and billboards filled the horizon. Readers got the message: they simply *had* to have a telephone, and other amenities, as well.

Business had been good in the twenties. New houses, new schools, new grocery stores, and new automobile agencies had all been built to accommodate the crowds moving to Montgomery County. Money flowed like bootleg whiskey in a Silver Spring speakeasy, and, if cash was not handy, a smart businessman borrowed it. There seemed to be no end to the rainbow.

The crash came as the twenties faded, and the early thirties bore the brunt of the despair that followed. Farmers who could not sell their crops could not make the payments on new tractors. The motor agent, in turn, could not send his regular check to Detroit. He mortgaged the family estate in order to get money to pay his bills, and the bank auctioned his homestead from the steps of the courthouse.

Editors urged their readers to give up foolish spending. On December 15, 1932, the *Sentinel* announced, "There is a very general agreement among people of all classes this year that they will not waste good money on foolish Christmas gifts. Ordinarily millions of dollars are thrown away as well-meant but really unjustified Christmas spending. The exchange of cards is not only a great expense but also a great nuisance to everybody. This year nearly all of this is being cut out."

Montgomery looked for happy days again, and it voted for FDR over Hoover, 11,804 to 8,257.

And New Deal experts poured into Washington, stopping first to buy houses in Montgomery County.

The CCC, the PWA, the CWA, the PWP, and the AAA were part of Montgomery life. The CWA (Civil Works Administration) and the PWA (Public Works Administration) built eighty-two school privies and a few for private homes. The PWA commissioned a new post office for Rockville complete with a mural. The PWP (Public Works Program) improved the road from Georgetown to Frederick under the federal Old Trails Highway program. The CCC (Civilian Conservation Corps) set up camp in Garrett Park and blazed trails and built picnic tables in Rock Creek Park.

The AAA (Agricultural Adjustment Act) was controversial. Montgomery farmers, ever independent,

Taken about 1930, this photo of Sarah Elizabeth Brown Hilton (1856-1941) tells the story of a lifetime of hard work in rural Montgomery County in the late nineteenth and early twentieth centuries. Mrs. Hilton lived on a farm in King's Valley near Damascus and contributed heavily to the support of her family by growing, storing, and preparing all their food. She also made most of their clothes out of feed sacks, preferably chicken feed sacks because of their varied patterns of flowers and stripes. After she cut out a dress or a shirt from the feed sack, she made quilts from the scraps. This photograph shows her hands, wrinkled and worn from work.

Sarah had chickens, turkeys, geese, and a large vegetable garden. She stored what she did not can (mainly dried beans and potatoes) in the root cellar. Whenever she decided to have a chicken for dinner, she slaughtered and picked the fowl herself, in self-sufficient, independent style. She always wore a big apron, as shown, tied with string from the feed sack. When she gathered eggs, tomatoes, or cabbage, the apron became a handy container. Courtesy of Jean King Phillips

did not want government interference. Under the AAA, they were paid to *not* raise wheat (a strange new concept) and the price soared from 50¢ per bushel to $1.20. But along with the carrot came the stick; not only wheat fields but also pigpens were allotted a specific harvest number. If a sow had piglets exceeding government regulation, some had to be destroyed. And cows were to give just so much milk and no more; so at a time when hunger was common, milk was poured into the streets as county commissioners passed controversial milk regulations.

For the most part, however, the new programs were helpful. The FCA (Farm Credit Association) lent money to farmers for seed, fertilizer, and feed, and the FHA (Federal Housing Administration) insured mortgages, thus contributing to the housing boom still going on in Montgomery County.

In general, Montgomery County was in the process of emerging from a pioneer society of individual farm families with little cash but sufficient ability to produce their own needs and barter for the rest.

In the early 1930s a new Ford cost $430, and a farm family of five could eat well on a total of $176 a year for the groceries they could not raise in their fields and

The Montgomery County almshouse in Rockville stood near the Montrose Road-Interstate 270 exchange ramp. The house was demolished to make way for I-270. Courtesy of Montgomery County Historical Society

pastures. Not everyone had even that much cash, however, and sometimes they advertised for work. For example, C. L. Stratmeyer (1932 telephone number 29W) published an ad that stated that she would do hemstitching and picoting for ten cents a yard. In the same column, Bertha Brown wanted laundry to pick up and deliver. Montgomerians knew a sense of responsibility to reach out in compassion and help those who were unable to help themselves, and ladies of the McDonald Chapel in Quince Orchard organized an aid society to help feed the county's hungry.

A social service league formed. Dr. J. W. Bird, the chairman of the league, explained the need for social workers and, in the same statement, revealed a tradition of the times, the relationship of a physician with his patients.

"Just as a doctor goes into a home, takes a history of his patient, examines the patients, talks with the family...trying to get a picture of the illness," in the same way social service work, too, requires involvement with the personality and family of the client. Bird cautioned, "A layman may go down in his pocket and give a hungry man a dollar, but unless he knows the man and what giving a man money means, he cannot be sure that he is not pauperizing him through his generosity."

In those turbulent times Montgomerians drew closer to God, looking for an answer in the times of stress. The Reverend Henry Pasma of Rockville wrote a weekly column for the local newspaper, and Governor Harry W. Nice proclaimed a National Universal Bible Sunday for the state of Maryland. Evangelist Homer Rodeheaver came to Montgomery, and more than one

This is the Montgomery County Welfare Board, circa 1935. Social workers with the new agency found it difficult to handle the problems of the Great Depression with limited finances. Money ran out quickly, although the ranks of poor and needy people seemed endless. The board used newspaper ads to attempt to locate homes for children, such as these dated March 6, 1932, for "winsome little Mary, age 5, with

blue eyes," and a "fragile boy of 14."
In 1937 the county's welfare board dealt with cases including 436 "old age assistance" clients, 454 families that needed "child aid to dependent children," and 15 "needy blind" people.
Pictured beside the courthouse in Rockville with the bank and the firehouse in the background are Mrs. Anna F. Rice (later Noyes), fourth from the left in the front row. Others

include Miss Bennie Rice, Clair Stacy, Gladys Benson, Ruth Hays, Richard Hall, Alice Hostetler, Claudia Kyle, Louise Whitney, Mary Rome, Anna Oursler, Gertrude Wolfe, Jane Freeman, Julia Montgomery, Eleanor L. White, Winnie Ricketts, A. O. Denham, Christine Bryan, Stephen C. Cromwell, Ruth M. Strother, and Lucille Kessler. Courtesy of William Fawsett Rice

thousand people crowded the chapel of Neelsville Presbyterian Church to hear him sing and call repentant sinners to the altar. Church officers Harry Hoskinson, A. R. Selby, and William Waters were overwhelmed and asked the police to come and direct traffic. More people came than would fit inside the church, and folding chairs were quickly borrowed from the Reuben Pumphrey Funeral Home and set up in the churchyard. Loudspeakers were placed on the chapel roof to enable everyone to hear.

Economics improved after Rodeheaver's 1935 revival. The New Dealers and other federal program personnel demanded more houses in Montgomery County. Homes sprouted in fields that had grown wheat the year before. The countryside bloomed with new roads, new schools, and new privies. Illustrated ads bombarded the people with new wants, and Montgomery County prepared for the 1940s.

Next door to Montgomery County, the city of Washington escalated in position during the forties and became not only the pivot of a nation, but a major world power. Central figures of the federal administration lived in the county and lent their expertise to develop good local government, too.

The county continued to shift political party dominance to a Republican majority until, in 1944, Charles Jamison was the sole Democrat elected to the Board of County Commissioners. In 1940 Montgomery chose FDR, but the citizens voted for Dewey in 1944 and 1948.

America went to war again, and all Americans were affected by it. From Montgomery County alone, 189 men died in World War II.

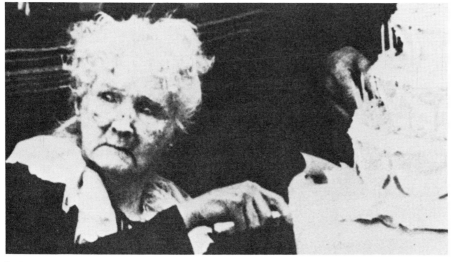

Mother Jones celebrated her 100th birthday on May 1, 1930 in Silver Spring. The ancient labor leader and union organizer stood amid masses of flowers beside a tall pile of congratulatory telegraph messages. She cut her huge pink and white cake with a withered, shaking hand, but she faced the cameras and gave a fiery speech for women's rights.

"America was not founded on dollars, but the blood of men who gave their lives for your benefit," she said. "A wonderful power is in the hands of women, too, but they don't know how to use it.

"Capitalists sidetrack women into clubs and make ladies out of them. Nobody wants a lady. They want women. Ladies are parlor parasites" (*Sentinel*, May 9, 1930).

A band played, refreshments were served all day long, and people streamed up the flag-lined, dirt road to congratulate the nationally known woman.

Mother Jones was born in Ireland, but she spent most of her life traveling the United States working for labor rights, particularly for miners. She lived her final months in Silver Spring at the home of a retired miner, Walter Burgess. Courtesy of *United Mine Workers Journal*

The consolidated Germantown School held classes for these fifth graders and for high school students, too. Courtesy of Ella Virginia Waters Gochenour

On the home front, ration stamps, not cash, determined how much sugar, coffee, fuel, oil, gas, and shoes the family would have. A new federal agency, the Office of Price Administration (OPA), regulated the project. Governor Herbert R. O'Conor appointed a local ration board, called the Montgomery County Commodity Rationing Board, which issued various ration books to residents. Blue stamps were needed to buy food and red stamps to purchase shoes. Sixteen stamps and eleven cents bought a can of corn; fifteen stamps and sixteen cents acquired a bottle of catsup; fifteen stamps and sixty-eight cents purchased three pounds of Spry shortening. Three gallons of gas or ten gallons of fuel oil could be exchanged for coupon five from "A Book," and purchasers of this amount of fuel were warned that it would have to last from March 7 to September 30.

Unemployment was, at last, eliminated. With the young men off to war and the crops to be harvested, every hand was needed. Schoolboys, Japanese-Americans, German prisoners of war, and the section crew from the Baltimore and Ohio Railroad were put to work on Montgomery's farms.

The world was in turmoil, and Montgomery County reflected the storm. The Farmers' Convention at Sandy Spring heard county residents John Muncaster, Carson Pope, and Roger Farquhar lead the call for county government reform. The farmers were soon joined by the League of Women Voters, the Civic Federation, and other groups.

The county was growing more urban and more vocal. Most of the citizens of Montgomery, it seemed, had complaints, and they mentioned them to their elected county officials. The commissioners, in turn, held public hearings, then sought professional advice from the Brookings Institution for Government Re-

The three-year-old Gaithersburg-Washington Grove Volunteer Fire Department and Ladies Auxiliary prepared for the annual big parade on the Fourth of July. Courtesy of Malcolm Walters

search. Led by Lewis Meriam, himself a resident of Kensington, Brookings recommended various changes. They suggested replacing the commissioners with a nonpartisan, nine-member city council, one from each election district and four at-large members to be elected by and represent the entire county. Brookings advised hiring a salaried county manager and county attorney, constructing better schools for the black children, abolishing the Liquor Control Board, and numerous other measures.

The notion of council districts was not universally appealing. Those living in the thickly settled suburban areas near the district line wanted a county council, but residents of the sparsely populated rural areas did not. The *Sentinel* did not, and the editor wrote that councilmanic districts "will completely destroy the balance between the agricultural and the suburban sections of the county."

By a very slight margin, the Home Rule Charter won in 1942, lost in 1944, won again in 1946, and was officially adopted in 1948. Thus a major decision-

making process was transferred from the state to the county level.

Outside of local politics, World War II was going on. On December 18, 1941, Lieutenant Colonel E. Brooke Lee, the commanding officer of the Seventh Battalion in the Maryland State Guard, called out the reserves and the Home Guard. The following year, 7,292 Montgomery men registered for the draft, includ-

When the department was first organized in 1922, the Montgomery County police were issued motorcycles. By 1930, however, officers graduated to fully-enclosed cars. Montgomery County policeman Jerry Hobbs stands beside his brand-new vehicle. Courtesy of Beverly Thompson Armentrout

Alongside the Rockville trolley tracks, the Majestic Company set out its traveling display in 1930, making good use of a converted steam engine and its cars. Shoppers could buy a radio or nickel sundries at the Rockville Paint and Hardware Company, groceries from any of three stores, or an ice cream soda. Courtesy of Malcolm Walters

ing 12 prisoners that Sheriff Leslie Carlin brought over from the jail. In 1942 another 5,914 men were inducted—4,370 white and 1,544 black.

Judge Charles W. Woodward and Wilton Tallen were appointed air-raid wardens for the county, and they delegated an official to perform this function for each neighborhood. If the warden noticed, lights of any sort could inflict a fifty dollar fine or thirty days in jail, and residents carefully covered their windows with tar paper. Outdoors at night one could not carry a lighted match, cigar, cigarette, or pipe.

Montgomery people sought to protect themselves from enemy bombs, fearing that the capital would be a prime target for invasion and that Montgomery County might be hit. To help survive such a catastrophe, the local government made free sand available for extinguishing incendiary bombs.

Housewives sealed water in gallon jugs and stored them together with canned food and blankets in the root cellar now ominously renamed the family bomb shelter. The army patrolled the county reservoirs and the bridge over the Monocacy River. Railroad bridges were guarded night and day.

Dorothy Troth Muir organized a project she named "Victory Exchange." In one room of her Washington

---

"Kounty J. Kuryosities"
by Hillbilly Hill

Old Tracks, old tracks, why are you here?
From Washington to Rockville fair
My limbs stretched out for many a year.
Across my ribs the streetcars flounced
The noblest of your sons I bounced
Until bus service was announced.
So now I lie here sore abused
Slowly to dust to be reduced,
Unwept, unhonored, and unused.

Courtesy of the *Sentinel*

The Janet Montgomery Chapter of the Daughters of the American Revolution placed a marker on the grave of Colonel Richard Brooke in 1932. Brooke (1736-1788), the son of James Brooke and a founder of Sandy Spring, fought in the American Revolution although it was against the principles of his Quaker religion. Courtesy of Roger Lamborne

Grove home, Mrs. Muir collected items to be sold on consignment for cash. The patriotic lady, however, paid the consignor in war stamps or bonds. Victory gardens replaced flower pots. However, rural skills had been forgotten in one generation, and residents needed classes in growing their own food.

Women were called on to join the armed forces as Women Army Corps (WACS) and Women Accepted for Volunteer Emergency Service (WAVES). "Let the Army experts discover your hidden talent," young ladies were urged by federal publications.

The local schools lost their teachers to the war effort. Superintendent Edwin Broome announced that he had "considerable difficulty" in finding enough personnel to staff the county's classrooms.

The Rockville Fair was suspended for two years.

But the lights went on again all over the world, and in Montgomery County as well. On December 22, 1948, the lights along Christmas Tree Lane in Rockville were turned on from Reed's Garage to the post office and Commerce Lane. Santa Claus came, and merchants offered their customers cash prizes just for shopping in their stores, thankfully stocked again.

After the war, the pent-up housing business exploded, and Montgomery's population increased nearly 100 percent between 1946 and 1950. ■

The class of 1932 of Rockville High School was photographed on January 7, 1931.

In the segregated school system, blacks were given secondhand books and leftover supplies. "It became a game to see who had the book with the most pages left," said Betty Talley Hawkins.

"We loved it! We loved to go to school," added Clara Luckett Talley, however.

This two-room building on North Washington Street in Rockville was built in 1927. It was the first high school in Montgomery County for black youngsters. Edward U. Taylor, the only teacher, taught part-time, reserving the hours he needed to perform his other job as supervisor of black education.

By the following fall two teachers were hired, and Mr. Taylor devoted all his time to his supervisory position, a job he held until his death in 1951.

Photographed from left to right in the first row are Mary Johnson, Martha Marr, Myrtle Hamilton (Thompson), Sarah Davis (Braxton), Corrie Alcorn Hodge, Mary Mercer, Edith Hill (Owens), Annie Jackson (Davis), Margaret Cooke, Maggie Prather (Gaither), Mary Jackson (Pumphrey), Amanda Jackson (Hart), Ethel Johnson (Graham), and the teacher, Queenie E. McNeill.

The girl standing on the first row of steps is unidentified.

In the second row are Alda Campbell (Taylor), Emma Holland, Russell Awkard, Mary Contee (Miles), Valerie Thomas (Burroughs), Zachariah Hart, Dewey Israel, Clara Luckett (Talley), Melinda Baker, and Helen Cooke (Bond).

In the top row are Howard Thomas, James Walker, and Arthur Frazier. Courtesy of Clara Luckett Talley

A men's basketball team from Bethesda poses in 1932. Courtesy of Malcolm Walters

Spring plowing at the Olney Inn was hard work. By the 1930s, Montgomerians had accepted the automobile, but draft horses were still used in place of tractors. Courtesy of Malcolm Walters

The Chevy Chase Dairy delivered the "Finest in Dairy Products" fresh to the door. Bill, Joanne, John, and Kelley Rice, and Orella Jane Beall of Montgomery County, along with Joanna Bell of Virginia and Brian Mulkerins of Washington, D.C., appeared to be in splendid health, therefore proving that the dairy provided "Safe Milk for Babies." Courtesy of William Fawsett Rice

Montgomery County hounds, their masters, and their friends prepare for a little coon hunting. Courtesy of Malcolm Walters

Left to Right
A. Riggs — F. S. Bradley — C. L. Gilpin — J. P. Smith — Walter Johnson — J. M. R. Lewis — K. Hobbs —
— R. Curran —

JUDGES

After a day of foxhunting, the following participants and judges posed for the photographer: A. Riggs, F. S. Bradley, C. L. Gilpin, J. P. Smith, Walter Johnson, J. M. R. Lewis, K. Hobbs, and R. Curran.

Although he was a baseball hero, Walter Johnson loved to foxhunt more than anything else. According to his son, Eddie Johnson of Comus, his father would open wide the window of his Germantown farmhouse in order to better hear the baying of his foxhounds.

Walter Johnson was a star pitcher with the Washington Senators from 1907 to 1927. He later managed the Senators and the Cleveland Indians. Johnson retired to Germantown in 1935 and participated in state and local politics as a member of the house of delegates in 1938 and as a county commissioner in 1942, leaving himself enough time to raise cattle and his beloved foxhounds. Courtesy of Malcolm Walters

Addison and Cecelia Noland Duffin sit beside Susie Smallwood and her baby dolls. The Duffin family lived in a red, frame, tenant house on the Benjamin Collinson Gott plantation near Boyds during the first years of their marriage. The Gott daughter, Daisy, taught the Duffin children their ABCs.

When the railroad brought prosperity to Boyds, Duffin bought land for himself and built a spacious home. He installed a parlor stove with heat-resistant windows, possibly obtained from Gilmore's mica mine near Kensington.

He farmed his land and worked, too, at James Darby's mill and Wade's Store in Bucklodge. Duffin became ever more prosperous, and helped build Saint Mark's African Methodist-Episcopal Church across the street from his home in 1893. (It is now Saint Mark's United Methodist Church.)

When the four Duffin daughters grew older, they left to work in other people's homes, and Cecelia and Addison invited the pastor's daughter, Susie Smallwood, to live at their big house. From the collection of Lorraine Duffin; courtesy of the Boyds/Clarksburg/Germantown Historical Society

The luxurious society wedding of Natalie Bowman and William B. Kuykendall, circa 1937, emphasized the end of the Depression in Montgomery County. Only the little flower girl, Carol Ann King, breaks the height pattern set by the five pretty bridesmaids and five handsome attendants of the groom.

From left to right, the bridesmaids were Polly Bergmann, Lois Marr, Jane Moore, Jean Pugh, and Marianna Howard. The groomsmen were Harry Canter Kuykendall, Hall Gibbons Canter, Harry Canter, Dewey Noland, and Joseph Kohen. Courtesy of Jean King Phillips

This young man's roots go back to the early history of Montgomery County. He is Roland Randolph, and his grandmother's grandfather was an American Indian.

Roland stands in front of the farmhouse built by his grandfather, Harry Thomas, on Hoyles Mill Road in Boyds. Courtesy of Valeria Thomas Burroughs and Carroll Greene, Jr.

Montgomery County agricultural agent O. W. Anderson instructs high school students before they go out into the fields to help local farmers in June 1942.

Miss Mae E. Howard, the manager of the United States Employment Service at Silver Spring, registered 125 high school students. They were given physical examinations and sent to nearby farms for the summer, where they tied their lunches in trees to protect them from dogs and ants. Their wages were twenty-five cents an hour. But Secretary of Agriculture C. R. Wickard told them that they could take satisfaction in knowing they were "helping to win the war and write the peace." Official War Information photograph by Liberman; courtesy of Library of Congress

Pictured is the Montgomery County General Hospital, circa 1939. Courtesy of Roger Lamborne

President Franklin D. Roosevelt participated in the ceremonial laying of the cornerstone for the United States Naval Medical Center in Bethesda that he had designed. Roosevelt considered himself an architect as well as a master politician, and he wanted the hospital to have an unusual design.

"I have very carefully studied hospital design," he wrote to Frederic Delano, the chairman of the National Capital Park and Planning Commission, "and, frankly, I am fed up with the type the Government has been building during these past twenty years....Therefore, I personally designed a new Naval Hospital with a large central tower of sufficient square footage and height to make it an integral and interesting part of the hospital itself...."

Delano, who was Roosevelt's uncle, replied, "OH! SIRE!...since the beginning of time the formula has been that 'the King can do no wrong.' However, from the time of Solomon and even further back, the King found it necessary to surround himself with soothsayers, astrologers, and other wise men to warn him of the pitfalls and dangers lying ahead of him" (Quoted by Lloyd Grove in the *Washington Post* on May 7, 1982).

Nevertheless, the hospital designed by a president was built, and on November 11, 1940, FDR was there when the cornerstone for the Bethesda landmark was laid. Courtesy of Franklin D. Roosevelt Library

President Franklin D. Roosevelt drove away in his 1939 Packard after the dedication ceremonies for the new United States Naval Medical Center in Bethesda on August 31, 1942. Courtesy of Franklin D. Roosevelt Library, National Archives and Records Services

Japanese-Americans worked in Montgomery County during World War II; here, some are shown at the Olney farm of Harold L. Ickes, the secretary of the interior. Mrs. Fred Kobayashi shoulders a hoe and her husband carries a bucket as Mrs. Ickes explains the operation and Roy Kobayashi and the Ickes's farm boss, Robert Lymburner, listen. Official War Information photograph by Hollem; courtesy of Library of Congress

Their dismay at relocation nearly veiled from the camera, William and Betty Kobayashi (left) and Giichi Omari (right) view Sam Rice's chicken farm near Olney as Rice assigns their duties. Rice, a former major-league baseball player, received the Japanese-Americans from the Colorado River Relocation Center. Official War Information photograph by Hollem; courtesy of Library of Congress

M. O. Chance graduated from Sherwood High School and left Montgomery County to pilot a plane in World War II. When he returned, he married his high school sweetheart and settled down in the peaceful, green valley of Unity to raise Romney sheep. Courtesy of M. O. and Nancy Chance

Bethesdans supported the war effort by turning in their aluminum pots and pans. Courtesy of Brooks Photographers

Rockville residents went to the center of town to celebrate VJ-Day with a big parade which moved west on East Montgomery Avenue past the intersection at Commerce Lane.

The old courthouse in the background is the sole building pictured that remains today. Although it's been moved from the center of town, the Confederate soldier monument remains in Rockville and still faces, appropriately, south. Photograph by Roy Perry; courtesy of Peerless Rockville

The war was over, and Montgomery County celebrated on the steps of a laurel-wreath-decked Montgomery County Courthouse in Rockville. Photograph by Roy Perry; courtesy of Peerless Rockville

Home at last, a soldier naps on the courthouse lawn with his pack for a pillow, just as he had in Algiers. Photograph by Roy Perry; courtesy of Peerless Rockville

Pictured is the Milo Theater on Commerce Lane, Rockville, in 1943.

"May its beauty live as long as the classic Venus," wrote Lionel Barrymore when the Milo Theater opened on October 10, 1935.

The local paper devoted nearly one entire issue to the occasion. Four pages contained advertisements and congratulatory messages from movie stars including Shirley Temple, Jean Harlow, Clark Gable, Robert Montgomery, Ronald Colman, Rochelle Hudson, Alice Faye, Freddie Bartholomew, and Warner Oland.

Rufus E. Milor owned the theater, and Sidney Lust was the proprietor when *China Seas* with Gable and Harlow opened to a capacity crowd of more than one thousand.

At one time, the Open Air Movie operated next to the Milo. After nightfall, patrons sat on benches and watched an outdoor screen. When Prohibition ended, a beer garden opened at the site of the Open Air Movie. Photograph by Roy Perry; courtesy of Peerless Rockville

The commissioners of Montgomery County, President Harry S Truman's neighbors, pay him a call at the Oval Office. By 1945, Montgomery's party politics had shifted; voters were electing Republicans to office. Truman, a Democrat faced with the same trend on a national scale, frequently complained about his Republican Congress.

Shown, from left to right, are Republicans George C. Esworthy, Oliver W. Youngblood, Brooke Johns, and Wesley Souders and Democrat Charles Jamison, the "Lone Wolf"; they stand around President Truman. Courtesy of Charles Jamison

Registered voters received paper ballots at the Grange Hall in Barnesville on November 7, 1944. Courtesy of Library of Congress Official War Information photograph by Lewis Walker

A prosperous farm in Montgomery County is pictured here circa 1940. Belonging to Julian Boyd Waters at the time this photograph was taken, the eighteenth-century manor house, five tenant houses, the former slave quarters, and numerous farm outbuildings on Waters Lane in Germantown resembled a small village.

The main brick house was built on property granted to William Waters in 1680 from King Charles through Lord Baltimore; the family has carefully preserved the deed.

Eleanor Cissell Waters, the woman of the house when this photograph was taken, was president of the Farm Women's Cooperative Market. She had graduated from the Andrew Small Academy in Darnestown and the State Normal School in Baltimore, and she had taught school before she married Julian Waters. Her participation in the Farm Women's Market in Bethesda added considerably to the family's income. She went to market every Wednesday and Saturday, taking with her pork, turkeys, eggs, sweet corn, tomatoes, and other fresh produce from her farm.

Her husband, Julian, shipped milk from his modern dairy, transporting the fragile liquid by train to the markets of Washington.

Violence exploded in the deep woods beyond the barn on November 17, 1920. Guy Vernon Thompson stole a keg of dynamite from Horace Waters's store and blew up one of Julian Waters's tenant houses; three people died, James Bolton, Evelyn Shipley, and Harold Shipley. Thompson, who had quarreled with Bolton, was tried and convicted of murder. He earned for himself the dreadful honor of being the last man to be hanged at the Montgomery County Courthouse. Courtesy of Ella Virginia Waters Gochenour

The Black Rock Mill used power from Little Seneca Creek to grind grain for residents of western Montgomery County. When steam proved a more efficient energy source, this wooden-wheeled mill was abandoned. The Maryland Historical Trust recently granted funds for an interpretive diorama at the site, now owned by Montgomery County. Courtesy of Idella Leaman

Leah J. Iglehart sold fresh eggs, jams, jellies, and even clown dolls at her booth at the Farm Women's Market in Bethesda. Courtesy of Neal and Marion Potter

Charlotte Waugh Potter found a good outlet for fresh vegetables, home-baked foods, and firewood at the Farm Women's Market. Courtesy of Neal and Marion Potter

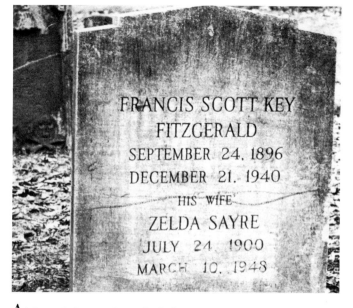

Although he was born in Saint Paul, Minnesota, and died in Hollywood, California, F. Scott Fitzgerald, the author of *The Great Gatsby* and many other books, is buried in Rockville, with his wife, Zelda Sayre, who was born in Montgomery, Alabama.

The tombstone pictured is the original burial site behind the Civic Center in Rockville; in 1976 the graves were moved to Saint Mary's Catholic Church. Courtesy of Thelma Osborne Gray

Photographed here is East Montgomery Avenue in Rockville, a street which no longer exists. It was replaced by a mall and urban renewal. Photograph by Roy Perry; courtesy of Peerless Rockville

Once common, signs such as this one at a store in Spencerville during the 1960s are no longer permitted in Montgomery County or anywhere in the United States. Courtesy of Barbara Knapp

Rockville boys play soccer behind the courthouse. In 1972 Rockville visionaries replaced the field with a shopping mall. Photograph by Roy Perry; courtesy of Peerless Rockville

Dwight D. Eisenhower joins the three other members of his regular foursome at the Chevy Chase Club: Floyd Parks, T. L. Fisher, and Frank A. Allen, Jr., Courtesy of the National Geographic Society

Here, the Bowman Brothers Mill, which had been rebuilt in Gaithersburg after a disastrous fire at their Germantown location, burns again. The Gaithersburg blaze was set by vandals. Courtesy of Jean King Phillips

Three generations of Montgomery's Lee family surround the family's newest member, future Montgomery County Councilman David Scull, born on May 10, 1943. He is held by his mother, Elizabeth Lee Scull; counseled by his great-grandfather, former United States senator Blair Lee; and admired by his grandfather, Colonel E. Brooke Lee. Courtesy of Blair Lee III

Shutters once framed the windows of this gracious Bethesda house with its jerkin roof ending in curved arches, its two-story bay windows, and its nicely turned porch rails.

But business was booming then, and it needed space for expansion. People moved out, several small businesses moved in, and vandals broke the upstairs windows. Courtesy of Brooks Photographers

Born a slave in Charles County, Richard Davis and his wife, Mary Davis, moved to Montgomery County and lived in a log cabin near Washington Street in Kensington. Mr. Davis was the sexton at Warner Presbyterian Church, where the members called him "Uncle" and gave him one thousand dollars when he retired at age ninety-six. Courtesy of Judge Alfred Noyes

This mural in the Montgomery County Post Office, along with the post office itself, was a Public Works Administration project. Judson White painted the mural in 1940. When this scene was chosen, controversy reigned because Sugarloaf Mountain is in Frederick, not Montgomery, County. Nevertheless, Montgomerians consider that it is *their* mountain because they can see it so clearly. Photograph by Anne Dennis Lewis

Rockville was still mostly farmland in the 1940s. Routes 28 and 355 and Veirs Mill Road are clearly defined. Courtesy of Air Photographics, Wheaton, Maryland

New industry, Montgomery County style, is nicely expressed by the 1969 National Geographic Society's Membership Center building with its park-like setting and its attractive architecture.

Alexander Graham Bell hired Gilbert Hovey Grosvenor, a Montgomery County resident, in 1899 to edit the *National Geographic Magazine*, a small, irregularly published technical bulletin of the National Geographic Society with one thousand subscribers.

By clever manuevers, skillful innovations, and a touch of genius. Grosvenor boosted the society to a membership of four million in the 1960s, each one receiving a subscription to *National Geographic Magazine*. Courtesy of the National Geographic Society

Chapter 8
1950-1969

By 1950 Montgomery County's reputation had blossomed into national recognition. Montgomery was named one of eleven All-American Communities. Plaudits included "outstanding accomplishments in providing good government for its citizens."

County leaders were working hard to adopt the reforms that had been recommended by Brookings Institution and, in addition to good government, took pride in good schools. In the early 1950s ten new elementary schools for white children were built, and Montgomery Junior College opened its Takoma Park campus for white students only. Black schools improved as well. Carver High School and Junior College began in a new, two-story masonry building in Rockville. Four black elementary schools opened between 1950 and 1952, and all small public schools in the county consolidated.

Blacks and whites did not mix at school, at work, or even at play at Glen Echo Amusement Park. During the summer of 1951, the school patrol was treated to a day at Glen Echo with lunch furnished by local businessmen. Jim Crow laws kept Glen Echo solidly white, and the black school patrol, sponsored by the police department, went to Emory Grove Campgrounds for lunch and games.

Montgomery County elected its school board for the first time in 1952, becoming the first Maryland jurisdiction to break away from a governor-appointed board.

Wheaton Plaza opened in 1954, and Congressional Plaza was built four years later on the site of the former Congressional Airport. Small, local shopping centers cropped up in the form of retail outlet stores grouped around paved parking lots. And Montgomerians began to frequent the malls. Established main-street towns throughout the county collapsed in the resultant exodus. Rockville shops were vacated, and the owners boarded up the windows. City officials responded by launching an urban renewal program. They relocated 180 families and demolished over one hundred buildings to make way for Rockville Mall, a move they were certain would bring the shoppers back.

Land development and building continued. The Capital Beltway was engineered and constructed, linking distant areas of Maryland and Virginia and creating a vast metropolitan region. Since everyone had a car and gas was cheap, Washington's work force could live in the Montgomery countryside and still get to work on time. Earlier in the century, land prices had soared near the district line. But during the 1950s rural property values exploded, too, in areas located within an easy commute of the new interstate highways.

Farms became subdivisions, and people worried that upcounty farmland would disappear altogether. M-NCPPC was involved in planning development only to the end of the sewer line, the jurisdiction of the WSSC, and dedicated planners such as Frederick Gutheim were concerned that the upcounty would be a victim of "the worst kind of spot development, with no plan for the entire county as a unit."

Clearly, a planning agency was needed for the more remote regions of the county. To answer this need, the Upper Montgomery County Planning Commission was formed in June 1950, dedicated to developing a master plan for the upcounty. The commission drew up an extensive zoning ordinance that would maintain the agricultural characteristics of the upcounty. In 1957, mission accomplished, the UMCPC dissolved.

The same year, M-NCPPC adopted a comprehensive general plan for the development of Montgomery and Prince George counties. Montgomery was divided into wedges and corridors with land designated for intensive development, open space, parks, and so on. Downcounty residents approved limiting development, but the farmers and land-owners upcounty considered it too restrictive.

Morrissee W. Swilling, a Rockville farmer, said that he resented anyone telling him what he could and could not do with his land. "I certainly don't want any group of people in Rockville spending my tax money and then having the gall and temerity to get up regulations that keep me from selling my property to whom I please," he wrote.

Mr. Swilling was in powerful company; Colonel E. Brooke Lee didn't like it, either. He called the ordinance "The first war against the location of new homes in Upper Montgomery County since the Indians were driven back across the Blue Ridge Mountains."

Despite the opposition, the council passed the ordinance with unanimous assent, and, except for Potomac and Comus, the upcounty was zoned in rural, residential, half-acre lots.

Farmers were hurt, too, when Interstate 270 swept through the northwestern part of the county. They found their fields split by the ribbon of highway. "To an

Shown with a map of Montgomery County and an ordinance for orderly development are members of the Upper Montgomery County Planning Commission in 1951. From left to right, they are Lathrop E. Smith, Marshall Davidson, Thomas C. Kelley, Kenneth Windham, and Frederick Gutheim. By law the group included two members of the Montgomery County Council. The commission was responsible for the zoning in the area north of Rockville, amounting to about 75 percent of the county.

These men had diverse back-grounds. Smith, the major conservationist on the county council, was a retired army colonel; the Lathrop E. Smith Environmental Education Center is named for him. Davidson had sold his family farm to the Atomic Energy Commission and retired his plow. Kelley was a retired judge and a member of the Montgomery County Council. Windham knew the county's farm communities well, serving as an officer in the Farm Bureau and Southern States Cooperative Association. Gutheim's background includes faculty appointments in history and planning at George Washington University, the University of Michigan, and Cornell University. He was a member of the editorial staff of the *New York Herald Tribune* and the *Washington Post*, the author of *The Potomac*, and the recipient of numerous honorary awards.

The commission had a staff of professional planners, including Harold Taubin, Patrick Cusick, and Nancy Grove. Merton Duvall, Ulysses G. Griffith IV, Wiley Griffith, and Charles Harris Jamison joined the commission later. Courtesy of Patricia Bailey Kelley

old farmer, land is dear," complained W. Lawson King, whose two Middlebrook farms were cut in two.

W. R. Rabbitt reported his cropland was cut off from his farm buildings. The superhighway "made it a tough proposition to continue farming," said Rabbitt.

But I-270 just hunkered down on its concrete footings, then shot ahead.

The most significant news story of the 1950s was the integration of public schools. In May 1954 the United States Supreme Court ruled that segregation in public education was unconstitutional under the Fourteenth Amendment. However, public schools in Montgomery County would not completely integrate until the next decade.

"Integration here will be a slow process," predicted school superintendent Dr. Forbes H. Norris.

Indeed it was. The board of education set up an Advisory Committee on Integration, composed of fourteen white and five black people. The committee recommended gradual integration of one grade each year, beginning with the first grade. The Farm Bureau applauded.

However, an executive committee from the Parent-Teachers Associations recommended swift integration. Also, the county's six black PTAs favored complete integration by September 1955.

Again, blacks protested when the board of education failed to hire any black teachers for the fall of 1955. Despite the large number of experienced black teachers with college degrees, the board chose 12 nondegree and 116 inexperienced white teachers to fill the positions.

One leading citizen said, "I believe the Negro child and the white child would be better off in segregated schools" because black youngsters are "as much as three years behind whites. . .and need problem classes. Integration. . .will be resisted with every force at our command."

At the same time, George Guernsey, an American Federation of Labor and Congress of Industrial Organizations (AFL-CIO) official, claimed full desegregation could be accomplished relatively quickly.

Everyone was mad at the school admininstrators. They were either too fast or too slow, too hard or too soft, too conservative or too liberal. In Poolesville, two hundred parents gathered in the school yard to protest integration, urging white pupils to stay home. Dr. Norris called for the county police to protect the fourteen black students wishing to enter and to ensure safe passage through the door and into the classrooms.

Pictured here is the Montgomery Junior College in Takoma Park. Originally constructed as the Seventh-Day Adventist Hospital and later used as the Bliss Electrical School, the building was purchased for a public junior college. The facility was opened in 1950 to white students only; the George Washington Carver Junior College opened for blacks at Lincoln High School in Rockville the same year.

Montgomery Junior College had begun, however, in 1946; classes had been held at Bethesda-Chevy Chase High School.

In 1962 a permanent, integrated college was proposed. It opened in Rockville in 1965. Courtesy of Edith Ray Saul

The superintendent himself held open the door and ushered the fourteen youngsters safely inside.

Petitions against integration were passed around the county, sponsored by the Montgomery County Chapter of the Maryland Petition Committee. Petition backers announced a meeting at Poolesville Town Hall, "in order to get this thing settled."

Gathering strength, the group went to Rockville and participated in a crowded meeting with the board of education, asserting their commitment to segregation. Superintendent Norris resigned.

Montgomery County's problems of the 1950s carried over into the 1960s.

The 1960s was a time of optimistic struggle in

Xander's Market on the corner of Georgia Avenue and Layhill Road in Silver Spring, shown here in 1950, has been demolished and the site paved to widen Georgia Avenue. Business property in Montgomery County often evolves from one function to another. Originally, the building was a roadhouse of the 1880s called High Steps. The wide veranda provided a pleasant spot to sit and sip along the Seventh Street Turnpike.

During Prohibition, the roadhouse business collapsed, and Charles Dwyer bought the building to use as a grocery store. The United States Postal Service opened its Glenmont office in one corner of the store.

From 1925 to 1953 the store was owned by Albert Xander. When Xander took over the business, he moved his operations to the ground floor to allow easy access to his newly installed gasoline pumps. Courtesy of Albert F. Xander and Peggy Elgin

Montgomery County. Widespread belief in the possibility of achieving equal rights for all Montgomerians seemed to blanket the county. Not everyone was secure within the fold, however. Crosses were burned in front of churches. Restaurants, recreational centers, and even some public schools remained segregated. Three black men, claiming innocence of a crime they did not commit, were convicted and sentenced to die upon the testimony of one white girl, and fifteen costumed members of the Ku Klux Klan visited the county seat. Montgomerians could smell smoke as Washington burned in the riots of the late 1960s.

Two memorable news stories filled the pages of the local press during this decade: the assassination of President Kennedy and the Giles brothers' criminal case.

More than half of Montgomery's schools were integrated by the fall of 1960. But forty-two elementary and two secondary schools remained white, "simply because no Negroes lived in their immediate area," said a spokesman for the board of education. Two all-black elementary schools, Taylor in Boyds and Rock Terrace in Rockville, were overcrowded, the spokesman announced, and he questioned opening them as integrated schools due to inadequate space.

Old houses were swept aside in the name of urban renewal and replaced with new shopping and housing projects. Housing standards were adopted by county officials, and homes not meeting the regulations were demolished.

Wheaton grew and grew. With 24,585 new units built in the 1950s, and 22,232 additional homes in the 1960s, Wheaton galloped into first place for new construction. Not only new houses but new ideas began in Wheaton. At Wheaton High School one thousand people swallowed the Sabin oral polio vaccine on the first Sunday the pink-coated sugar cubes were offered.

Just a short distance away from Wheaton High School, the nation's first home radioactive fallout shelter was put on sale. Inside the cozy, underground room, advertised the builder, a family of six could live for two weeks with no outside aid. The chilling thought attracted thousands to an open house.

In 1962 a new organization called the County Above Party elected the entire county council. The bipartisan County Above Party favored less restriction on growth. CAP claimed the county's master plan for development was unamerican. Although numerous residents signed a petition against it, the General Plan for Orderly Development, conceived by professional planners, was adopted in 1964. The lame duck County Above Party, however, countered by rezoning thousands of acres to permit higher-density construction.

Montgomery County's growth continued. Planned communities appeared, including New Mark Commons, Montgomery Village, and Rossmoor Leisure World. Two shopping malls opened in 1968: Montgomery Mall and Gaithersburg Square.

With all this construction going on, more and more farmers sold their land to developers and moved away. Montgomery farmland declined 21 percent during the 1960s as the average price of one acre shot from $301 in 1954 to $4,302 in 1964. Land in neighboring counties was not nearly as expensive, however. In 1964 farmland in Frederick and Carroll counties averaged $370 an acre.

The federal space program sparked development and Montgomery County, with its proximity to the capital, was a natural site for new buildings. Montgomery welcomed these industrial developments, which led to the growth of many attractive structures with park-like settings. IBM came to Bethesda and Rockville in 1959 and consolidated its Washington operations with a move to Gaithersburg during the 1960s. Other technological firms that came to Montgomery County during the 1960s included Fairchild-Hiller; Comsat Corporation; Gillette Research Institute; Control Data Corporation; Xerox-Scientific Data Systems; Tracor; Hydrospace-Challenger; NUS Corporation; Comress; Bechtel Corporation; Kodak; Weinschel Electronics; and the National Geographic Society membership center.

John F. Kennedy came to Montgomery Blair High School on a Sunday evening in October 1960; his visit was arranged by one of his campaign managers, Blair Lee III.

The Shady Grove Music Fair opened with Dorothy Collins in *Brigadoon*. Critics praised the summer tent show and predicted a long life and success to the county's theater-in-the-round performances.

But the biggest news story in Montgomery County during the 1960s was the case of John and James Giles and James Johnson. The Giles brothers became a cause celebre involving every liberal group in the nation; their story led to many books and magazine features.

The three men were sentenced to death based on the testimony of a sixteen-year-old white girl who had a history of promiscuity. She claimed that the three men

had raped her. County intellectuals Dr. Harold Knapp, Mrs. Frances Ross, and other civil libertarians joined forces and stood in the path to the gas chamber. Due to their intervention, the discovery that the prosecutor had withheld information from the jury, and the eventual failure of the complaining witness to appear in court, all charges against the Giles brothers were dropped in November 1967. Governor Spiro Agnew pardoned James Johnson in February 1968. Civil liberty for blacks in America grew closer. ■

Montgomery County children learned to canoe and fish in the quiet waters of Camp Echo Lake, founded by Judge Alfred Noyes. The camp was located in Frederick County, but it was operated for Montgomery County youngsters. Today Interstate 81 bisects the former camp. Courtesy of Judge Alfred Noyes

President Harry S Truman participated in the ceremonial laying of the cornerstone at the Research Clinic of the National Institute of Health in Bethesda on June 22, 1951. Courtesy of Harry S Truman Library, National Park Service and Abbie Rowe

At an IBM employee picnic, Martha Dangler accepts a balloon creature from a friendly clown. Courtesy of Barbara Dangler

President Dwight D. Eisenhower lays the ceremonial cornerstone for the Atomic Energy Commission building in rural Germantown on the brand-new interstate highway in 1957. Courtesy of Dwight D. Eisenhower Library, National Park Service

The Montgomery County school board considers the integration of the public schools in 1958. Courtesy of Harrison and Gladys King

Champ Birely plans to vote for Richard Nixon and has convinced his master, Bill Birely, to do so as well. Champ campaigned at Wheaton Plaza in 1959. Courtesy of Avis Birely

While he campaigned to be elected president of the United States, Senator John F. Kennedy visited Montgomery County, shaking hands and signing autographs freely. Courtesy of the *Sentinel*

Integration worked at Gaithersburg Elementary School in May 1962. Under the gentle touch of a teacher with wisdom and experience, Mrs. Mary Rice, children of various skin colors learned their ABCs together. Photograph by Rideout and Stapp; courtesy of William Fawsett Rice

Outspoken radio commentator and columnist Drew Pearson, although fearless and undaunted before his typewriter, lacked aggression when faced with his runaway buffalo cow. Pearson raised bison and green beans at his Darnestown farm. Courtesy of the *Sentinel*

During the spring of 1966, Nola Birely, Montgomery County's Miss United States, stands in front of the new Maryland-National Capital Park and Planning Commission headquarters at 8787 Georgia Avenue in Silver Spring. Courtesy of Avis Birely

As late as the mid-1960s, children in rural Montgomery County ran errands to the general store and exchanged visits by pony cart. Shown is George Mauser visiting the home of naturalist Lathrop Smith in Buck-lodge. Courtesy of Elaine Mauser

Carolyn Birely campaigned for Barry Goldwater in 1964 and worked as a volunteer in his Montgomery County headquarters. As a result, she got her picture in the *Saturday Evening Post*! From the collection of Avis Birely; courtesy of the *Saturday Evening Post*

President Lyndon Baines Johnson greets Vice-President Hubert H. Humphrey in 1965. Sargent Shriver and his wife, Eunice Kennedy Shriver, applaud beneath the flowered canopy set up on the lawn of their Rockville home. Photograph by Okamoto; courtesy of Lyndon B. Johnson Library

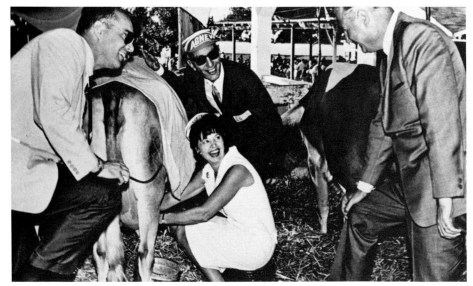

Avis Birely demonstrated an unusual skill to Spiro Agnew at the Montgomery County Fair in August 1966. Both people were campaigning for election, and both won, which may say something about milking cows in Gaithersburg. Avis Birely became chairman of the Montgomery County Council and Agnew became vice-president under Richard Nixon. Courtesy of Avis Birely

With a Confederate flag waving from the antenna and KKK painted on the rear window, the Ku Klux Klan came to Rockville in August 1966. From left to right are Xavier Edwards, an unidentified KKK member, David Harris, and an unidentified KKK member. Boasting a Montgomery County membership of two hundred and a klavern in Gaithersburg, Edwards advised white onlookers to buy guns to defend themselves, and threatened to come back with "the American Nazis and Minutemen and every right wing organization we can." As he talked, the other Klansmen handed out booklets entitled, "The Negro— Animal or Human."

Business continued as usual, however, with Rockville left to wonder why the hooded visitors came and what it was they were supposed to buy guns to defend themselves *from*. Courtesy of the *Sentinel*

One hot, sultry summer night, three young black men left their homes to cool off in the Patuxent River. Before they made the journey home again, an event occurred that would wash in a wave of controversy to swell from shore to American shore, crest in newscasts and publications throughout the land, and result in two hearings before the United States Supreme Court. The men would be faced by certain death and be rescued by a white man—a man slight in stature, but with a heart big enough to understand the struggle of human rights and a spirit strong enough to quell a tide of their violations.

On July 20, 1961, Joseph E. Johnson, Jr., twenty-three, John G. Giles, twenty-one, James V. Giles, nineteen, and John Bowie, twenty-five, drove past the end of Batson Road to the Rocky Gorge reservoir on the Patuxent, less than a mile from their homes in Spencerville. By 11:30 p.m., cool and comfortable again, they loaded their fishing gear into Bowie's car. Bowie volunteered to drive his friends home, but the Giles brothers and Johnson told him they would cut through the woods and reach home more quickly on foot.

On this eve of the civil rights upheaval, however, fate had something else in store. About the same time the four black men were climbing out of the river, four whites were wending their way down the lonely road to the dam. They parked, then two of them left the area. The remaining couple, Joyce Roberts, sixteen, and Stewart Foster, twenty-one, were in the back seat when they saw the lights from Bowie's car. The road was narrow, and Foster called out, "Do you have room to get by?"

Bowie did, and he drove off, revealing James Johnson, who asked Foster for a cigarette. Foster replied with a racial epithet, an obscene word that seared the muggy blackness like a match thrown casually at a thimbleful of gasoline.

Johnson threw a rock at Foster and smashed the car window. Foster got out and hit Johnson. James and John Giles appeared in the darkness and came to their companion's defense.

This round was won by the black men, who admitted they broke a car window and fought Stewart Foster.

Meanwhile Joyce Roberts went into the woods, and when the Giles brothers and Johnson left Foster, she met them. And here is the great dichotomy. Truth is neither black nor white, and two distinctly different versions of the ensuing incident were reported. John Giles swore he never touched the girl. His brother and Johnson said they were enticed. Roberts said she was raped. However, a Montgomery County circuit court jury convicted John and James Giles as well as James Johnson of rape. The judge, James H. Pugh, sentenced them to the gas chamber and sent them to the state penitentiary.

And that was the end of the story. Or so it seemed, until Dr. Harold A. Knapp, a government scientist living in Germantown, became involved in the case. Knapp found that Leonard T. Kardy, the state's attorney for Montgomery County, and the chief prosecutor had withheld information from the jury. Knapp made this fact known. Nonetheless, Judge Pugh stood firm.

But the movement for civil rights

was gaining momentum, and the Giles-Johnson Defense Committee formed in Silver Spring with an impressive list of sponsors.

The cause began to snowball. Nearly ten thousand signatures for clemency were collected by the committee. Former Secretary of State Dean Acheson lent his support. Harold Knapp sent Governor J. Millard Tawes a thick document of new evidence. The defense was unwittingly helped by Joyce Roberts, who was arrested at a teenage brawl shortly after the Giles's trial. Because she had a previous record of offense, Roberts was committed to the Montrose School for Delinquent Girls. Her associate, Foster, Knapp discovered, was a known racist with a criminal record. In addition, Knapp turned up evidence showing that Kardy had been aware of their records and reputations when he pressed for conviction of Giles, Giles, and Johnson.

America picked up the beat. Edward P. Morgan devoted two of his nationwide newscasts on ABC to defending the Giles brothers and

Johnson. National magazines, including *Jet* (1967), *Esquire* (1968), and *The Reporter* (1968), featured stories on the case. Editors of the *Washington Post*, the *Sentinel*, the *Evening Star*, and WWDC radio proclaimed that the three men should be set free.

But the Giles family had received yet another blow. Mary Frazier Giles, the grief-stricken mother of James and John, died. Her sons were not permitted to attend her funeral. They were escorted from the penitentiary for a brief look at their mother's casket, and final services for Mrs. Giles were held at the Round Oak Baptist Church in Spencerville on March 31, 1964.

The United States Supreme Court heard the Giles's case twice and ruled for a new trial in November 1967. When the complaining witnesses did not appear, all charges against the brothers were dropped.

On February 10, 1968, James Johnson received a full pardon from Governor Spiro Agnew. And after six long years in jail, most of them spent on death row, the three men were home again.

Without Dr. Knapp's quest for truth, the end of this story would have been quite different. He is shown in the foreground of the photograph, which was taken at his Germantown home during a visit with James and John Giles. Photograph by Mike Mitchell; courtesy of the *Washingtonian Magazine*, October 1967

Mr. Montgomery,'' E. Brooke Lee, retired to his farm in Damascus to raise Hereford cattle. From the collection of Blair Lee III

Montgomery County people watch the Laytonsville bicentennial parade on June 5, 1976. Photograph by Roger Lamborne

Unlike the centennial of 1876, the bells of Rockville rang in glorious profusion for America's bicentennial. Montgomery County was caught up in a spirit of pride and patriotism. Twenty-six communities throughout the county received national recognition as bicentennial communities. The list included Barnesville, Bethesda-Chevy Chase, Boyds, Brookeville, Burtonsville, Cabin John, Chevy Chase View, Clarksburg, Damascus, Gaithersburg, Garrett Park, Kensington, Laytonsville, Montgomery College, Montgomery Village, Olney, Poolesville, Potomac, Rockville, Rossmoor, Sandy Spring, Silver Spring, Somerset, Takoma Park, Village of Friendship Heights, and Wheaton Woods. A group of citizens came together in each of these communities to write a history of their part of Montgomery County. In so doing, they recognized the wide scope of their local culture and realized that important architectural landmarks were already lost.

As a result of these studies of neighborhood history, local historical societies formed, including Boyds/Clarksburg/Germantown Historical Society, Capitol View Park Historical Society, Friends of the Great Falls Tavern, Friends of Historic Hyattstown, Friends of "In the Woods," Historic Medley District, Historic Takoma, Kensington Historical Society, Peerless Rockville, and Takoma Park Historical Society. Montgomery County Historical Society had already formed in 1944.

Public agencies celebrated the bicentennial as well. M-NCPPC published an atlas identifying historical sites. Sugarloaf Regional Trails formed with grants from the National Endowment for the Arts and the Montgomery County Planning Board. This agency, led by staff members Gail Rothrock and Eileen McGuckian, planned biking, hiking, rail, and canoe trails and delved into an ambitious study of old homes with volunteers doing the research. From the project grew a countywide masterplan and ordinance for historic preservation.

Montgomery County's two hundredth anniversary was September 6, 1976, and Montgomerians commemorated the event with band concerts, ethnic dances, horse shows, and parades.

The Montgomery County Council president, Elizabeth Lee Scull, gave a speech. She said that she loved the rolling hills and the green stream valleys of her native county. Yet, she also recognized and yearned to help the county's poor. She addressed the county's

The Reverend Edward Voorhaar leaves Sunshine for Brookeville in 1976. For the bicentennial, Voorhaar recreated the role of his predecessors, the Methodist circuit riders who preached three times on Sundays while commuting on horseback. Photograph by Roger Lamborne

bicentennial celebrants, saying, "We cherish the beauty of our remaining rural areas," and expressed the hope that "our community will include a more harmonious economic mix" in the future.

Council member Jane Anne Moore added similar remarks. She said that she hoped that "Potomac will become as well integrated as Takoma Park."

With fine speeches reflecting on the high quality of its leadership, Montgomery County began a third century. A new executive position was created by a vote in 1968. The voters of 1970 chose James P. Gleason, a Republican, as the first Montgomery County executive. Gleason's position was similar to that of a strong city mayor. He had executive and administrative powers and significant veto authority over the council, plus the duty of administering all departments of the county government.

The county council of 1970 had seven members, five from councilmanic districts designated by area population, and two at-large members. Election was countywide for all members. Their function was to make laws dealing with zoning, subdivisions, and planning; to set tax rates; and to approve budgets.

Montgomery County school students have been performing in skits for a long time. Here, Virginia Sutton's fourth and fifth grade classes at Olney Elementary School sing together about the Boston Tea Party.

Photograph by Roger Lamborne, January 15, 1976

In 1984, Montgomery has 37,042 acres of public park land, about 500 additional acres in private parks, 126,000 acres of assessed farmland, an excellent public school system, shopping malls both elegant and practical, a subway, trains, an interstate highway, social services, and recreational programs for every taste and interest.

The 1981 population was 579,053. Montgomery measures about twenty by twenty-five miles, and it contains 316,800 acres. Tobacco, once the king of local commerce, grows on four acres.

Montgomery has fine public schools. In 1980, 117 students were chosen as National Merit semifinalists, more than all the remaining Maryland schools combined. Nearly half of the county's budget goes to the board of education. The nonpartisan, elected school board is responsible for 95,587 students in 177 public schools. (Twenty-eight schools are scheduled to close by 1984). Educational facilities include 8 special, 122 elementary, 4 middle (grades five through eight), 21 junior high, 1 combination junior/senior high, and 21 senior high schools. In addition, Montgomery College has three locations with campuses in Takoma Park, Rockville, and Germantown. The two-year academic program has an enrollment of 18,753.

Montgomery has a splendid public library system with America's second highest per capita circulation of books. Library headquarters are in Rockville, and nineteen neighborhood branches contain a total of approximately 1,333,000 volumes.

Montgomerians participate in local government. More than three hundred associations represent the grassroots of Montgomery County. Members often attend public hearings to present the views of a specific community or special interest group. These meetings may be administered by a number of governmental agencies or officials, including the Maryland-National Capital Park and Planning Commission, the Montgomery County Planning Board, the Washington Suburban Sanitary Commission, the board of education, the county executive, and the county council.

During the past thirty years, civic groups have protested many county issues, such as the completion of Interstate 270 through Chevy Chase and the razing of Forest Glen Seminary to make way for high-rise apartments, as well as low-income housing, halfway houses,

211

landfills in Norbeck and Laytonsville, sludge in Germantown and Dickerson, and the closing of the neighborhood schools. The governing bodies involved listen to all the voices, but strive to make their decision to benefit the majority of Montgomery residents.

Montgomery County is a nice place to live. It is still green and the citizens participate in the government. The countryside is close to the people, and the town house dwellers can bicycle to a pick-your-own orchard or a local farmers' market. Children of the rich and the poor have the privilege of an excellent education.

Montgomery's past has provided the pattern for the 1980s. Today is the result of decisions made yesterday. Our county government, our schools, our race relationships—we owe them all to Montgomery County residents of the past. To know them and to recognize their traumas and their choices is to gain a glimpse of insight into the 1980s.

Our children and grandchildren will know our successes and our failures just as we know so well, by looking back through history, the successes and the failures of past Montgomery County citizens. By unfolding the ongoing history of Montgomery County, we contribute our chapter, our lives, our participation. ∎

GARDEZ BIEN

The Montgomery County seal borrows heavily from Richard Montgomery's family coat of arms, including the broken spear, the armor-encased forearm, the fleur-de-lis, the rings in two quarters of the shield, and the motto itself, *Gardez Bien* ("serve well").

The Maryland coat of arms is reflected in the two flags at the top of the crest. Tying the emblem to Montgomery County alone is the turretlike crown with its indented line, repeated in the center of the shield to represent the borders of a local government.

The design was arranged and approved for Montgomery County by the College of Arms in London, England. Courtesy of the Maryland Municipal Room, Rockville Library

The soda fountain at Vinson's Drug Store with its copper fittings, marble top, and huge mirror with carved trim, lent an elegant note to Rockville's past. When the store was dismantled for urban renewal, the soda fountain was purchased and moved to the Kelley farm in Darnestown, where Michael Kelley (standing) and Darien DiCamillo (seated) enjoy a cold drink on a hot summer day. The stools as well as all the glassware came from Vinson's. Photograph by Anne Dennis Lewis

The names of 105 Montgomery County residents are inscribed on the Vietnam Veterans' Memorial in Washington, D.C., including Robert W. Abernathy, Frederick A. Barclay, Harold E. Barnard, Martin J. Begosh, John A. Bifareti, Jr., Harold D. Biller, William R. Bissell, William J. Boehm, John M. Bowers, Richard B. Bruce, Lance D. Brunson, Charles G. Butler, Jr., John H. Call III, Francis E. Camden, Jr., Darrell E. Campanello, John A. Capasso, Robert M. Carlozzi, Lewis E. Casner, Jr., William H. Christman III, Larry M. Clark, Ernest W. Cole, Jeremiah F. Costello, Kevin M. Coyne, Gerald L. Crosby, James R. Cumberpatch, Jr., Henry D. Custen, Kenneth J. Cymbalski, Charles R. Dale, Tommy E. Dickerson, Carroll S. Dieudonne, Robert D. Donaldson, Walter L. Drosd, Bruce C. Ducat, Leslie M. Dyson, Jr., George L. Ellis, Charles L. Flott, Clayton E. Fraley, Robert M. Gaffigan, Robert W. Gardner, Stephen J. Geist, Robert R. Groom, James B. Hall, Steve W. Harris, David M. Hart, Eugene W. Hartman, Terrin D. Hicks, Robert M. Higginbotham, David L. Hodges, William J. Hodges, William K. Hopkins, John M. Joyce, Jon A. Julia, Wayne A. Keller, Anthony K. Kercoude, Thomas E. Kessing, Jr., Harold J. King, Jr., Arthur G. Klippen, Albert O. Krausser, Kenneth R. Lancaster, John C. Liverman, James E. Love, Wayne T. Lundell, Balfour O. Lytton, Jr., Theodore E. Mangum, Jr., Harold D. Martin, Robert D. Mason, Robert E. Mentzer, Jr., Thomas C. D. Moffitt, Richard K. Morrison, Thomas W. McCarthy, John A. McGinn, William L. McGowan, Frederick R. Neef, John L. Nielson, Gerald E. Neiwenhous, Jr., Frances F. Novello, Roy T. O'Keefe, David F. Osborne, Ernest Postorino, James W. Prather, Edwin H. Pumphrey, James P. Purkey, James A. Reid, Robert H. Shields II, Ralph Simon, Victor A. Smith, Paul W. Smithson, William R. Spates, Jr., William A. Stacy, Jr., Frank M. Streeks, Jr., Allen R. Stroud, Robert H. Swain, Richard E. Swab, Akos D. Szekely, John R. Tine, Thomas G. Turner, Austin R. von Kleist, Donald W. Ward, James P. Ward, George B. Waring, Donald E. Weisman, William A. Wilk, Lorne J. Wilson, Terry Wintermoyer, and Larry A. Woodburn.

In a sad moment of history, one of Montgomery County's finest young men, Terry A. Mote, twenty-three, died in Vietnam on July 1, 1970.

Terry Mote graduated from Richard Montgomery High School and received the Young Adult Award of the Montgomery County Press Association for his varied activities. He entered Montgomery Junior College and earned an associate of arts degree in 1966. According to a dean of students, James H. White, Mote was "one of the finest students" at the college.

The young man joined the service and was twice selected as the outstanding trainee. He was assigned to the assault helicopter platoon of the 189th Aviation Company and sent to Pleiku, Vietnam. Courtesy of Jane Mote

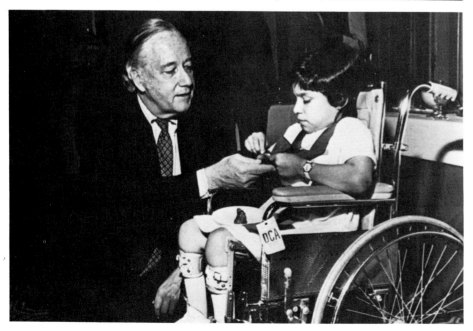

Senator Charles "Mac" Mathias, Jr., visited one of his Montgomery County constituents. Courtesy of the *Courier*

The Damascus High School
marching band struts down the street
in Saint Lo, France, on June 6, 1979,
led by their drum major, Bobby
Corazza. The Damascus band, under
the direction of Matt Kuhn, has two
glass cases full of trophies and certifi-
cates of award.

Shown is the band during Operation Friendly Invasion, an occasion
commemorating the thirty-fifth anniversary of United States's troops
landing in Normandy during World
War II. Although twenty-six bands
throughout the United States were
selected to participate, Damascus was
the only one that accepted. But in
order to attend, the band needed
money. Through a series of fund-
raisers and private donations, the
group raised $61,160.45, and all 146
members went overseas.

The Damascus band returned to
Normandy for the 1984 Operation
Friendly Invasion. Courtesy of the
Courier

Governor Harry Hughes presented
the 1979 Good Neighbor Award to
Gladys King in appreciation of her
friendship and help to hundreds of
Montgomery County residents over a
lifetime of service to her community.
Courtesy of Gladys King

Montgomery County boys leave their town houses to play little league baseball in Rockville. Photograph by Roy Perry; courtesy of Peerless Rockville

"Preservationist" was a word practically unknown in Montgomery County until 1976 when the nation's bicentennial celebrations awakened a sense of patriotism and pride in the past. Communities established historical societies to research local history and preserve significant aspects of the neighborhood architecture. Then, preservationists multiplied, delighted with the special something that made their towns unique.

County Executive Charles Gilchrist and the Montgomery County Council appointed a preservation commission and approved a masterplan and ordinance for historic preservation in Montgomery County. Capitol View Park became the first historic district to apply for and be granted a place on the masterplan.

Historic Medley District in Poolesville restored the mid-nineteenth century Seneca Sandstone Schoolhouse with grants from public agencies. Shown is the ceremony rededicating the schoolhouse as a school museum. Steve Tregoning and his Poolesville High School band performed for visitors, who were also attracted to the ancient school bus in the background.

At the present time, Seneca Schoolhouse is booked solid with classes of Montgomery County schoolchildren eager to experience the way it used to be. Photograph by Margaret Marshall Coleman

Overlooking the Capital Beltway The Church of Jesus Christ of Latter Day Saints Washington Temple illumines the evening sky. Photograph by Anne Dennis Lewis

Montgomery citizens protested. Royce Hanson, chairman of the Maryland-National Capitol Park and Planning Commission, is specifically criticized. Photograph by Anne Dennis Lewis; courtesy of the *Courier*

With help from The Maryland Historical Trust and the Community Development Block Grant, the Boyds/Clarksburg/Germantown Historical Society Inc. restored the one-room Boyd Negro School and re-opened it to the public on May 16, 1982. Special guests were former teachers and students. The teacher pictured here is Miss Lillian Giles and students, names arranged alphabetically, are Mary Frances Butler Carter, Mae Doy Coates, Randolph Diggins, Deacon Gonza Duffy, Virginia Hawkins, Louise Coates Hebron, Ollie Holland, Mable Irvin, Manuel Jackson, Georgiana Johnson, Ivy Johnson, Louise Moore, Ella Moseley, Mary Nailor, Edna Luckett Prather, Lillie Suggs Proctor, Addie Quonn, Henrietta Thomas Randolph, Lucile Sidney, Ella Wims Smith, Louise Snoiere, Clara Talley, Cleve Talley, Howard Talley, Addison Eugene Thomas, Arline Suggs Thompson, and Mary Turner. Photograph by Anne Dennis Lewis

It is frequently said that prices are high in Montgomery County. Not often, however, does cake sell for $265. At the 4-H baking auction at the Montgomery County Fair in 1981, John King has just bid $265 and won a cake baked by Laura Bessier. His father, Harrison King, and his wife and son laugh as Miss Bessier hands him his cake. Courtesy of Harrison and Gladys King

Betty Scull speaks out for her top-priority issue: housing for low- and moderate-income families in Montgomery County. Elizabeth Lee Scull was the most influential woman in Montgomery County for several years. Her strong leadership qualities persuaded many who opposed her liberal policies. She was elected to the county council in 1970; was voted president in 1977; and was serving her third four-year term when she died on May 29, 1981.

Mrs. Scull's son, David Scull, was appointed to complete his mother's term of office. Courtesy of Blair Lee III

They're Montgomery County boys—they love a challenge, cheer a winner, and eat plenty of junk food. Photograph by Roy Perry; courtesy of Peerless Rockville

Michael Barnes, a Democrat from Bethesda, represents the eighth congressional district and tries to shake hands with a potential future voter who remains, however, quite noncommittal. Courtesy of Michael Barnes

Earl and John Glaze prepare to market their tobacco. The brothers cultivate two of the four acres of tobacco currently grown in Montgomery County. Photograph by Anne Dennis Lewis

Today the Chesapeake and Ohio Canal is owned by the National Park Service and is a charming place to stroll, jog, hike, ride bikes or horses, watch birds, fish, canoe, or enjoy a voyage on the *Canal Clipper*, a replica of an old wooden barge.
   Dressed in period costumes, park employees lead the mules, sail and dock the boat, and entertain guests with songs, dances, and tales once a part of canal culture. Photograph by Anne Dennis Lewis

Police officer Joan Preller stands in front of the Hillandale Shopping Center. Today's Montgomery County police officers number 756 and will increase to 783 by the spring of 1985. An additional support staff numbers 191. Of the officers, 74 are women and 138 are members of minority groups. Photograph by Anne Dennis Lewis

Chapter 10
Montgomery County in the 1980s

From quiet, peaceful farmland, to the new industry of high technology and a thriving metropolis—Montgomery County in the 1980s had it all. In a harmonious blend of progress and conservation, high density development and plentiful parks and countryside, Montgomery County planned for today and tomorrow and attained international recognition in the new industries of biotechnology, telecommunications, and space exploration. Long strides were made toward the renaissance of two cities and the preservation of farmland. Controversy surrounded the disposal of solid waste. In equally noteworthy but more personal affairs, two county leaders quit politics, one to help the poor and homeless and the other one to serve God. A youth from the streets of Vietnam arrived in Montgomery County speaking no English and graduated a few years later near the very top of his class.

In Montgomery County anything can happen. Sometimes progress meant turning backward a page or two of county history. In 1873, the Baltimore and Ohio Railroad swept across Montgomery County from Dickerson to Takoma Park bringing with it the wonder of rapid transportation. In the early 1900s, trolley cars wove together the suburbs near the district line. Modern Montgomerians bought automobiles and tracks were replaced with macadam. In the 1980s, a state-of-the-art subway made fast transit a reality between Shady Grove and Washington, D.C. Three passenger shelters opened on the old railroad tracks and even the trolley—that old-fashioned people mover—received funding as traffic gridlock was a daily routine, and residents wearied of driving their own cars to work every day.

Kids got smarter; 154 of them were national merit scholarship semi-finalists in 1989, nearly half of all the scholarship winners in Maryland. Their schools got computers and two prestigious universities built permanent branches in Montgomery County.

Connecting the burgeoning city of Germantown with the farmland of Boyds and Barnesville, the Maryland-National Capital Park and Planning Commission (M-NCPPC) designed and built Black Hills Regional Park with its 505-acre lake. Fit Montgomerians now paddle their Grummans from the brisk town with its new condominiums and

Montgomerians enjoyed the many recreational opportunities offered by the county including horses at Wheaton Regional Park (above), and a quiet canoe at Seneca Creek (shown on previous page).
Photograph by Charles McGovern

houses, its super markets, two malls, and building cranes, to the quiet farmland where Jimmy Lawson raises corn on the hill above the fields and barns of his mother's farm, now buried far beneath the waters.

But the big event of the decade was the arrival of high technological industries. Montgomery jetted into the future on the wings of high achievement and international recognition.

Perhaps it was the proximity to the nation's capital, the federal agencies already established, the good schools and housing, the highly educated, scientifically-oriented population, the clear streams and peaceful meadows, the parks, or a combination of all those attributes. Whatever the springboard, the intricate, tantalizing, incredibly amazing era of high technology landed in Shady Grove.

No question there was a need for the products of high tech industry. For along with the million dollar, tinted glass architectural delights came the whisper of solutions to world problems ranging from AIDS and Alzheimer's Disease, to bug-free, spray-free sweet corn in Bethesda back yards, to go-anywhere pocket phones carried about like a credit card. Protein engineering, information technology, and space exploration became the

Considered one of the best competitive pools in the nation, the new Montgomery County Aquatic Center has a 50-meter pool, five diving platforms with an 18-foot-deep diving well, a "leisure pool" with a playful giant mushroom that sprinkles endless raindrops, and a 200-foot water slide. Located near White Flint in Bethesda, the pool is alternatively a training spa for Olympic contenders, a safe spot to learn to canoe, a court for water polo, and a place for family fun.
Photograph by Brien Williams

Madonna of the Trails returns to a new view of Bethesda. (See page 157.)
Photograph by Margaret Marshall Coleman

Montgomery County's twelve mile, Red Line Metro rail was officially complete on December 15, 1984, with the opening of the Shady Grove station. The adjacent parking area of 7,500 spaces was called the world's largest transit parking. About 100,000 people rode Metro daily, arriving by Ride-On and Metrobus as well as private auto. At this time Metro stations were already completed in Friendship Heights, Bethesda, Grosvenor, Twinbrook, and Rockville.
Photograph by Brien Williams

buzzwords of the decade.

In 1981, the Office of Economic Development promoted Montgomery County as in the forefront of high technology, establishing the county as a center of research and development facilities. Already the county had a solid base of over 250 high technology firms and the National Institutes of Health, National Bureau of Standards, David Taylor Naval Ship Research and Development Center, Food and Drug Administration, and the National Oceanic and Atmospheric Administration.

The High Technology Council was formed, a non-profit corporation aimed at bringing resources to the high technology community of Montgomery County. Major universities were actively wooed and two of the best came, The Johns Hopkins University and the University of Maryland. The National Institute of Standards and Technology contributed staff and loaned valuable computer and telecommunications equipment to the efforts.

With the arrival of the new industry and its stylized buildings, the face of mid-county Montgomery changed considerably. "Tell me where this place is," said an NIH biologist and 20-year county resident recently, "I want to go there! But I don't know where it is."

He had just watched a new video of Montgomery County and found it hard to recognize. Handsome new structures lined the I-270 corridor and the new roads at Shady Grove. The cities, too, were changing.

By the late 1970s, the retail giants had abandoned Silver Spring. Smaller shop owners followed. But the 1980s saw a reversal in this trend as the OED and private industry cooperated and waged an aggressive campaign to bring business back. The Silver Spring renaissance began in 1982 when Lloyd Moore completed the office building at 1100 Wayne Avenue. Moore was acclaimed as the pioneer of the new Silver Spring. Other developers followed, building 8484 Georgia Avenue in 1984, Silver Spring Business Center in 1985, and two big projects in 1986, Lee Plaza and the Metro Center Plaza.

Each building cost millions of dollars. Metro Plaza for example is a $100 million, 750,000 square foot project of three buildings tied together with a mall of retail shops and restaurants and connected directly to the Red Line Metro. County executive Charles Gilchrist called it a balance of the best of the old with the new and an example of government/citizen partnership.

E. Brooke Lee III built Lee Plaza in *art deco* style and included a museum of Silver Spring memorabilia. The black granite and limestone structure with its shoeshine parlor, interior glass brick, and rose neon light was designed to reflect the heritage of Silver Spring architecture. Crisfield's, long a Silver Spring favorite, opened a restaurant on the streetside.

About the same time, the Petrie Corporation proposed another project, City Place. The abandoned Hecht building would be incorporated into 300,000 square feet of leasable space and become a four-story interior mall with an eatery, six movie theaters, retail shops, and offices.

Residents began to rebel when Moore proposed his "Silver Triangle." It would be a massive retail/office complex with apartments, two major department stores, shopping mall, hotel, and office space on both sides of Georgia Avenue, which it would span with multi-stories.

Heydays would come back to Silver Spring. But not everyone liked it. Planning Board Chairman Norman Christeller voted against it. He feared massive traffic gridlock. The Art Deco Society wanted the old buildings restored and included as the cornerstone of Moore's plan. Ten civic associations in conjunction with the Allied Civic Group regrouped as CPOSS, Citizens to Preserve Old Silver Spring.

Nothing happened. By the decade's end, City Place was still just a fanciful signboard on the corner of Colesville and Fenton, and there were lots of places to park at Crisfield's.

Bethesda planners used a different approach. Dubbing it a "beauty contest," they initiated a competition for space available and chose developers who offered pleasant amenities that would be of greatest benefit to the public. Higher density office space was awarded winners who included artistic devices in their plans.

Metro Center began in 1982 and a year later a rush of building applications swamped the professionals at M-NCPPC headquarters. Since the county council had already set a traffic capacity ceiling, development would be limited. Keeping in mind the total cars to be allowed, planners initiated a competition and chose nine projects, resulting in a state-of-the-art city core with gardens, artworks,

Train service increased dramatically during the eighties. The Dickerson station of 1891 was restored in 1986 and Metropolitan Grove shelter was built in 1987. But Germantown was the most fortunate. Once it had a fine red frame station like the one in Dickerson, but in 1978 it was burned by arsonists. In the early 1980s, more and more people moved to Germantown, rode the train, and needed a place to wait. In 1983, the Germantown Bank building of 1922 became a station waiting room. But in 1989, a new station was built, an exact replica of the 1891 structure, with an adjacent, free parking lot. From 150 passengers in 1982, ridership increased to more than one thousand. The MARC Brunswick Line carried 4600 people daily between Point of Rocks and Union Station. Here, MARC (Maryland Rail Commuter Service) zooms into Germantown on the tracks of the old B & O.
Photograph by Margaret Marshall Coleman

Silver Spring Center on Georgia Avenue was once the Woodside Elementary School. During the eighties, school buildings no longer needed were rehabilitated to new use such as homes for the homeless, private schools and academies, or other purposes. Woodside became a government services center, containing recreational facilities, medical services, meeting rooms, and information desks.
Photograph by Margaret Marshall Coleman

and brick-paved walkways.

Nothing was left to chance. Street lights were to be the "Bethesda lantern" style. Trash receptacles had to be cast iron and the sidewalk was specified as "Watsontown 'Garden Blend.'" Even the tree planting wells were carefully prescribed. Bethesda was colored green. To achieve a quick canopy of foliage, the London Plane Tree (*Platanus Acerifolia,* 'Bloodgood') was to be placed every thirty feet along major streets and within the median of Wisconsin Avenue, Old Georgetown Road, and East-West Highway. In planters ("lightweight concrete, tan in color, sandblasted"), flowers would transform the city into a beautiful garden.

The presence of art was emphasized. *Madonna of the Trails* came back to a Bethesda greatly changed. By the end of the decade, more than forty separate pieces of new art had been approved, ranging from an architectural fountain to brick relief sculpture to neon lights.

Throughout the process, the major objective of planners was to create a city for walking. Interesting paths were drawn. Parking was placed underground. Retail shops were to relate to the streets with decorative doors and other attractions, opening outside with vitality and life. Metro Center was the core of Bethesda commerce and granted the highest zoning density, reflecting its status. The tallest buildings were located at this crossroads. Residents wanted their favorite shops retained and plans included some of these. Streets were to be lined with trees, twelve different varieties, but mostly the London Plane. In all, M-NCPPC achieved a pleasant aura in Bethesda—a garden that is not a garden really, but a major new city, a lively downtown with new restaurants, retail stores, offices, and residences served by mass transportation.

Sweeping from east of Silver Spring to west of Shady Grove, Montgomery County traced a green line, establishing the only agricultural preserve in the metropolitan area. This major set-aside of 89,000 acres meant all residents of today and tomorrow could find green pastures, quiet stream valleys, and fresh farm products growing within a short drive. According to the Functional Master Plan for the Preservation of Agriculture and Rural Open Space in Montgomery County of October 1980, land in this area will not be subdivided into lots less than twenty-five acres.

Futurists compared the preserve to Central Park in New York City. The Commission on the Future of Montgomery County predicted in 1988, "As the entire Northeastern corridor becomes one vast megalopolis, we see Montgomery County's rural areas as a refuge for wildlife, for people longing for fresh air and scenic beauty, and for a vital agricultural industry that would otherwise be crowded out by high land prices. It will be the 'green lung' of the Washington metropolitan area filtering our air . . . Montgomery County's agricultural reserve is our Central Park, and just as vital to the health of our county."

It was a great day for many people when this ordinance was passed. To the upcounty farmer, however, it was a disaster. For this was his retirement income. His children's heritage. With that stroke of a pen, farmland value plummeted. Just a week earlier, a farm could be sold to a developer for more than a million dollars. But now land could be sold only to another farmer.

What the county broke, the county could also fix. By the end of the decade, the farmer had three options to provide considerable benefit. The Maryland Agricultural Land Preservation Foundation, the Montgomery County transferable development rights, and agricultural easement programs paid farmers for their development rights. By paying him the difference between the price of his acreage as farmland and its value for real estate development, county officials made the downzoning more equitable to the landowner.

The county helped in other ways. Markets were set up in Silver Spring, Bethesda, and Gaith-ersburg. City governments opened markets in Rockville and Takoma Park. An Agricultural History Park was developed near Needwood. A Farm Market Association and Agricultural Products Council were encouraged and supported by the Office of Economic Development.

Farmers continued to plant, and plants continued to grow. As dogwoods bloomed along the country roads of the agricultural preserve, vegetable, fruit, and wool growers welcomed city dwellers yearning for a whiff of country air and a glimpse of young foals and little lambs, as well as the fresh local products. As the decade drew to a close, farms continued to operate and more than five hundred high technology companies were located in Montgomery County. National and international publicity attracted visits from Japan, Germany, France, England, China, and Brazil, as well as other areas of the United States. The private sector had invested more than $1 billion in the development of the Shady Grove Research and Development Village. Ancillary projects were nearing completion in the corporate focus area of the Village as well as the Shady Grove Executive Center, the Key West Corporate Center, and Decoverly Research and Development Park.

Population increased from 579,053 in 1980 to about 704,400, and at the same time, registered vehicles increased from 445,000 to 549,000. Roads were increasingly congested. The widening of I-270 to twelve lanes was undertaken and nearing completion by the end of the 1980s. New roads were built at Shady Grove. Great Seneca Highway, Midcounty Highway, and the Sam Eig freeway were almost finished.

From Shady Grove to Silver Spring, Montgomery County underwent rapid growth during the eighties, accelerating between 1985 to 1990 when 75,000 new jobs were generated. By the end of the decade, 60 percent of Montgomery's working residents worked within the county and unemployment was only 2.3 percent. Household incomes averaged $68,100, ranking eighth among counties across the nation.

Many things changed in the 1980s. But one factor remained the same: Montgomery County was still a nice place to live.

The old and new of Silver Spring is seen here at Colesville Road and Wayne Avenue.
Photograph by Margaret Marshall Coleman

Ten Mile Creek Stream Valley is shown here in September 1982. This entire valley was soon to disappear far beneath the waters of Little Seneca Lake.
Photograph by Charles McGovern

Black Hills Regional Park and Little Seneca Lake connect Germantown with the farmland upcounty, shown here in August 1986.
Photograph by Bob Powell

A·N·N·U·A·L
Harden & Weaver
TOURNAMENT
Benefitting Children's Hospital

Official 1987 Souvenir Program

Montgomery County's favorite radio performance is the Harden & Weaver Show. Every day except Sunday for nearly thirty years the twosome delights listeners with their friendly good humor, a march, and a hymn. Every year they play host to a golf and tennis tournament at the Montgomery Village Golf Club and the Aspen Hill Racquet Club and Fitness Center. Children's Hospital in Washington, D.C., benefits and everyone has a great time.
Courtesy of Mary Corcoran

Over two thousand horses live in Montgomery County. In the early 1980s, they began dying of a new disease at the rate of sixty to seventy a year. Veterinarians were alarmed. Equestrians were disconsolate. One year all horse shows in the county were cancelled and bridle trails deserted as owners withdrew their mounts into seclusion and watched for fever, diarrhea, lethargy, and colic, symptoms of the horrible disease. It was called Potomac Fever.

Horse owners were terrified. Among them was veterinarian Jean Sessions. She began to examine blood serum of horses infected with the new disease. One night she saw microbial forms resembling *Rickettsia,* a bacteria she recognized from her work with army guard dogs who were dying following symptoms of fever, diarrhea and lethargy. *Rickettsia,* she theorized, caused Potomac Fever.

There followed consultations with researchers at Fort Detrick, the University of Illinois, and the Virginia-Maryland Regional College of Veterinary Medicine. The research was confirmed; treatment and a vaccine were recommended. For her part, Dr. Sessions was named the 1984 Veterinarian of the Year by the Maryland Veterinary Medical Association. And horse trails from Potomac to Brighton were occupied once again. Dr. Sessions is shown here with Molly. Photograph by Dale Leatherman

Widened to twelve lanes, I-270 is overlooked by One Washingtonian Center and Sam Eig Highway. Collector-distributor, or C-D ramps, facilitate entrance and exit points. A high tech wall, aided by freshly planted trees, provides privacy and softens highway noise in nearby homes.
Photograph by Brien Williams

Montgomery County's new high tech industry blooms beside a field in Shady Grove.
Photograph by Brien Williams

229

Few of Montgomery's towns are incorporated. University of Maryland professor of architecture and columnist Roger K. Lewis gently suggested that residents of Silver Spring might consider the idea.
Courtesy of Roger K. Lewis, FAIA, from his column, "Shaping the City," in *The Washington Post*

The December 1985 meeting of the Mutual Improvement Association, the oldest continuously meeting women's organization in the United States, is pictured here.

In 1857, ladies near the Quaker settlement of Sandy Spring decided to meet once a month for intellectual discussion and a simple lunch. Each one would contribute a bit of poetry, literature, or a thoughtful idea. Sometimes one read from an old family diary.

Today they still meet and still keep meticulous minutes so that future generations will have these ties to treasure also. Shown here are Chris Kolstad and Wendy Lawrence, sitting on the floor. In chairs are Helen Nesbitt Farquhar, Sylvia Woodward, Jocelyn Woodward Shotts, Elizabeth Hartshorne Ligon, Caroline Brown Schauffler, and Sylvia Nash. Standing

behind them are Mary Lillian Moore, Margaret Gibian, Nell Ligon Johnsen, Rose Hutton, Caroline Hussman, Louise Young Canby, Henrietta Riggs

Bregliano, Elizabeth Bullard, Elizabeth Jones Grey, Jane Stabler, Mary Moore Miller, and Kay Metcalfe.
Courtesy of George Kolstad

The oldest such organization in the world is the Farmers Club of Sandy Spring.

In Montgomery County, agriculture is big business, producing sales of $30 million a year. But in 1844, it was the business of nearly everyone who was responsible for a roof overhead and bread on the table. With no U.S. Department of Agriculture and no University of Maryland Extension Service, there was no information on new products and methods. In answer to this need, a group of local landowners became the agricultural experimental station for the country.

On February 12, 1844, the Farmers' Club of Sandy Spring was officially organized.

According to the original charter, the improvement of agriculture was the major goal. They would meet monthly

at each farm in alphabetical order, inspect as a group the crops and stock, "farm improvements and contrivances," and return to the farmhouse for tea.

Members of the Farmer's Club of Sandy Spring in 1990 were George

Lechlider, Fred Lechlider, Stanley Stiles, Chris Stiles, Donald Hobbs Sr., Donald Hobbs Jr., Jimmy Barnsley, Harry Fraley, Ellis Hood, Robert Hilton, David Martin, Robert McAlister, Douglas O'Keefe, Robert Smith, Fred Maier, and Gene Iager.
Photograph by Caroline Lechlider

230

Sam Eig died in 1981. A few years later a major road from the Metro to the Shady Grove corporate area was built and named for him. But then, Sam Eig was a most unusual person.

Years ago when he was fourteen, Sam Eig left Russia by himself. A lifetime later he was a millionaire and had donated over $10 million to charities crisscrossing ecumenical lines from Methodist to Catholic to Jewish, and to secular institutions such as Kiwanis and the American Red Cross. *Fortune* magazine selected him as one of ten Americans who had made outstanding contributions to their communities as well as their own business interests.

From a small liquor store on Georgia Avenue, "Mr. Sam" as he was called, built houses in Silver Spring's Rock Creek Gardens in the late 1930s and donated adjacent land for a Jewish Community Center. With his profits he turned to commercial development and constructed the Silver Spring Shopping Center at Georgia Avenue and Colesville Road and the Eig Building. Looking westward, he put up Shady Grove's first big facility, the Washingtonian Towers with its motel and surrounding golf and country club, and created the Shady Grove Music Fair.

Considering all this it seemed most appropriate for his name to soar over the entrance to the new Shady Grove —Sam Eig Highway.
Courtesy of Elizabeth Birnman Eig

Lots of people go to the county fair the third week in August to see the exhibits and watch the animal shows. During the eighties, they had a new instant favorite, pig races. Cheered by the crowds, little pink porkers raced for their oats. None was left out, but one got his dinner first.
Photograph by Tim Warman

The family car of the eighties for Montgomery County families is the van, like the one shown above with Houston Miller and his son, Garrett, of Barnesville. Miller, a NIST environmental chemist and professor at George Washington University, likes the van for the roominess and the safety features for his three small sons.
Courtesy of Dalis Davidson

Jessica Bright, Cara Judson, Lindsey O'Neal, Jennifer Bright and the baby, Molly O'Neal, play with their Cabbage Patch kids on the front porch of the O'Neal home in Quince Orchard. Ian O'Neal plays with transformers, the number one favorite of little boys, and Brady O'Neal gets an unexpected visit from his cat. Like most little girls of the eighties, Molly is wearing her favorite footwear, pink "jellies." Her mother, Carol O'Neal, quit teaching school when her children were born and stays at home with them. Clifford O'Neal is a biochemist with Gillette.
Photograph by Margaret Marshall Coleman

231

These little lambs as well as the burro, mare, geese, border collies, jersey cow, chickens, and sometimes turkeys of Springdale South Farm don't know it, but their days are numbered here on busy New Hampshire Avenue near Ashton. New houses, glimpsed through the trees, begin to line their pastures and fill with city folks. Soon the lambs will be moving and there will be one less farm near Silver Spring. In this area of eastern Montgomery County development was rampant during the eighties.
Photograph by Margaret Marshall Coleman

Elena Stamberg is an artist. With the wool from her sheep and llama, she spins yarn and knits it into incredible garments of unique design.

Elena's view won't suddenly sprout with houses. Her farm, In Sheep's Clothing, lies within the master plan for the preservation of agriculture, keeping the herefords next door forever.

In 1989, the Montgomery County Agricultural Products Council formed to help market her yarn as well as other local crops. Staffed by the Office of Economic Development, the council distributed a farm directory, listing about a hundred farmers wanting customers at the farm.
Photograph by Greta Stamberg

Montgomery County lies gently between the Potomac on the west and the Patuxent on the east. The area described in the Functional Master Plan for the Preservation of Agriculture and Open Space in Montgomery County is outlined in orange. Development rights have been purchased from farms colored green. Individual properties listed in the Master Plan for Historic Preservation in Montgomery County are represented by red dots; yellow colors represent historic districts.
Photograph by Margaret Marshall Coleman

Enjoying the Ethnic Heritage Festival at Wheaton Regional Park, 1985, are Montgomery County Executives during the eighties, Sidney Kramer and Charles Waters Gilchrist.
Photograph by Charles McGovern

Four of Montgomery County's major decision makers form a candid group at the 1985 opening of a new park and conference center, Woodlawn Manor House. Left to right they are Sidney Kramer, David Scull, Norman Christeller, and Neal Potter.

By the end of the decade all but one had a new job. State senator Sidney Kramer became the county executive in December 1986. David Scull, like both his parents, was a member of the Montgomery County Council. He would return to his private office in December 1986, to practice law and write a book. From 1981 to 1989, Norman Christeller was the chairman of the Montgomery County Planning Board. He is now the president of the Montgomery County Housing Partnership.

Neal Potter is a Montgomery County Council member. Elected to the council in 1970 and in every succeeding election, Potter served as council president three times.
Photograph by Charles McGovern

Andrew Schultz, 13, of Ashton wearing a handsome wool tallis from Israel and velvet yamulka, holds the torah as he practices for his Bar Mitzvah with Rabbi Phillip Pohl at B'nai Shalom of Olney synagogue. Following the traditional Sabbath morning ceremony his parents, Dr. and Mrs. Morris Schultz, hosted a party, inviting friends and relatives to join in celebrating the occasion.
Courtesy of Norlaine Schultz

Skye and Patrick Handler slide down a hill at The Oaks Sanitary Landfill. Just over the ridge is their home, Oaks II. This historic log and frame house was moved across the road and an archeological dig completed at the site before construction of the landfill began.

During the 1980s, the prime subject of protest in Montgomery County was the location of a facility for the disposal of solid waste. In January 1981, Laytonsville residents disputed the choice of their neighborhood and contended that a landfill should not be built anywhere at all.

Despite the protests of many civic associations and individual citizens of Laytonsville and Olney, The Oaks Sanitary Landfill opened in June 1982, scheduled to close in July 1989. But as July of 1989 turned into fall and then winter, 2100 tons of trash were added each day and it was clear The Oaks would not be closing soon.

Upcounty residents were just as adamant as those in Potomac and Shady Grove. No one wanted the new landfill. And as the decade drew to an end, there was none. The Laytonsville landfill continued to receive more trash and little boys went sledding in the weekend quiet of its slopes. Photograph by Hank Handler

Ed Stevenson of Travilah likes tractors although he's only two years old. His big sister Sarah watches nervously as Sue Coleman hugs baby Kathryn dressed—like most Washington metropolitan area babies in the spring of 1983—in her Redskins jacket. Photograph by Margaret Marshall Coleman

In the 1980s, all things Gaithersburg got a new appearance. Each street and avenue, each city park or facility was marked with a logo, consisting of a big "G" around the town's historic tree, the Forest Oak. Shown here, the logo denotes the newly purchased Summit Hall Farm Park that once was the Summit Hall Turf Farm. Courtesy of the City of Gaithersburg

Montgomery County people can attend live performances at Burn Brae Dinner Theatre in Burtonsville, in Rockville at the F. Scott Fitzgerald Theater, at the Washington Jewish Theater, and at the Harlequin Dinner Theatre. At the Olney Theatre, Silver Spring Stage, and the Round House Theatre in Silver Spring, and at the Montgomery Playhouse in Gaithersburg, theater may also be enjoyed. Courtesy of the Office of Economic Development

Steven Muller of The Johns Hopkins University, and Dyan Lingle Brasington pose with the Montgomery County flag at the official opening of the university's Montgomery County branch.

Dyan Brasington is the director of Montgomery County Office of Economic Development. In this position she represents the women of the eighties who have achieved success in the profession of their choice. According to the U.S. Bureau of Labor Statistics, the Washington metropolitan area had a greater percentage of professionals than any other region. In 1988, nearly 40 percent of working women held professional jobs. Courtesy of the Office of Economic Development

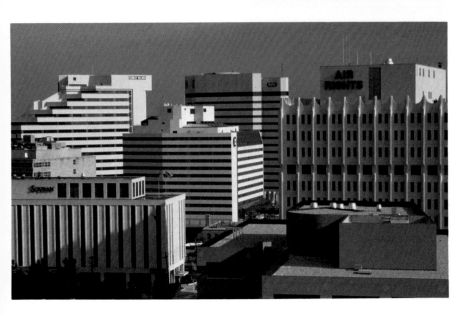

Downtown Bethesda steps up to Metro, July 1986. Community Paint and Hardware, looking like a little yellow buttercup in a forest of giant oaks, remained in its original location. It was about to be moved to a new site in Potomac by the Chevy Chase Savings and Loan Association. Photograph by Robert C. Shafer, courtesy of the Office of Economic Development

The biochemists of Shady Grove wanted a good high school for their kids. And they got one. Quince Orchard High School, shown here, opened in 1988. It was immediately termed state-of-the-art. Since 90 percent of the students had college plans, Quince Orchard was loaded with the very latest in educational frills. Principal Tom Warren said, "We will have the most computerized system of probably any school in the nation," and installed 350 computers, mostly IBM PC-2s.

The same year several new elementary schools opened in the eastern and up-county areas for a total of 160 public schools and approximately 100,000 students. Shown is the S. Christa McAuliffe Elementary School in Germantown.

Private schools and foreign language institutions were laced throughout the county with a combined enrollment of about twenty thousand students. The Japanese Language School in Rockville held Saturday classes for five hundred students. The French International School in Bethesda enrolled more than one thousand full-time students from pre-kindergarten through grade 12. In Potomac, the German School had six hundred full-time students from kindergarten through grade 12. Other schools taught children from Spanish, Chinese, Ukranian, and Arabic countries. Photographs by Margaret Marshall Coleman

Tramp, tramp, tramp the boys are marching! Right down the street in an old Barnesville much changed from the days of long ago. But no matter the air conditioner in the asbestos-framed window or the hybridized begonias along the walk, each costume and rifle is either an authentic reproduction or a genuine antique.

Civil War re-enactments were popular events during the 1980s. The one pictured was part of a large performance taking place over Labor Day 1988 in the picnic woods behind St. Mary's. Troops from Delaware, Pennsylvania, and Georgia were there as well as men from Maryland and Virginia.
Photograph by Dalis Davidson

One Washingtonian Center and the Washingtonian Towers flank an old farm at Shady Grove.
Photograph by Brien Williams

When Michelle Reilly was growing up in Garrett Park her mother often took her to Glen Echo Amusement Park to swim in the Crystal Pool and ride the carousel. Michelle grew up to be a fiber artist. In her mind she could still see the ever-changing kaleidoscope of the Crystal Pool and bright, twinkling, mirrored lights of the carousel, hear the lilting organ music, and feel the motion of the prancing, wooden horse with his painted saddle and tossing mane and tail. With needle, thread, scraps of cloth and her own childhood memory, Michelle Reilly pieced together a quilt for the Glen Echo Park Foundation.

The Glen Echo Park Foundation, Inc., had formed a partnership with the National Park Service in 1987 to rehabilitate what remained of the nineteenth century resort whose rapidly deteriorating infrastructures had outpaced the park's budget. With a goal of $3 million to raise in five years, membership jumped from nineteen to eight hundred members. No one wanted to see the Spanish Ballroom, Adventure Theater, and stone pillars disappear like castles in the sand. The foundation started a fundraising campaign. They sold stoneware vessels created by resident artisans. They held "Big Band" dances in the ballrooms, and sold raffle tickets for Michelle's quilt. By the end of the eighties, Glen Echo was still there and all Montgomery's children could ride the magic carousel.
Photograph by Michelle Reilly

During his administration, Charles Gilchrist initiated the Ethnic Heritage Festival to coincide as often as possible with the county's birthday, September 6. He asked Missy Warfield to serve as chairman and she got together representatives from each of the parts of Montgomery's rich and varied cultural heritage. Shown here is one of the acts performing at the Ethnic Heritage Festival in Wheaton Regional Park, September 1985.
Photograph by Charles McGovern

In 1987, Paul McGuckian was appointed judge of the circuit court in a courthouse considerably different from the one shown on page 104.

No open windows to catch the summer breezes in the 289,000 square foot judiciary highrise of 1981! With nine floors of courthouse space plus a basement terrace and two levels of underground parking, the building has several nice features. It has its own law library and cafeteria but no court stenographers. Judges and jury sit in a circular, raised well surrounded by excellent acoustics; proceedings are picked up by electronic recordings. The sheriff holds prisoners in an interior jail with its own exclusive elevator which travels non-stop to the holding cell of each individual courtroom. A cell door opens directly to the assigned seat, providing security for public and prisoner alike.

By the time he donned his long black robe, Judge McGuckian was already well acquainted with county law and lawyers. During most of the decade he was the Montgomery County Attorney.
Courtesy of Emily McGuckian and her father

McCrillis Gardens, in Bethesda, was donated to Montgomery County in the 1980s and quickly became a favorite spot with its flowering trees and shrubs and quaint statuary. The house interior became an art gallery.
Photograph by Charles McGovern

Brooke Johns died in 1987; he was ninety-three. He is shown doing his favorite thing, entertaining.

Brooke Johns was born to entertain. During a span of three generations, he was Republican county chairman, county commissioner, racing commissioner, real estate broker, and father of six. He married Hazel Barnsley of Sandy Spring and lived with her in a Georgia Avenue mansion of seventeen rooms on 207 acres. They called it Brooke Manor. Years later, all but the house and twenty-three acres became the Brooke Manor Country Club where Brooke Johns' banjo was often heard.

The banjo was signed by four presidents and the Prince of Wales. He loved to play it and sing. Years ago he was a singer, dancer, orchestra leader, emcee on stage, screen, radio, and television. He performed with Al Jolson, Ginger Rogers, Eddie Cantor, Ray Bolger, and Gloria Swanson, among others. Billed as "6 foot 3 and oh, so different," Johns starred in the

Ziegfield Follies in New York and Palace Matinees in Washington.

A third well known Montgomery County man died during the 1980s, Gen. Albert C. Wedemeyer. A four-star general, Wedemeyer was the World War II theater commander of China. During his distinguished career he worked directly with Great Britain's Lord Louis Mountbatten and China's Generalissimo Chiang Kai-shek.

The Wedemeyer home, Friends Advice, is the ancestral home of Elizabeth Dade Emrick Wedemeyer, the general's wife. It is an historic site, included on the Master Plan for Historic Preservation in Montgomery County.
Photograph by Charles McGovern

It was during this decade that the Montgomery Chamber Orchestra formed. Piotr Gajewski, music director and conductor, spearheaded the organ-ization. He is shown here performing in the auditorium of Montgomery College, Rockville. Later, Gajewski changed the name of his group to National Chamber Orchestra.
Photograph by Joseph Bailey, courtesy of the National Geographic Society

In 1985, Suburban Hospital built an addition for their shock/trauma facility and a helicopter landing pad for emergencies.

Here, highly skilled physicians like Dr. Brajendra Misra and his team of health care specialists work wonders. The unit is one of ten in Maryland and has a survival rate that is two-and-a-half times greater than that in other states. Over ninety percent of the critically injured patients brought to the emergency care survive their injuries.
Courtesy of Suburban Hospital

Montgomery County trend-setting weddings and receptions often took place at public mansions, such as Strathmore Hall, shown above.
Photograph by Barbara Glaeser

Chapter 11
Profiles in Leadership

Counties are in large part a reflection of the quality and success of their economic and cultural institutions and the people who manage them.

From the earliest times Montgomery County has been blessed with people and institutions of foresight and tenacity. Their collective story is reflected in the preceding pages. The detailed stories of some of the best are told in the following pages.

The Publisher

Montgomery County Office of Economic Development

The Shady Grove Life Sciences Center, a 288-acre site, is the nation's first R&D park developed exclusively for biotechnology industries, life sciences service, and university education and research.

Einstein said that the only universal constant is change. This aptly describes Montgomery County's economy. It grew and changed from an agricultural economy to a major employment center in its own right, dominated by advanced technology enterprises. It will change again, but one thing is certain: its healthy and steady growth has enhanced the county's quality of life.

The Montgomery County Office of Economic Development is fortunate to have played a part in charting and directing the course of the county's economic growth. In recent years, the office has broken out of the traditional bounds of industrial development and expanded into helping the county shape and implement its vision. Thus the office's theme: "Montgomery 2020: Share the Vision." Its director, Dyan Brasington, put it this way:

"Since our vision is one of continued prosperity and balance, we have sought to develop a healthy mix of economic enterprises, and to position the county in the forefront of technological changes. Business diversity and technological innovation set the pace for achieving our goals for the year 2020."

Like the county's economy, the office has changed over time, reflecting the government's commitment to spurring balanced economic growth. During the 1950s and 1960s, the office did little more than distribute information and let economic forces take their natural courses. It was the county's "passive stage" of economic development.

Coping with a stagnant economy in the last half of the 1970s, the county upgraded its economic development efforts in 1978. The office was split away from the Department of Housing and Community Development and charged with the mission of revitalizing the county's economy. Aggressive economic development efforts soon turned the tide and succeeded in transforming the county into a community with a vibrant and fast growing economy. This was the "active stage" of economic development.

As early as 1984, the county's economic development efforts entered a "visionary stage." Long-term plans were implemented to ensure the continued economic prosperity of the county in the twenty-first century. The biotechnology initiative was adopted. The R&D Village was born,

and major universities expanded into the county.

Today, the county's economy is like a many-faceted gem. As the county and its corporate community turn toward new fields of development, like a revolving gem, new economic facets appear and old ones capture new light in previously unseen ways.

Just as the county economy is diverse, so are the services provided by the Office of Economic Development. It offers a wide variety of programs to serve businesses. Its technical and financial assistance, site search, export development, and many other services are aimed at helping companies to start, prosper, grow, and expand. And through many of its public-private partnerships, such as the Economic Advisory Council, Conference and Visitors Bureau, and Agricultural Advisory Board, it has contributed to the realization of the county's long-term vision.

"Unlike communities that pursue economic development solely for revenue enhancement, Montgomery County follows development strategies that will improve our lifestyle as well," said Montgomery County Executive Sidney Kramer. And these strategies have the active support of many community leaders. Their profiles on the following pages illustrate how diverse and multi-faceted Montgomery County really is.

Montgomery County is one of the premier site locations for high technology industry in the nation. More than six hundred technology related companies are located in the county.

242

The Montgomery County High Technology Council

The Montgomery County High Technology Council is a non-profit, educational organization, established in December 1985 by members of the county's high technology business community, federal laboratories, and Montgomery County government. Initially the council was composed of a core of twenty-three firms and federal laboratories. Today, it numbers over two hundred members from several high tech industry sectors, including biotechnology, computers, tele-communications, and information technologies.

In the early 1980s, the high technology business community and the county government discussed a critical missing ingredient needed to assure a competitive posture, both on a national and a global level: a major university presence in Montgomery County. As a result of these discussions, the council was formed and, charged with serving as a broker for the high technology community in representing its needs to higher education institutions and government.

Satellite centers of The Johns Hopkins University and The University of Maryland have been established in Montgomery County and Montgomery College, and other colleges and universities throughout Maryland and the District of Columbia have increased their offerings and presence in the county.

The High Technology Council also serves as a catalyst to bring together entrepreneurs, large firms, venture capitalists, and university faculty, helping to establish networks that bring people and resources together to assist in building working relationships. The council sponsors monthly "network" breakfast meetings for both the biotechnology and information technologies sectors. It also has quarterly CEO Roundtable dinner meetings, quarterly board-sponsored luncheons with guest speakers and special business seminars and conferences. The council publishes a bi-monthly newsletter, a directory of Montgomery County high technology firms, and reports based on studies and surveys conducted by the council.

Finally, the High Technology Council helps educate public officials on the needs of the high technology

A council member makes a presentation at one of the council's network meetings.

Winners of the council's annual Montgomery County High Technology Council Awards in 1990 are from left, Larry Cunnick, Lewis Shuster, Joseph Sciulli, Dennis Curtin for John Puente, Dan Goodman, and Jack Harris.

community. In the past two years, the council has helped in the formation of the state of Maryland's Office of Technology Development, and several of the council's members serve on its Advisory Committee. The council monitors legislation and regulations at the federal, state, and local levels affecting the high technology community. The council recently received a grant from the state of Maryland to undertake a feasibility study for a statewide Maryland Information Technologies Center.

The council continues to work to increase the higher education presence in the county through new programs such as software engineering, biotech-nology, and telecommunications offer-

ings. State government in Maryland has awakened to the importance and presence of high technology to its future economic well-being. With nearly one-third of the high technology employment in the state and 40 percent of its recent growth, the health of the county's high technology community and the health of the state are inextricably linked. Montgomery County is one of the leading high technology centers in the country and the council remains committed to its role in maintaining this position of leadership.

Conference and Visitors Bureau of Montgomery County, MD Inc.

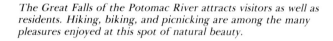

One of the most colorful spots in Montgomery County is Brookside Gardens, a 50-acre garden open to the public year-round.

The Great Falls of the Potomac River attracts visitors as well as residents. Hiking, biking, and picnicking are among the many pleasures enjoyed at this spot of natural beauty.

In the early 1980s, business and government leaders in Montgomery County realized the need for a county-wide organization to promote tourism to Montgomery County. Through the cooperation of the private and public sector, the Montgomery County, MD, Travel Council, Inc., was created as a non-profit membership association dedicated to the promotion of travel to and within Montgomery County. The council's purpose was multifaceted: to promote and develop travel and the travel industry in Montgomery County; to unite private organizations and public agencies concerned with the economic benefits of the travel and convention business; to pool resources, exchange ideas, and share experiences so that members might participate in the development and expansion of the travel industry; and to undertake cooperative promotional efforts to increase travel and convention business in Montgomery County.

As part of the organization's marketing strategy, leisure travelers, group tour participants, business trav-elers, and conference and meeting attendees are targeted through trade shows, direct mail campaigns, market-place exchanges, and advertising. The organization has also reached out to the local community by exhibiting at local trade and community shows, pre-senting slide show programs of county attractions to civic organizations, service clubs, and senior centers, and providing brochures in response to phone and mail requests for informa-tion about county attractions and accommodations.

In 1989, the organization offi-cially changed its name to the Con-ference and Visitors Bureau of Montgomery County, MD Inc., in order to stress the organization's em-phasis on bringing small meetings and conferences, as well as tourists, to the area. The bureau is an active member of both the National Tour Association and American Bus Association and works closely with tour operators bringing groups of tourists into Washington, D.C., and its surrounding suburbs. Since 1988, the bureau has aggressively pursued both the group travelers coming into the area as well as government, association, and corpo-rate meeting planners. The bureau also holds memberships in the Society of Government Meeting Planners, Professional Convention Management Association, and the Greater Washing-ton Society of Association Executives.

Membership within the bureau has grown to nearly one hundred busi-nesses and organizations representing accommodations, restaurants, attrac-tions, tour and transportation com-panies, meeting and event planners, relocation companies, and professional services. Membership is open to busi-nesses and organizations who share the desire to promote tourism to Montgomery County.

Through its myriad marketing activities, the Conference and Visitors Bureau strives to meet the needs of the hospitality industry in Montgom-ery County and to serve all travelers to Montgomery County with informa-tion to make their stay both pleasant and memorable.

Prospect Associates, Ltd.

Founded in 1979, Prospect Associates provides health sciences research and communications support for organizations striving to improve public health. Prospect works with scientific, health, and technical clients to help them solve the nation's foremost health problems, including AIDS, cancer, heart, lung, and blood diseases, diabetes, digestive diseases, kidney and urologic diseases, arthritis, mental disorders, and problems of the aging population, including Alzheimer's disease.

The company's high quality services and direction are driven by a staff of more than 150 professionals who come from science, health, and technical disciplines. Through these individuals, the company offers "thoughtware," the culmination of staff members' experience, expertise, knowledge, and interests, and their ability to apply this combination to health issues. On-staff Ph.D.'s, scientists, nurses, dieticians, biostatisticians, and epidemiologists work together with staff experts in health education, public health, health promotion, information dissemination, and media to provide comprehensive support.

Using a multidisciplinary approach, Prospect tackles each project with an understanding of science and technology and knowledge of how to interpret, translate, and disseminate information to scientists, health professionals, patients, and the public. This combination of science and communications makes Prospect unique in offering clients comprehensive support for health-related projects.

Prospect's broad spectrum of services parallels the needs of the science and health communities: each day, as the amount of research and scientific data increases, this information is synthesized and disseminated to appropriate audiences. Many of Prospect's projects use the company's complete range of support, beginning with science-based and technology services. Prospect assesses the state of science by collecting, analyzing, evaluating, and interpreting scientific and technical data. The resulting information is used for various purposes, such as the development of strategic plans and public health policy on crucial health topics.

Prospect Associates President Laura Henderson.

Prospect's communications experts translate this information into messages for health professionals, patients, and the public. Using mechanisms such as teleconferences, television and radio ads, and printed materials, Prospect reaches each audience with information on the prevention, diagnosis, and treatment of disease. The end goal may be to try to change a doctor's medical practice to use state-of-the-art treatment, modify a person's behavior or attitude about unhealthy habits, or provide information to allay fears or change attitudes about a disease.

Prospect has supported hundreds of health-related projects for clients in the public and private sectors, including all twelve of the National Institutes of Health; other agencies and departments of federal, state, and local governments; research institutions; universities; professional and voluntary associations; hospitals; and private industry. Through this depth of experience, the company has gained credibility in the scientific community and has won awards for its technical, creative, and economic excellence.

Among its awards, Prospect received the 1988 Maryland Award for Economic Excellence, the state's highest award for economic development. Also in 1988, Prospect was selected as Montgomery County's Small Service Firm of the year.

Part of the company's success is due to its location in Montgomery County, which is in the heart of the nation's biomedical and health research community. Prospect's interest in health and related issues also extends to local and state initiatives aimed at improving public health education, care, and practice. Within the county, Prospect's volunteer affiliations include the Commission on Health, the Economic Advisory Council, and the Education Exchange. In addition, Prospect's President, Laura Henderson, is a member of Maryland's Office of Technology Development advisory group and an active board member of the Corporation Against Drug Abuse.

Prospect's greatest asset has always been its people.

GTE Government Systems-NCSD

The largest telephone exchange company in the United States had total annual revenues in 1988 of over $16.5 billion. It has been listed by *The Wall Street Journal* as one of the top ten corporations "poised to lead business into the 1990s." It has also established Montgomery County, Maryland, as a key location for development of its U.S. Government business base.

GTE is a multinational corporation operating in forty-six states and forty-one countries, whose price share appreciation and shareholder return are one of the highest in American industry. GTE chairman, James L. "Rocky" Johnson, has set an objective for GTE to be recognized as a world leader in all three of its core businesses: Telephone Operations, Telecommunication Products and Services, and Electrical Products. GTE president, C.R. "Chuck" Lee, has noted that it requires "Top quality, top technology, and most of all, top people to make this kind of thing happen." The top people and high tech commitment of the Montgomery County, Maryland, local community led GTE Government Systems to locate its National Center Systems Directorate (NCSD) in Rockville at 1700 Research Boulevard in January 1983. This office was established to give GTE Government Systems Corporation a strong Washington, D.C., presence and, to provide excellence in software and systems engineering support in transport, processing, distribution, analysis, and dissemination of intelligence data.

Frank Gicca, President of GTE Government Systems Corporation, has stated that "GTE is in the business of providing quality solutions to satisfy requirements of the U.S. Government, its military services, and allied governments around the world." Noting GTE's commitment to high ethical and professional standards, Mr. Gicca has also stressed, "We shall operate our business competitively and with dedication to the professional well-being of our employees, and with support to our local communities."

Don Littler, vice president and general manager of GTE's Strategic Electronic Defense Division, selected the Montgomery County location for GTE's Government Systems Washington Operations. He hired A. Roy Burks who retired as Director of SIGINT Operations from the Central Intelligence Agency to lead the newly established National Center Systems Directorate. In late 1984, NCSD was awarded a very large government contract which has made it the focal point for Voice Processing research in GTE. It has also established GTE as one of

Growth in sales has been accompanied by increases in personnel and facilities. GTE employed over four hundred personnel in Montgomery County in 1988. GTE occupies approximately 150,000 square feet of Montgomery County real estate of which eighty thousand square feet are Special

The GTE/NCSD Integration and Test Building at the Decoverly complex on Key West Avenue.

GTE/NCSD Montgomery County Headquarters at 1700 Research Boulevard, Rockville, Maryland.

the nation's leaders in computer security, mass library storage of digital data, workstation design and engineering, and database management systems. GTE is a leader with the intelligence community in Ada methodology, and software reuse and productivity. GTE also maintains communications databases which allows it to provide the very best in C3I analytical support to the Washington, D.C., agencies.

GTE/NCSD in Rockville has grown rapidly. Average annual sales growth was a spectacular 140 percent from 1984 to 1988 with annual sales in excess of $50 million in 1988.

Compartmented Intelligence Facilities (SCIF). In 1987, NCSD took occupancy of a uniquely designed integration and test building with a seventeen thousand square foot shielded enclosure, one of the largest such contractor facilities in the Washington area.

In Rockville, Burks is now SEDD Director of Business Acquisition - New Ventures. Gerry Roth, a long time GTE employee and one of the original group of personnel transferred from California, is now the new Director of NCSD. Mr. Roth had been the manager responsible for GTE's large Voice Processing win.

The Johns Hopkins University Montgomery County Center

Situated on a 36-acre campus, in a 44,000-square-foot instructional facility with seventeen classrooms, a 300-seat auditorium, and study areas—donated by Montgomery County—the Montgomery County Center serves as a base from which Johns Hopkins responds to the continuing professional development and research needs of government, business, education, and high technology.

The Johns Hopkins Montgomery County Center—located at Shady Grove in Rockville—is the site of Montgomery County's newest education complex. A cooperative venture of Montgomery County government and the University, the Center provides graduate degree and professional development opportunities in engineering, business, education, and public health to thousands of adults living and working in the greater Montgomery County area. Local organizations use Center space for special training programs and professional activities. Regular lecture series, free and open to the public, also bring leading scientists and Hopkins researchers to the county to discuss evolving issues in science and advanced technology.

The G.W.C. Whiting School of Engineering offers one of the largest graduate engineering programs for part-time students in the nation. Complete master's degree programs are available in computer science, electrical engineering, and technical management. Select courses are also offered in applied mathematics, applied physics, and mechanical engineering. With the proliferation of high technology firms and govern-

ment agencies along the I-270 corridor, part-time graduate education has become an integral part of the region's economic development goals. Hopkins engineering is pleased to be a partner in that development.

When the Hopkins School of Public Heath was founded in 1916, it was the first institution of its kind to combine research and education. Today, it is the largest school of public health in the world. It awards more doctoral degrees than any other American public health school and trains graduate students from more than seventy countries. Through its ties with Montgomery County, the School of Public Health reaches Washington-area professionals who want to increase their expertise in a variety of health related areas. Physicians, dentists, nurses, and veterinarians are among the students who earn public health degrees at the Montgomery County Center. The program in Montgomery County gives those students access to faculty members from the Baltimore campus and a range of courses dealing with policy, statistics, epidemiology, maternal and child health, and other specialties from the ten academic departments.

For more than eighty years, the School of Continuing Studies has pro-

vided advanced educational opportunities for adult, part-time students. At the Montgomery County Center, the School offers business professionals master's programs in management, financial management, information technology, and human resource/ organization development. Educators and human services practitioners may enroll in master's programs with concentrations in counseling, special education, and rehabilitation, or in courses in curriculum and instruction. And those pursuing careers in science or science-related fields may apply for the master's program in interdisciplinary science studies. The School's Center for Management and Professional Development offers certificate programs in marketing communications and real estate development at the Rockville campus. Corporations may call upon the Center's business specialists to design customized programs for delivery on site or at the Montgomery County Center.

Hopkins has also acquired the Banks' Farm, which is adjacent to the Shady Grove Life Sciences Center and within easy walking distance to the Montgomery County Center. It is anticipated that this special, historic environment will become the home of the Johns Hopkins Belward Research Campus, and ultimately integrate Hopkins research with that found in Montgomery County's broad corporate and institutional research and development community.

The Johns Hopkins University Montgomery County Center campus will accommodate future research facilities, expand the number and size of classrooms, increase space for faculty and professional staff, and improve student support services. The approved overall master plan will accommodate 375,000 gross square feet of building construction to be completed in seven phases.

The Gillette Company

King Camp Gillette, the company's founder.

The story of the international company that now bears his name began with the remarkable imagination and talents of King Camp Gillette.

Born in 1855, Gillette began his career at the age of seventeen as a traveling salesman at the Baltimore Seal Company. There, he met William Painter, the inventor of the crown cork, still used to cap bottles today. Painter urged Gillette to concentrate his creative talents on developing a product that could be used over and over again by satisfied customers.

The idea of inventing such a product intrigued Gillette. He went through the alphabet doggedly, considering all the things that people used frequently, searching for inspiration. Nothing clicked until one summer morning in 1895. As Gillette began to shave, he found his razor

edge so dull he couldn't use it. His irritation grew as he realized the razor would require professional sharpening. Suddenly, as he told the story years later, the idea of an entirely new razor and blade flashed into his mind.

He quickly saw a sequence of parts: a very thin piece of steel with an edge on both sides, a handle and a clamp to center the blade over the handle. He was certain that this product—one that would be purchased over and over again—was the great invention he had been looking for.

In 1901, a mutual friend outlined Gillette's safety razor idea to William Nickerson, an MIT graduate and successful machinist. Nickerson was unimpressed with Gillette's idea, but after some badgering, agreed to study the idea more closely. A few weeks later Gillette had a partner.

Nickerson estimated they would need five thousand dollars to tool up sufficiently to manufacture the razor on a commercial scale. To raise the money, Gillette formed the American Safety Razor Company on September 28, 1901. While Gillette tried to sell stock, Nickerson began creating machinery in a friend's shop in Boston. By the end of his first full year in operation. Gillette had sold fifty-one razor sets and 168 blades.

The year 1904 was more encouraging. Gillette received a U.S. patent on the safety razor, and the company bought a six-story building on First Street in South Boston, where all manufacturing took place. By the end of 1905, production had grown to 250,000 razor sets and nearly 100,000 blade packages containing a dozen blades.

For the next ten years, during which razor sets continued to sell at a rate of between 300,000 and 400,000 per year, blade sales soared to 84 million.

Millions Learn to Shave at Home

As American soldiers entered the war in April 1917, U.S. military commanders worried about the unsanitary conditions of trench warfare. Then they learned that French soldiers, who had fought in the trenches for three years, relied on the Gillette safety razor to keep clean shaven. The U.S. government placed an order unprecedented in its size—3.5 million razors and 36 million blades—enough to supply the entire armed forces.

The government's sales order not only boosted the company's business enormously, but also irrevocably changed American attitudes toward shaving. Self-shaving had been introduced to millions of men who previously depended on barbers. More specifically, the Gillette Safety Razor Company now had a vast pool of new customers, especially those who were buying blades to fit the safety razors they received in the service.

Ironically, another war, World War II, prompted more changes for Gillette. Because of manufacturing restrictions, no new products were introduced until after 1945. During the War, the Gillette research and development staff prepared for the postwar market by developing the first dispenser for double edge blades. The dispenser was a considerable improvement on the waxed wrappers and outer envelopes in which blades had been packaged previously.

New Opportunities in the Postwar Years

The war years had produced a tremendous backlog in demand for the company's products, and record shipments of razors and blades were made during 1946. To meet this demand, manufacturing facilities were expanded with factories opening in Argentina, Brazil, France, and Switzerland.

In 1948, following several years' deliberation on its future direction, the company decided to broaden its product line, thereby attracting a wider range of consumers. That same year, Gillette acquired the Toni Company, a home permanent manufacturing firm. The following year, the Toni product line was expanded with introduction of White Rain shampoo and Prom home permanents. In 1957, the company introduced Adorn Hair Spray, which soon became the leader in the hair spray market. The company's second acquisition, the 1955 purchase of the California-based Paper Mate Company, marked Gillette's entry into the writing instrument field.

The decade of the sixties opened on a high note with the full-scale introduction of the Gillette Super Blue Blade, the company's first coated edge blade. Gillette also introduced Right Guard aerosol deodorant in 1960.

The company's two acquisitions also were doing well. Paper Mate's sales grew, and the popularity of Toni's line of shampoos and hair sprays more than balanced the declining demand for home permanents.

In 1964, to further stimulate growth in the shaving and personal care industry, Gillette created a new corporate research facility, The Gillette Medical Research Institute. The Institute was formed from a nucleus of R & D personnel from the Toni Company and the Gillette Safety Razor Company. The Institute's purpose was twofold: to conduct applied research in areas relating to the company's interests and to ensure the efficacy and medical safety of all Gillette products. Today, these functions continue to be the responsibility of the Gillette Research Institute and the Gillette Medical Evaluation Laboratories, located in Gaithersburg, Maryland.

In 1971, the company's Safety Razor Division introduced the Trac II twin blade shaving system. The razor quickly became the top seller in the United States, and its success prompted the development of two more twin blade products—both disposable— the Daisy shaver for women and the Good News! razor. Later, shaving systems that would revolutionize shaving were introduced—the Atra razor in 1977 and Sensor in 1989.

The Gillette Company Today

The Gillette Company today bears little resemblance to the firm founded by King Camp Gillette at the turn of the century. The Gillette Company has grown to a diversified international corporation whose personal care and personal use businesses yield annual sales of about $3.5 billion. Gillette employs 29,600 persons. The company's policy is to recruit, hire, train, and promote employees at all levels without regard to age, race, color, religion, sex, or national origin.

Manufacturing operations are conducted at sixty-two facilities in twenty-eight countries, and products are distributed through retailers, wholesalers, and agents in over two hundred countries and territories.

The Gillette Company's overall success stems from a carefully executed product and diversification effort, coupled with an acquisition program to position Gillette in new businesses with attractive growth and profit potential. In addition, throughout the company's history, the commitment to make and sell products that give sound value to consumers and that are safe for intended use has remained constant. Excellence in this task has resulted from the skillful and consistent performance of Gillette employees whose great store of talent and initiative will serve the company well in the future.

The first Gillette razor, circa 1901.

Boehringer Mannheim Pharmaceuticals Corporation

Boehringer Mannheim Pharmaceuticals Corporation in Rockville.

Boehringer Mannheim Pharmaceuticals Corporation (BMPC) is the newest member of a 130 year-old health care company, Boehringer Mannheim (BM). Founded during March of 1859 in Mannheim, Germany by Christian F. Boehringer, the company is still solely owned by his direct descendants. In the early part of this century, BM was a large manufacturer and marketer of quinine, an important drug at that time. In the 1950s, BM grew to an international company by opening sales offices and new companies on many continents around the world.

Boehringer Mannheim came to the United States in 1964 when the first office was opened on East 44th Street in New York City. Today, the Boehringer Mannheim America, Ltd., (BMA) family of companies manufactures and sells health care products to a wide variety of market segments. They supply reagents and diagnostic systems in chemistry, hematology, and immunology. BM provides diagnostic and biochemical companies with the basic ingredients for innumerable tests, assays, and surveys. Further, Boehringer Mannheim provides pharmaceutical and industrial manufacturers with the raw materials for their products and is among America's leading producers of dry chemistries. BM also works through its subsidiary, DePuy, Inc., with orthopedic surgeons and teaching hospitals by developing and marketing the best in orthopedic implants, instruments, and surgical appliances.

All of the BMA companies have grown dramatically over the past decade. Collectively, sales were more than $500 million in 1988 making BMA a leader in the U.S. health care industry.

BMPC was founded during the summer of 1984 in Rockville, Maryland. Rockville was selected as the site for the new company because of its proximity to the Food and Drug Administration (FDA) and the National Institutes of Health. Dr. J. Richard Crout, vice president of Medical and Scientific Affairs, led the new division in its goal of conducting the clinical research and regulatory work required by the FDA to obtain approval of Boehringer Mannheim compounds for marketing in the United States.

BMPC is dependent upon its "mother company" in Mannheim, Germany, for the discovery of new drugs and initial testing. When data on a new, promising drug becomes available from Mannheim, an Investigational New Drug (IND) application is submitted to the FDA, along with a research plan for studying the drug in the United States. Upon completion of the clinical research, a New Drug Application (NDA) must be submitted to, and approved by the FDA before the drug may be marketed.

A partnership was formed in June 1987 with SmithKline Beecham to gain the aid of a major company in the U.S. pharmaceutical market in order to develop and market two important new Boehringer Mannheim compounds. One of these compounds will be used in the treatment of hypertension, the other for the treatment of coronary artery disease.

In December of 1988, Mr. L. William McIntosh joined the company to lead the newly formed Marketing and Business Development group. March of 1989 found BMPC moving to its new corporate headquarters consisting of twenty-seven thousand square feet of office space in the Decoverly Office Park in Rockville. Today, BMPC employs over sixty employees with full staffs in clinical research, pharmacokinetics, regulatory affairs, pharmaceutical operations, marketing, business development, and administration. It is our goal to build a fully integrated pharmaceutical company before the turn of the century.

As a company dedicated to the development and marketing of novel, innovative, high-quality prescription drugs, BMPC will continue to expand its research efforts. This expansion has begun and will result in efforts to develop products for a variety of diseases including hypertension, congestive heart failure, angina, diabetes, and cancer.

Boehringer Mannheim Pharmaceuticals Corporation is proud to be part of the international expansion of Boehringer Mannheim worldwide. Soon, pharmaceutical products from BMPC will join the highly successful line of Boehringer Mannheim diagnostic and biochemical products marketed in the United States. Pharmaceuticals, diagnostics, and biochemicals—better health care through technology from Boehringer Mannheim.

Center for Advanced Research in Biotechnology

In 1985, the University of Maryland, the National Institute of Standards and Technology (NIST), and Montgomery County jointly established the Center for Advanced Research in Biotechnology (CARB), a unique forum for collaborative research among academic, government, and industry scientists.

Located on the University of Maryland's Shady Grove Campus at the Shady Grove Life Science Center in Rockville, CARB lies in the heart of Maryland's thriving biotechnology community and is near all Maryland's major university research campuses and several government laboratories, including the National Institutes of Health. The 40,000 square foot facility that houses CARB was designed to meet the specific needs of the biotechnology community in the field of protein structure, function, and design.

CARB, with sophisticated state-of-the-art instrumentation, provides an exceptional environment for training graduate students and post-doctoral fellows in fields critical to the future of biotechnology. CARB also offers a Visiting Scientists Program that allows researchers from industrial, academic, and governmental laboratories to work at the facility for extended periods.

Basic to all research at CARB is the ability to clone and express genes to produce large quantities of engineered protein and nucleic acids for detailed biophysical studies. CARB has established molecular biology laboratories with state-of-the-art facilities for DNA chemistry and genetic engineering and has small-scale fermentation capabilities as well as access to a large bioprocessing facility on the College Park Campus of the University of Maryland.

Some of the most important biotechnology products now emerging are genetically engineered proteins that are used in a variety of medical and commercial applications. Many are hormone-like molecules with significant potential as therapeutic agents. While genetic engineering will continue to produce a variety of natural proteins for medical, industrial, agricultural, and other commercial uses, the rapidly advancing field of protein engineering will significantly enhance

CARB moved into its new headquarters in November 1989.

CARB's ability to produce novel proteins with improved properties.

Protein engineering, the specific modification of the atomic structure of a protein, can be used to alter and enhance the properties of the molecule. To advance the field, CARB has established programs in five critical research areas: molecular biology, macromolecular crystallography, nuclear magnetic resonance spectroscopy, physical biochemistry, and computational chemistry and modeling. The combined efforts of scientists in these areas, working toward the common goal of understanding protein structure and function, will help ensure that protein engineering becomes a commercial reality.

In addition to the outstanding laboratories that have been established at CARB, there are facilities for seminars, workshops, and scientific meetings. The CARB building contains a 100-seat auditorium and several seminar rooms that can be used for programs and short courses to communicate the latest advances in protein engineering. These exceptional facilities are available for scientific meetings by special arrangement with CARB.

One of CARB's primary missions is to narrow the gap between discoveries in the research laboratory and the practical needs of industry. Working closely with industry to help determine the direction of research, CARB's goal is to enhance the transfer of technology to strengthen Maryland's and the nation's industries in protein structure, function, and design.

Booz · Allen & Hamilton, Inc.

Thirty years ago, one of Booz, Allen & Hamilton's Washington area offices was based in a Bethesda storefront that eventually became an Italian restaurant. Today, that restaurant would run out of pasta long before it ran out of Booz, Allen mouths to feed.

Now occupying most of East West Towers on East West Highway in Bethesda, Booz, Allen is securely at the forefront of Montgomery County's burgeoning high technology community. With more than 1300 people in East West Towers, 3000 in the Washington area, and 4500 worldwide, the firm stands as a leader in providing technology and management consulting services to government and industry.

In fact, it helped pioneer what has become known as the professional services industry—engineering, research and development and technical services companies whose growth propelled Montgomery County into a fertile ground for technology development.

"When I joined the firm in the 1960s, the professional services industry was still in its infancy," says chairman R. Michael McCullough, who served as one of the first presidents of the Professional Services Council, a large, national industry trade group. "We're very proud to have been part of it from the beginning."

"There's no question in my mind that firms like ours are home to many of our country's best and brightest engineers, scientists, and technologists," says William Stasior, president of Booz, Allen and board member of the Montgomery County High Technology Council.

Booz, Allen, long known as management consultants to senior industry management, performed its first assignment for the U.S. Navy in 1940. By 1948, it had a permanent office in Washington. Today, some 60 percent of its nearly $500 million annual sales derives from helping organizations develop, acquire, use, and manage

technology.

In the 1950's the firm's technical activities were managed out of a series of offices in Bethesda's Woodmont Triangle. Later, the firm consolidated these activities into what was known as the Booz, Allen Building on Bethesda Avenue before outgrowing that site in the early 1970s. Important projects performed by the firm in the 1950s and 1960s in such areas as space, ship systems, computers, and communications were precursors to what Booz, Allen is doing in the same fields today.

"The work back then was extremely interesting. There always was something new to do and learn. The same is true today," says Peter Mettam, a thirty-year veteran of the firm.

Then, as now, the role played by the firm's Bethesda-based Technology Center was that of system engineer—working as a catalyst to help government and industry design, manage, and implement solutions to complex problems. An important difference today is that Booz, Allen has extended the concept to system integration and implementation, working hands-on with clients on projects ranging from Space Station to computer security.

"Some firms help formulate a strategy, others do the nuts and bolts work. We cover the ground by helping a client develop a strategy, deliver a solution, then ensure that it works successfully," says Gary Mather, president of the firm's Technology Center. "We call our approach interdisciplinary —the combination of people with technological skills, expertise in key organizational functions, broad industry perspectives."

Adds Stasior, "Our success is due, foremost, to our people. But it also comes from our ability to walk in the client's shoes, then work the problem from top to bottom."

As a result, the growth of the Technology Center has been spectacular, averaging more than 20 percent

per year during the 1980s. Today, Technology Center staff work in such areas as aerospace, defense, communications, information systems, environmental science, transportation, manufacturing, human resources, ship systems, and more. Booz, Allen is helping cities like Los Angeles engineer and build a new subway system; it's also helping the Navy design,

develop, and launch a new satellite communications system.

"What we basically sell is the talents and abilities of our people," Mather says. "Providing them with the tools and training they need to do the job, as well as a vibrant quality of workplace life, are fundamentals of our strategy."

Accordingly, Booz, Allen provides

staff with more than two hundred training courses, including satellite links to academic consortia; computer resources, including 7.5 gigabytes of minicomputer capacity and a microcomputer to staff ratio of 1:1.5; and a Local Area Network woven together by more than eighteen miles of coaxial cable.

In 1989, the firm also opened a Systems Resource Center in East-West Towers that serves as a testbed and R&D facility for advanced computing technologies. "The SRC provides the firm with enormous leverage," Stasior says. "It's already been responsible for $40 million in new business."

What's ahead? "Ours is a legacy of leadership," says Stasior. "We plan to keep growing as an integrated provider of technology and management consulting services."

"Increasingly, we're working on a global basis," says Mather. "This is what our clients demand of us, and this is how we're going to serve them. I think the 1990s are going to be the most exciting decade in our history."

Mettam agrees. "Booz, Allen's a magnificent company with many opportunities. If I had to do it all over again, I wouldn't hesitate to stay thirty years at Booz, Allen."

IBM in Montgomery County

IBM, the world's largest computer company, traces its beginnings in Montgomery County to 1959 when a handful of employees began work at a temporary location in Rockville's Congressional Shopping Center. These employees were part of IBM's Military Products Division, a group that developed special information handling systems for the U.S. government. The division was establishing its headquarters in the Washington metropolitan area.

Later that year, the division moved into its first permanent Montgomery County location at 326 East Montgomery Avenue in Rockville. Also, the division was renamed the Federal Systems Division. The new division combined the engineering, manufacturing, and systems management capabilities of the Military Products Division with the Washington Federal Data Processing Division marketing office.

Within a short time, the company had spread to several buildings in the county. That changed on June 13, 1966, when IBM opened a new facility in Gaithersburg. The Gaithersburg facility consolidated many of the division's offices in the county under one roof. More than one thousand employees relocated to the new facility at night and over weekends to avoid disruptions and delays in work. To get large pieces of furniture to the second floor, the movers took a window out of the second floor, put in a hoist and brought the furniture through.

Today, IBM's nine thousand employees in the county occupy 3.6 million square feet of leased and owned space and are located in thirty-two buildings. The majority of the county's employees work in the Federal Sector Division which focuses on IBM's work for the federal government. Other county employees are involved in development of commercial systems integration solutions and the marketing, servicing, and administration of IBM products, both nationally and worldwide.

One of IBM's most visible programs in the county is its work for the Federal Aviation Administration (FAA). IBM installed new computers in the nation's twenty air route traffic control centers for more efficient

In the early sixties, the IBM Gaithersburg site was 121 acres of farmland.

handling of air traffic. The new computers feature increased capacity, improved reliability, and faster computer speed.

IBM employees are presently working on an FAA contract to develop, deploy, and service the Advanced Automation System (AAS), a major modernization of the nation's air traffic control system. The contract combines advanced hardware and software that has been designed to make air traffic controllers more efficient.

AAS will provide the FAA with the reliability, flexibility, and additional computing power needed to meet increases in air travel into the next century.

IBM believes in being a good neighbor in the communities in which it does business. Besides being a member of such organizations as the Chamber of Commerce and the Montgomery County High Tech Council, the company supports the county with a wide variety of contributions, grants, funds, gifts, and personnel programs.

At IBM, surplus equipment and furniture doesn't collect dust in warehouses. Charitable non-profit organizations can receive chairs, desks, lamps, and other office equipment. Montgomery College receives

technical equipment the company no longer needs. Even surplus food from company picnics and celebrations is donated to local soup kitchens.

IBM also encourages its employees to be active in their communities. Through its Fund for Community Service program, IBM supports employee volunteer efforts with grants. In Montgomery County, funds have been used for everything from purchasing computers for educational programs to buying food processing equipment to feed the poor. Company employees may also take a paid leave of absence to work for a nonprofit organization.

Many of IBM's community programs began as an employee suggestion. In 1970, IBM employee Rupert Curry had a simple idea. Why couldn't the company help still the pangs of hunger? Out of that idea came Project Thanksgiving. Every November since then, hundreds of Montgomery

IBM Federal Sector Division headquarters in Bethesda.

Today, Gaithersburg is IBM's largest facility in Montgomery County with 2.4 million square feet of space and more than four thousand employees.

County IBM employees have worked packing grocery bags, loading trucks, and distributing food to community service agencies.

Over the years, IBM has contributed nearly twenty-one thousand dinners—more than 125,000 meals—to needy families, and more than six thousand IBM employees have donated their time to help make the project a success.

Education is another area in which IBM and its employees take a keen interest. IBM has been an active partner with local schools in the Adopt-A-School program. Employees work with students giving them an opportunity to learn about business and discover possible careers. They also tutor students and serve as positive role models.

IBM was a strong supporter of creating an education center in the county to provide coursework for advanced degrees. Montgomery County has recognized the company for its help in establishing the University of Maryland Education Center in the county.

IBM is proud to have been a part of Montgomery County for more than thirty years.

COMSAT
Communications Satellite Corporation

Shown above are the headquarters of COMSAT Laboratories, COMSAT Systems Division, and COMSAT Video Enterprises.

COMSAT Corporation was created by President John F. Kennedy when he signed the Communications Satellite Act into law in August 1962. From this beginning, COMSAT has put satellites to work linking people and businesses around the globe—"helping the world work." These vital satellite connections allow us to make international telephone calls, send and receive data and facsimile, and view live international broadcasts.

In 1964, COMSAT formed the International Telecommunications Satellite Organization (INTELSAT) to facilitate international communications between fixed points by satellite, and was named the U.S. representative to that treaty organization. Initially, Intelsat had eleven participants. It has since grown to 119 member-countries.

In 1976, COMSAT developed the MARISAT System which later evolved

into the International Maritime Satellite Organization (INMARSAT). COMSAT is also U.S. representative to this fifty-nine member international cooperative, through which the maritime community benefits from satellite communications services. In early 1991, COMSAT will begin providing satellite communications services to airliners in international flight. COMSAT's international and mobile communications services are carried out through its World Systems Division in Washington, D.C.

COMSAT Laboratories

COMSAT Laboratories, the research and development center of COMSAT, was formed in 1967 to help meet the technical challenges of managing the global INTELSAT system. Initially located in Washington,

D.C., the Laboratories moved to its present site in Clarksburg, Maryland, in 1969. The Laboratories is housed in a 400,000 square foot facility on 210 acres of land along route I-270 north of Gaithersburg.

The Laboratories employs approximately three hundred people, including some of the most experienced communications engineers and scientists in the world. These professionals, in their diverse areas of expertise, conduct research on devices, subsystems, technologies, and techniques related to telecommunications, with a strong emphasis on communications via satellite.

COMSAT Laboratories' reputation for excellence in advancing communications is reflected by the customers that rely on its expertise. For example, as a subcontractor for NASA's Advanced Communications Technology Satellite (ACTS) program that will usher in the next generation of communications satellites, COMSAT Laboratories is designing, developing, and implementing the NASA ground station and Master Control Station.

Many of the Labs' projects are performed for and directed by COMSAT's major lines of commercial business, including COMSAT Video Enterprises and COMSAT Systems Division, which are also located at the Clarksburg site.

COMSAT Video Enterprises

COMSAT Video Enterprises

A researcher works with experimental optimized dual-polarized global coverage antenna in the anechoic chamber at COMSAT Laboratories.

(CVE) is the second largest provider of in-room video entertainment services to the lodging industry. It serves more than seventeen hundred hotels nationwide (more than 300,000 hotel rooms), with pay-per-view and free-to-guest programming. It also provides electronic guest room services, special events programming, and video-conferencing.

Delivered to hotels via satellite, COMSAT's video entertainment ser-

A technician observing plasma deposition of materials at COMSAT Laboratories.

vice offers hotel guests the chance to see pre-home-video movies in the comfort of their hotel rooms.

CVE's electronic guest room services system is the most advanced technology of its kind available. It provides everything from video room checkout and housekeeping status to a video magazine, while minimizing the demands placed on hotel staff and operations.

COMSAT Systems Divison

COMSAT Systems Division (CSD) specializes in the engineering and integration of systems and networks for the movement and management of information. Its systems integration expertise encompasses the total spectrum of telecommunications and information systems technology and services. CSD's capabilities, backed by the world class COMSAT Laboratories, include expertise in all aspects of information and communications networks and systems. COMSAT General, the satellite operations arm of CSD, operates a satellite–based television distribution network under contract to the NBC television network,

and provides satellite engineering and technical support services around the world.

Today, CSD provides systems and services to government, commercial, and international customers. Ongoing programs include contracts with various elements of the U.S. government, Voice of America, governments of Federal Republic of Germany, Cote d'Ivoire, Turkey, Japan, Republic of Korea, Italy, USSR Academy of Sciences, Geostar Corporation, and others.

COMSAT is proud to have been a solid citizen of Montgomery County for more than twenty years. It looks forward to playing a significant role in the county's continuing vital growth and development.

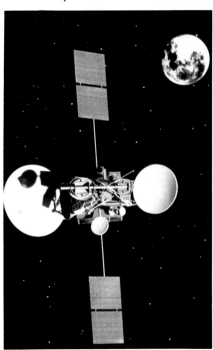

COMSAT Laboratories is one of the principal private sector contractors for NASA's Advanced Communications Technology Satellite (ACTS).

BIOCON, Inc.

Research for a healthier tomorrow.

BIOCON, Inc., is a biomedical research laboratory specializing in animal-related services. Equipped to provide all phases of animal care, including quarantine and routine health screening, BIOCON's goal is to provide a wide range of research animal-related services to both private and government clients.

Since its incorporation in 1978, BIOCON has managed on-site animal colonies for several federal agencies. BIOCON has also performed, in our own facility, product safety evaluations, long and short term carcinogen studies, as well as the production and manipulation of monoclonal antibodies *in vitro* and *in vivo*. Our animal breeding experience includes the production of over forty congenic mouse strains and twenty transgenic mouse constructs for the National Institutes of Health. Additionally, BIOCON provides histology, veterinary pathology and animal health screening services.

Staff members routinely care for approximately nine thousand animals of various species on a daily basis both on and off site. Specializing in Animal Holding and Breeding, Acute and Subchronic Toxicity Testing, Animal Disease Diagnostic Services, Contract Management Services for Animal Facilities, Contract Antibody Production, and Contract Technician Services, BIOCON also provides assistance to clients in the selection of appropriate animal models which meet their research needs.

Each contract, regardless of its size, is considered important to BIOCON. Depending on the type of services required, a team is formed and held responsible for all phases of animal care and technical manipulations under the direction of the project manager, who interacts directly with the client. Additionally, the project receives routine inspections from BIOCON's Quality Assurance Unit to ensure compliance with approved research protocols.

BIOCON has continued to expand each successive year and is adding 60 percent more facility space in 1990. Additionally, sales volume has doubled over the preceding three years and similar growth is expected over the next three to five year period.

Some of BIOCON's present activities include breeding of congenic, transgenic, and inbred mice; breeding rabbits; holding mice, rats, hamsters, guinea pigs, and rabbits; hybridoma maintenance; surgical procedures on rodents such as fat pad clearing, transplantation of preneoplastic tissue, cell grafting, solid tumor transplants, and collection of samples for DNA analysis; and antibody production in mice and rabbits.

BIOCON is also capable of performing comprehensive health profile screenings in-house. The ready availability of three, board certified veterinary pathologists has proved to be a distinct advantage when emergency diagnoses are needed for quick response to real or potential disease outbreaks, and is a key asset to the laboratory animal health program. Additionally, these consultants respond to daily health observations; advise and implement procedures to prevent, control, and treat disease occurrences and animal injuries; provide training and guidance to animal technicians in proper animal handling and restraint; monitor surgical procedures in-house where required; and remain available for consultation with investigators.

In keeping with a commitment to quality in research, BIOCON adheres to and often surpasses the guidelines for animal care and facility requirements as described by the Animal Welfare Act; the *Guide for the Care and Use of Laboratory Animals*; and the *Principles for the Use of Experimental Animals*. BIOCON also has an approved Animal Welfare Assurance Statement on file with the Office of Protection from Research Risks (OPRR); is accredited by the American Association for Accreditation of Laboratory Animal Care (AAALAC); and is registered with the U.S. Department of Agriculture (USDA).

Contel ASC

Contel ASC was founded in 1972 as a subsidiary of Fairchild Industries. The company, then known as American Satellite Company and based in Germantown, Maryland, was one of the first communications companies to provide transmission and network services via satellites.

The ability to launch and position communication satellites in space opened the door to new approaches for communicating both nationwide and worldwide. Prior to space-based communications, the primary means of transmission was either copper cable or radio frequencies.

During the 1970s, Contel ASC introduced a number of innovative applications that were firsts in this young industry. In 1975, Contel ASC successfully implemented the first high-speed facsimile remote printing of a newspaper. The customer was *The Wall Street Journal.* Similar satellite-based services are used today by *The New York Times* and *USA Today* for transmitting photos and copy to regional printing facilities.

In 1979, the company first used Cryptoline for Western Bancorp in a specialized network application, which provided for the secure transmission of sensitive financial information. During the same year, Contel ASC introduced the first integrated digital communications controller.

The company came under dual ownership in 1980, when Contel Corporation of Atlanta, Georgia, reached an agreement with Fairchild to enter into a joint ownership of American Satellite Company. Contel Corporation acquired sole ownership of the company in 1985, and two years later changed its name to Contel ASC. During the same year, the company launched its first wholly-owned communications satellite, ASC-1. In addition to ASC-1, the company uses 50 percent of the Galaxy III satellite, and holds a significant interest in the Westar IV and V satellites. A major event for the company will be the launching of its second satellite, ASC-2, in the first quarter of 1991.

Contel Corporation provided the financial backing for Contel ASC to grow and expand its satellite-based

Contel ASC employs more than four hundred people at its headquarters in Rockville.

communications services. In 1987, Contel ASC acquired Equatorial Communications Company, and the VSAT business of Comsat Technology Products. Equatorial has a number of major achievements in VSAT technology including the first data broadcast network, patented spread spectrum technology, and the first interactive VSAT network.

These acquisitions positioned Contel ASC as a major force in both the interactive data and broadcast data markets. The company presently operates and maintains an installed base of thousands of domestic data network sites. Contel ASC also operates the National Network, a shared service available in fifty cities nationwide, and a number of private high speed data and video networks. In addition to this broad-based domestic communications

business, the company is a major data network provider to customers in Brazil, India, Australia, Spain, Sweden, and a number of other countries.

Contel ASC continues to increase its customer base by providing the users of data networks with reliable and efficient systems solutions. Among its major corporate customers, the company serves leaders in the energy, banking and finance, insurance, and retailing industries. Headquartered in Rockville, Maryland, along the I-270 technology corridor, the company employs more than eight hundred employees. In addition to its head-quarters' location, the company has offices in Los Angeles, California; Mountain View, California; Atlanta, Georgia; Chicago, Illinois; Detroit, Michigan; Houston, Texas; New York, New York; and London, England.

Hughes Network Systems, Inc.

HNS headquarters in Germantown, Maryland.

Hughes Network Systems, Inc., (HNS), a wholly-owned subsidiary of Hughes Aircraft Company, is a major supplier of communications networks and products for commercial and government organizations. HNS has been a pioneer in advanced, digital communications technology for over nineteen years.

Located in Germantown, Maryland, with an additional manufacturing facility in San Diego, HNS supports sales offices throughout the United States, and its subsidiaries, representatives, and distributors provide worldwide sales and service coverage. HNS presently employs approximately twelve hundred people, almost half of whom are software and hardware engineers.

Hughes products include Very Small Aperture Terminals (VSATs) for data, voice, and video networking via satellite, turnkey packet switching networks, mobile satellite communications equipment, digital radio telephone systems, Time Division Multiple Access (TDMA) equipment for domestic and international use, and a complete line of digital satellite modems and encryption equipment.

As part of its comprehensive approach to providing reliable, cost–effective communications network solutions, HNS has developed significant strength in each of the key

areas associated with turnkey system design and implementation. These areas include network modeling, design, engineering, manufacturing, program management, and field support. HNS is acutely aware of the importance of these disciplines to successful delivery of high performance systems in a timely, economical, and reliable manner. As a result, HNS has committed significant resources in each of these areas to offer customers state-of-the-art communications systems tailored to their specific requirements.

Hughes Network Systems, Inc., was founded in 1971 as Digital Communications Corporation (DCC) by a team of engineers at the forefront of digital satellite communications technology. The objective was to take their vision and research experience into the real world and develop a new industry based on satellite networking.

Initially, DCC designed, developed, and manufactured a variety of sophisticated digital satellite communications networks used primarily in international applications for INTELSAT and INMARSAT. These large networks preceded today's digital technology explosion and, therefore, required DCC to develop a variety of technologies ahead of the industry.

In 1976, DCC was selected by

TELENET to develop the world's first multi-microprocessor packet switch. This design has served as the mainstay for TELENET for over a decade and propelled DCC into the forefront of data communications networking.

DCC was acquired by Boston-based M/A-COM in 1978 and began an aggressive expansion program to take advantage of its technological lead. M/A-COM, with its microwave and fiber technologies, began a variety of joint programs to develop digital-based communications systems. From 1978 to 1987, the telecommunications division grew rapidly, with the expansion of the computer industry and its dependence on data networking.

Hughes Aircraft Company, a division of General Motors, and the largest manufacturer of satellites in the free world, recognized this market revolution and decided to acquire M/A-COM's telecommunications division so that Hughes could become a complete turnkey network supplier, vertically integrated from an equipment manufacturer to a service provider. Today, Hughes Network Systems, Inc., along with Hughes Communication, Inc., and Hughes LAN Systems, Inc., represents an unparalleled force in the private networking market.

Trammell Crow Company

Phase III at Metro Park North features a five-story barrel vaulted atrium.

Trammell Crow Company's Phase V at Metro Park North was preleased, designed, built and occupied in fifteen months.

Privately held by its 155 partners and employing more than fifty-five hundred people, Trammell Crow Company has evolved from a local Dallas development firm into a diverse real estate investment and management firm that is active in every significant market in the United States, and in several major markets abroad. As a principal or a fiduciary, the company owns and manages an $11 billion portfolio of real estate projects, including 170 million square feet of office buildings, warehouses, and retail space internationally. In addition, the firm manages 70 million square feet of commercial space for third party institutional investors.

Trammell Crow Company is the largest commercial real estate development and management firm in the United States. Each office is managed by a local operating partner. These offices operate as autonomous, full-service companies that acquire and develop industrial, retail, and office real estate. Each Trammell Crow Company office manages and leases property for its own account and for third parties. The company operates from ninety such offices located throughout the United States and abroad.

From long-term experience,

Trammell Crow Company knows that real estate is a cyclical industry. In the midst of an ever-changing world market that opens new opportunities as well as new challenges, the firm will continue to seek and embark upon new ventures where it has significant competitive advantages.

What will remain the same is Trammell Crow Company's adherence to a strong working philosophy that ensures value to its customers, investors, and lenders, and provides the highest-quality working environment for its partners and employees.

Trammell Crow Company has been an active member of the Montgomery County business community since 1975. From offices in Rockville, the Suburban Maryland Division owns and manages over three million square feet of office, R&D, and industrial space in four Maryland counties.

The crown jewel of these properties is the Metro Park North office park located in the I-270 corridor in Montgomery County. Currently comprised of 900,000 square feet of office and R&D buildings, Metro Park North has a projected total buildout of 1.8 million square feet.

In keeping with the Trammell Crow Company tradition of providing value to its customers, the Suburban

Maryland Division has created a complete working environment at Metro Park North, and pioneered the amenity center concept in the Maryland market. Tenants enjoy the benefits of a fully equipped fitness center complete with stair-master, free weights, cross-country ski machine, air-dyne bike, universal weights, hot tub, steam, and locker rooms. They also are served by a free conference center, delicatessen restaurant, dry cleaners, jogging trail, and an on-site Trammell Crow Company professional property management team.

Metro Park North is within a mile of the Shady Grove Metro Station and is served by the Montgomery County Ride-On bus system. The buildings feature superior design, ample parking, state-of-the-art HVAC systems, and the lowest operating expenses in the county for comparable quality space. In all respects, Metro Park North is a first-quality office park providing superior accommodations and service to tenants.

Synthecell Corporation

From left to right, James W. Hawkins, Ph.D., President, and E. Courtney Hoopes, Vice President and Chief Financial Officer, are the company's founders.

Synthecell Corporation, a Rockville-based company founded in 1986, is already making a big mark in the field of biotechnology.

One of only a handful of companies devoted to "antisense technology," one of the newer areas of biotechnology, Synthecell's unique niche in the marketplace has the potential of creating entirely new approaches for the treatment of diseases.

Synthecell uses four nucleic acids to make a synthetic DNA. DNA is the fundamental component in the cells of all living things and is needed for organisms to live and grow. Using synthetic DNA to "program out" defective genetic information, the company eventually hopes to identify products that would block the development of various cancers, AIDS, sickle cell anemia, or any genetic diseases. Meanwhile, Synthecell continues production of new types of DNA and supplies synthetic DNA to a steady group of clients for research.

Synthecell's initial resources were oriented toward the development of scientific protocols and a modest productive capacity targeted to the needs of individual researchers. The rapid development of more demanding customer relationships such as pharmaceutical houses and large research

institutions necessitated not only expansion but reorientation of Synthecell's production strategy. Accordingly, Synthecell committed significant effort to reconfiguring its laboratory to the high output production of synthetic DNA and developing product documentation to support the highest level of quality assurance.

In its effort to set the highest standards for itself in custom DNA systhesis, Synthecell has set a standard for the industry. New product development has been a keystone of Synthecell's strategy from the outset. The company's first product line was developed around the synthesis of conventional oligonucleotides, or O-oligos, the form of DNA with a chemical composition identical to that found in nature. As basic applications for synthetic DNA have developed, Synthecell has identified several emerging requirements for the specialty synthesis of modified forms of O-oligos, the first company to do so. Synthecell is still the leading commercial source of this product.

The most recent focus of Synthecell's ongoing product development program is the synthesis of peptides. In the future, Synthecell will continue to focus in two areas: DNA and peptides, and hopes to market diagnostic kits

for genetic and infectious diseases to the clinical diagnostic market.

The company now occupies space in the Shady Grove Life Sciences Center, the nation's first R&D park developed exclusively for biotechnology industries, life science service, and university education and research. Synthecell expects that this facility will be one of the premier biotechnology centers in the world.

From left to right, Linda A. Chrisey, Ph.D., Senior Scientist, Robert L. Somers, Ph.D., Vice President-Science, and Gong-Huey Shiue , Ph.D., Peptide Scientific Director, are seen here in the lab.

Westat

Westat is its staff—more than one thousand researchers, data technicians, and field workers who apply modern statistical survey methods to the information needs of U.S. government agencies and business clients. Most of this staff live in Montgomery County, home to Westat's corporate offices for over twenty-five years.

A typical day at Westat begins hours before dawn as the night computer operator finishes the backup of Westat's data files from the previous day and resets its extensive network. By 9:00 a.m., 530 full-time staff and 600 part-time staff arrive at the company's offices in Rockville. Reports and presentations are being finalized for U.S. government clients; data collections are being designed for studies that range from epidemiological medical research to energy consumption; data clerks are keying and editing interview forms for more than fifty different projects; the telephone research centers' staff are preparing for another day of calls to households, employers, schools, and health providers across the country.

In rural Ohio, a Westat technician draws a sample of drinking water to be tested as part of a nationwide survey of pesticides in water supplies. In a New York City hospital, a Westat nurse checks the charts of patients as part of Westat's management of an NIH-sponsored clinical trial of a new drug. In Los Angeles, a Westat survey management team is beginning the five-day training of sixty-five experienced interviewers on the details of collecting student financial aid data from 1,200 colleges and schools nationwide. In west Texas, a team of Westat health professionals begins another day of medical examinations and nutritional assessments in Westat's mobile health center that will move from site to site across the country throughout a six-year period.

Throughout the day and early evening, Westat field interviewers collect survey data from individuals and institutions in over one hundred locations across the United States. Their interviews cover a wide range of topics: expenditures for health care, the results of federally-funded job training, and experience with foster care programs. It is well past midnight in

Senior Officers of Westat in the 1980's - Standing left to right are vice presidents Doris Northrup, Stephen Dietz, and Thomas McKenna; seated are Edward Bryant, chairman emeritus; Morris Hansen, chairman of the board; and Joseph Hunt, president.

Maryland when Westat's telephone interviewing center in California shuts down and the daily closeout of computer databases in Rockville begins again. It has been another day of service to clients and another day on the long path to becoming one of the ten largest private survey research organizations in the United States and the world.

The path for Westat began in Denver, Colorado, in 1961 as a partnership of statistical consultants. In 1965, the young company moved to Washington and found new opportunities in contract work for the U.S. government. By 1970, when Westat was acquired by the Information Technology Group of the American Can Company, the company had about fifty full-time employees. The appeal of employee ownership never disappeared, however, and eight years later, an employee stock ownership plan (ESOP) purchased the company from American. At present, 725 employees own Westat stock. Employee ownership plays an important part in the company's success; it contributes to employee participation and motivation, and it gives Westat the freedom and the incentive to make long-term investments that enhance its reputation for quality and survey integrity.

As the company grew, expertise

was developed in a broad range of government program areas. Senior statisticians who are internationally recognized authorities in sample survey design joined the company. Broad experience was acquired in data collection methodologies and computerized data systems. A custom market research organization, Crossley Surveys, was acquired. A nationwide field data collection organization and three modern telephone interviewing centers were established.

Since its beginning, Westat's growth has reflected the increasing importance of timely, high-quality information to researchers, to business and government program managers, and to government policymakers. For federal government agencies, information developed through statistical research serves a broad range of needs: assessing the educational achievement of students, understanding health and environmental risks, gaining new knowledge of the causes of disease, monitoring the performance of social programs, developing recruiting strategies for our armed forces, and supporting the development of policy and regulations in many areas of government. In meeting these needs, Westat combines a well-established experience and reputation with a constant effort to innovate and build new capabilities.

ANT Telecommunications, Inc.

ANT Telecommunications' headquarters are in Gaithersburg, Maryland.

ANT houses its own Computer Aided Engineering (CAE) Center.

ANT Telecommunications, Inc., officially opened its doors in Gaithersburg, Maryland, in late 1985. Unlike most new companies though, ANT brought with it over eighty years of corporate experience, solid financial backing, and a worldwide reputation for technical excellence.

This is due to the fact that ANT Telecommunications is the U.S. subsidiary of one of Europe's leading telecommunications manufacturers, ANT Nachrichtentechnik GmbH, headquartered in Backnang, West Germany, and a pioneer in worldwide communications since 1903.

Originally founded under the name Telefunken, ANT's roots go back to the very beginning of electronic communications. Not only has the company grown up with the industry, it has contributed greatly to that growth as well—from developing Germany's first carrier-frequency system in 1919, to leading the way in today's fiber optic systems, digital transmission, and satellite communications.

ANT now employs over eight thousand in its German headquarters and four production plants, has agents and representatives on every continent on the globe, and generates annual revenues of over $900 million.

Further strengthening its position, ANT became part of the Bosch Telecom group of companies in 1989. Bosch Telecom is a business sector of Robert Bosch GmbH, best known around the world as a manufacturer of electronic equipment for the automotive industry. Worldwide, Bosch employs 170,000 people and has subsidiaries, affiliates, and representatives in more than 130 countries. Annual sales revenues during 1989 totalled $17 billion.

Much of ANT's success in the telecommunications industry during the past eight decades is a direct result of its strategic persistence. Throughout its existence, ANT has concentrated its efforts on enhancing and expanding its capabilities solely in the field of communications systems, serving a very defined market segment. As a result, ANT has built a worldwide reputation for stability, reliability, and outstanding quality in its products.

ANT Telecommunications brings to the United States the background and experience of its well-established, technology-oriented parent company. ANT's commitment to the U.S. market is demonstrated by its decision to develop and manufacture its products in the United States, specifically for that market.

ANT's main focus is business development based on engineering, manufacturing, and customer support activities. The company provides sophisticated telecommunications equipment primarily to major carriers in North America with the first products being introduced to the American market in 1988.

Working closely with its parent company on all efforts, ANT also provides technical assistance to its German colleagues and marketing support for relevant German products in the United States.

According to the company's president, Jost A. Spielvogel, ANT's size is ideally suited to the company's target market segment. The Gaithersburg office employs approximately sixty professionals in its engineering, sales, marketing, and operations departments. Compared to its larger competitors, ANT can be more flexible because of its size and can therefore better serve the unique needs of its customers in a quick, responsive manner.

ANT's commitment to the U.S. telecommunications market is to continue its tradition of technical excellence originally set over eight decades ago. Armed with a combination of U.S. technology and the highest standards of German engineering, and backed up in expertise and solid financial support by a large, well-established parent company, ANT Telecommunications has all the ingredients for a long and successful future in the U.S. market.

WEST GROUP

WEST*GROUP, a leading commercial real estate developer in Montgomery and Fairfax counties, introduced the concept of the quality office park to the Washington Metropolitan area nearly thirty years ago. That concept begins with the selection of a prime site on major transportation arteries and is enhanced by a beautifully landscaped campus. The success of the concept has been realized in award-winning parks such as WEST*GATE and WEST*PARK office parks in Tysons Corner, Virginia, as well as WEST*FARM Technology Park in Silver Spring, Maryland, the largest office park offering R&D/flexspace in Montgomery County.

The WEST*GROUP portfolio now includes more than 9 million square feet of commercial, residential, and retail space including several premier office centers along the I-270 corridor. Among these are Executive Plaza, Research West Corporate Center, WEST-X Building, Research Park, and Executive Office Center.

Originating in the early 1950s with Mr. Gerald T. Halpin's initial real estate venture for Atlantic Research Company in Gainesville, Virginia, WEST*GROUP has evolved into one of the nation's outstanding developers. The firm continues to provide expertise in land acquisition as well as development, design, construction, leasing, and management services.

In 1960, Mr. Halpin and Mr. Thomas Nicholson formed a private real estate investment company, Commonwealth Capital, Inc., which helped to plan, develop, and manage the 680,000 square foot Landmark Shopping Mall in Alexandria, Virginia. In the early 1960s, Mr. Halpin and Mr. Nicholson were joined by Mr. Charles B. Ewing, Jr., and by Mr. Rudolph G. Seeley, owner of adjoining land in Tysons Corner, to form the WEST*GATE Corporation, which established its headquarters in McLean, Virginia. The organization was incorporated in 1970 as Management Associates, Inc., with a name change to WEST*GROUP in 1984.

WEST*GROUP enjoys a major presence in Montgomery County not only at its Rockville office centers, but also through its distinctive

The Harford Buildings at WEST*FARM Technology Park in Silver Spring: winner of a National Honor Award for Excellence in Design and Development. WEST*FARM is the largest office park offering R&D/flexspace in Montgomery County.

WEST*FARM Technology Park, located near the intersection of Cherry Hill Road and Route 29 in Silver Spring. The 250-acre flex/tech park is presently being developed by WEST*GROUP into low-rise research and development office buildings. Eight attractive single-story buildings offering more than 300,000 square feet of office/flexspace have been completed by WEST*GROUP with another five buildings currently under development. Each of the buildings has been named after Maryland counties, such as the Harford Buildings (winner of the 1989 National Association of Industrial and Office Parks Honor award) and the Allegany, Dorchester, Talbot, Garrett, Kent and Somerset buildings.

In addition, Gannett Corporation (*USA Today)* has constructed a major computer facility at WEST*FARM; Altek Corporation has established its headquarters there; and Kaiser Permanente has purchased twenty-eight acres where it is locating a regional headquarters, data center, storage facility, and new medical center.

Other WEST*GROUP projects include: Dulles Corporate Center, Dulles World Cargo Center, Spring-field Tower Shopping Center and The Shops at WEST*DALE, all of which are located in Northern Virginia. In addition, WEST*GROUP has recently entered into a joint partnership with Westinghouse, the largest private employer in Maryland, to develop a high-technology office and retail complex on thirty acres in Anne Arundel County.

As a local corporation with a stake in the progress of the Washington area, WEST*GROUP fosters its reputation for developing and constructing high-quality projects on time and on budget. That reputation is documented by long-term relationships with more than 150 leading corporations that have operations in WEST*GROUP properties. WEST*GROUP has gained the knowledge and track record for developing superior office, retail, and residential environments as well as for expert property management by a team of top professionals. Yet the company itself has remained relatively small in order to provide its clients first class personalized service and to ensure WEST*GROUP's tradition of excellence.

Shady Grove Adventist Hospital

Since it opened in 1979, Shady Grove Adventist Hospital has been committed to providing excellent, affordable health care to the growing communities and businesses along the I-270 corridor.

Area businesses were among the first to realize the need for a new hospital close to I-270's burgeoning corridor of commerce, and business and community leaders banded together to strengthen access to medical care for upper Montgomery County. As a result, in 1974 the first applications were filed for a new community hospital to be called Shady Grove Adventist Hospital, one that would become a recognized health care leader in the Washington area.

Construction of the new hospital, located on the campus of the Shady Grove Life Sciences Center, began in September 1977, and two years later the hospital was officially dedicated. The first patient arrived on December 16, 1979, and the new Shady Grove Adventist Hospital opened with forty-one beds, two operating rooms, and a surgical day care unit. In its first week of operation, 240 patients were served in the Emergency Department.

By 1980, generosity set the tone for the new hospital. Volunteers numbered 160, and $696,000 had been donated toward the first $1 million fund-raising goal. Throughout its short history, sizable donations from employees, volunteers, and businesses —along with sponsored 5-K runs, golf tournaments, horse shows, and other unique fund-raising events—have helped the hospital raise vital funds for advanced technology and expansion of services.

Even the gift shop plays an important role in fund-raising for the hospital. Named by the Hospital Auxiliary, the gift shop is called "The Crab Apple" for the seventeen crab apple trees saved from the bulldozer during construction. Now the trees are planted along the median strip at the hospital entrance. The gift shop has been very successful in raising money for such projects as expansion of the Same Day Surgery area, surgical lasers, and a room in the Emergency Department just for children.

Throughout the entire hospital, registered nurses give all the direct patient care. Skilled in assessing patient needs and certified to handle the complex equipment born out of today's technology, these registered nurses are able to consistently observe the progress of each patient. And the resulting continuity of care has paid off in two areas. First, the incidence of hospital-acquired infections is dramatically lower than the national average. And second, the patient length of stay is short. The average stay—which includes the long-term visits—is only 4.7 days.

By 1990, Shady Grove had grown to a 233-bed comprehensive, acute-care hospital with major outpatient diagnostic and treatment services. Technology available in the newly expanded Same Day Surgery and Laser Center and in the regular surgical suites gives Shady Grove one of the broadest range of surgical laser capabilities in the metropolitan area. Other outstanding medical services include the family-centered maternity program backed by an intensive care nursery with 24-hour neonatology coverage, an orthopedic surgery specialty program backed by excellent physical therapy, an oncology unit which includes humor therapy and family education in the treatment of cancer, and a Medical Special Care Unit which provides acute substance detoxification and a family support program. Shady Grove also provides critical care, hyperbaric oxygen therapy, a gastroenterology laboratory, and a sleep disorders center, as well as the general medical surgical units of the hospital.

In addition to advanced medical treatment, healing at Shady Grove involves education and prevention. Members of the hospital staff emphasize principles of healthful living— guiding patients, their families, and friends toward a healthier lifestyle.

In the ten years since it opened, Shady Grove has worked jointly with an innovative medical staff to create a health care institution with an excellent reputation in the community it serves. Many services have reached capacity and the hospital is currently doubling the size of its Emergency Department, expanding the support services such as radiology and the laboratory, and proposing the addition of new beds. As the communities and businesses along the I-270 corridor grow, Shady Grove Adventist Hospital is committed to build for your future.

The I-270 Partnership

More than 150,000 persons work in the I-270 Technology Corridor.

The I-270 Partnership looks at Interstate 270 and sees a bright future.

Once the heavy machinery is removed, the mountains of dirt leveled, and the detours dismantled, I-270 will emerge as a sleek expressway, ferrying people easily to homes, shops, and businesses.

When that happens, the I-270 Corridor will be recognized for what it is: Montgomery County's new center of commerce. Even now, in Maryland, it ranks second only to Baltimore in the number of people who work there.

When the I-270 Partnership was established in the mid-1980s, its leaders were determined to focus attention on the Corridor's advantages and assets. It was no small task. Traffic congestion was taking its toll on the thousands of commuters who used the highway daily. The widening and reconstruction only made matters worse. I-270 was maddening—and maligned—and it was difficult to look beyond the next traffic backup.

But the I-270 Partnership remains fixed on its goal.

It encourages careful development, promotes a high-technology flavor, and fosters cooperation among competitors, governments and businesses. State and county governments are spending more than $1 billion on roads and public facilities. More shopping is coming, new higher educational institutions are opening, and recreation and housing options are abundant.

The I-270 Partnership is proud to be part of Montgomery County's future. It expects twelve thousand new residents will locate in the corridor during the next decade. Major companies will line its expanse, from Bethesda to Frederick, giving it a broader corporate image.

Through its marketing efforts, the I-270 Partnership will continue to raise the visibility of the Corridor. Once the dust clears, the I-270 Corridor will assume a prominent profile in Montgomery County's future and in business circles everywhere.

Twelve thousand new residents are expected in the next decade.

Seldeen Development Corporation

Martin Seldeen, founder of Seldeen Development Corporation.

Martin Seldeen, President of Seldeen Development Corporation (SDC) was an unlikely player in the real estate development field when he first arrived in the Washington, D.C. area in 1946. With a B.S. degree in Pharmacy, earned ten years earlier, and ignoring a well-wisher who had commented "the only thing goin' on out there in Wheaton is fox hunting," he opened the Wheaton Pharmacy. Early on, his determination, hard work, and his penchant for success proved itself, as four years later five pharmacists were kept busy filling more prescriptions than any other drug store in the entire metropolitan area. Searching for an appropriate location, he discovered a piece of property which seemed to him, an ideal place for a shopping center—in which he would have his second drug store.

Partnership formation, zoning, and building, is a slow, laborious process. Having sold his drug store in order to raise capital, he soon found himself employed at his formerly owned Wheaton Pharmacy—"to put bread on the table"; but, contrary to his desires for a grand new drug store within a shopping center, approval was given for him to develop the property as a large apartment complex. This became the turning point in his career.

Seven years later, he quit pharmacy to pursue the fascinating world of Real Estate Development. In 1965, together with John J. Grady and others, he was a founder and investor in Grady Management, Inc., now one of the largest property management companies in the area. He is still a board member of that organization.

The I-270 Industrial Park, the first business park in Montgomery County specifically designed to attract High Tech companies was developed by The Seldeen Organization.

Although over the years Seldeen has developed many communities and projects, he takes the most pride in his planned 192-acre Traville research and development complex, the executive conference center, and the adjacent 710-unit residential community, Willows of Potomac, slated for the site on Route 28 and Shady Grove Road. Seldeen is acutely interesting in research and development in Montgomery County and is an avid supporter of educational facilities, in particular, Johns Hopkins University's Montgomery County Campus and the University of Maryland.

Seldeen is well known for his financial support for various charities and civic organizations. He has been appointed to many commissions and task forces concerned with issues facing county citizens. He has been in the forefront of efforts to provide the county's much needed affordable housing.

Seldeen is a member of the Montgomery County High Tech Council, Montgomery County Chamber of Commerce, Suburban Maryland Building Industry Association and Urban Land Institute. He is trustee of the Maryland College of Art and Design and has served on various boards of directors of public companies and banks.

Born in Boston, he and his wife of fifty-one years have lived in the Woodside area for thirty years; they have five children and four grandchildren. . . . At seventy-four years of age, he still has no intention of retiring.

Mulligan/Griffin and Associates, Inc.

The National Association of Securities Dealers' Operations Center at Decoverly, one of Mulligan/Griffin's award winning projects in Montgomery County.

Mulligan/Griffin and Associates, Inc., is a privately held real estate development, investment, and management firm with headquarters in Rockville, Maryland. The firm has substantial experience as the developer of quality commercial properties throughout the Washington, D.C. metropolitan area. Mulligan/Griffin is best known for the fast-track development of both signature corporate headquarters facilities and complex office and research and development facilities for large technology-driven corporate and institutional users. During its first ten years of operation, Mulligan/Griffin has developed approximately 2,500,000 square feet of commercial property.

Mulligan/Griffin is comprised of a small number of dedicated and highly skilled individuals with broad experience in the coordination of design, development, leasing, financing, property management and asset management. The firm conducts the design and development process through the assembly and coordination of a team of professionals with extensive collaborative experience in the development of large and complex office facilities. The development team for each project is carefully selected by Mulligan/Griffin to match each team member's experience and expertise with the needs of the project.

Although most office buildings are designed only to satisfy the office and light support requirements of the office market generally, Mulligan/Griffin's projects are carefully designed and developed to accommodate both the present and future needs of a rapidly changing workplace. Both the physical structure and the environment are designed to economically accommodate the tenant's work force and the often complex mechanical and electrical systems required for efficient performance and productivity.

During the 1980s, Mulligan/Griffin helped to shape the working environment for many major employers in Montgomery County. Headquarters facilities were developed by the firm for NUS Corporation, a division of Haliburton, and for Computer Data Systems, Inc., The Prudential Home Mortgage Company, and Contel ASC. In addition, major computer centers and operations facilities were completed for the National Association of Securities Dealers and GTE Government Systems. Mulligan/Griffin has also developed multi-tenant facilities which are occupied by other prestigious Montgomery County firms, including Boehringer Mannheim Pharmaceuticals Corporation, Marriott Corporation, and IBM.

Mulligan/Griffin's careful attention to architecture, building material selections, landscaping, signage, asset management, and property maintenance all combine to create quality business environments. The firm's commitment to tenant satisfaction continues long after the completion of a project. In recognition of its commitment to quality, Mulligan/Griffin has received numerous awards from the National Association of Industrial and Office Parks, the Maryland Building Industry Association, and a variety of other industry groups.

Mulligan/Griffin has a history of active support and participation in social and community-related endeavors. Significant support was given by the firm to the Wells/Robertson House, a facility offering temporary shelter to homeless men and women in the city of Gaithersburg. The firm consistently and actively supports the activities of the Children's Hospital National Medical Center. Mulligan/Griffin is perhaps most proud of its role in initiating and implementing the development of the Washington area's first single-room occupancy (SRO) residence for the homeless. Completed in 1989, this project was co-sponsored by So Others Might Eat (SOME), a non-profit interfaith organization which serves the homeless, the destitute, and the elderly in the Washington area. Mulligan/Griffin provided seed capital and other substantial resources for site selection and evaluation, design, financing, and the organization of the development and construction team.

Mulligan/Griffin hopes to build on its past successes and continue to serve Montgomery County and its businesses well into the next century.

Miles & Stockbridge

"The Jefferson," a Rockville landmark.

Although 1932 was not a particularly auspicious year for the U.S. economy, it was, in retrospect, a fine year for founding law firms. In that year the firm today known as Miles & Stockbridge was founded in Baltimore, Maryland, and began its practice at 10 Light Street, in the still-beautiful art deco monument now known as the Maryland National Bank Building, where the firm still maintains offices.

For the past fifty-eight years Miles & Stockbridge has prospered while serving Maryland's largest manufacturing and banking interests in their growth. At the same time, the firm has devoted a significant part of its efforts to smaller endeavors, community enterprises, state, county, and municipal bond issues and virtually every sort of undertaking that accompanies the continuing growth of the state of Maryland.

At the beginning of the last decade, the firm's leadership noted the growing need of its clients for representation around the state. To accommodate this need, the firm undertook a program of growth resulting in offices in the prime commercial areas of the state and neighboring jurisdictions. The enlargement of the firm has been achieved primarily through mergers with well-established, experienced practitioners in each location. At the beginning of this decade, the firm finds its practice more varied than ever and handled by approximately two hundred lawyers in eight offices located in Baltimore, Towson, Easton, Cambridge, Rockville, Frederick, Washington, D.C., and Fairfax County, Virginia.

The Rockville office has its roots deeply in the past of Montgomery County practice. On January 1, 1982, Miles & Stockbridge established its Rockville presence by merging with McKeever, Fitzpatrick & Canada, a group of lawyers active and well-known in the Montgomery County and Washington, D.C. area, particularly in the fields of real estate development, banking, commercial transactions, and litigation. In the years following the merger, this office has broadened and deepened the scope of its practice, drawing upon the resources found in the offices of the firm, while helping others in the firm in an interoffice practice unique to Miles & Stockbridge by reason of its metropolitan market.

The Rockville office reflects the diversity of the rest of the firm, encompassing many areas of practice, including real estate acquisition, its sale and development, as well as title and land-survey issues, zoning, community planning, homeowner and condominium organization, and home-building and commercial construction of all sorts. Banking, both from the corporate and transactional aspects, is an important part of the work of the Rockville office. Litigation of a wide variety, particularly matters of land use, construction, foreclosure, creditors' rights and, increasingly, environ-mental concerns engage this office. Corporate undertakings ranging from the incorporation of small, family-owned enterprises, through the efforts of entrepreneurs of high technology and biotechnology, to multimillion dollar international transactions are also accomplished.

The firm's Rockville office is fortunate to be quartered in The Jefferson, a gracious, Georgian, brick building at 22 West Jefferson Street, near the old Court House, in the Historic District. The Jefferson is as much envied for its commodious parking amenity as for its graceful line and comfortable offices. Before the firm occupied The Jefferson, it had long been the home of the much esteemed and widely known law firm of Betts, Clogg & Murdock, as well as to many other lawyers in the community for the past thirty years.

Like The Jefferson, Miles & Stockbridge has become a part of Rockville.

Miles & Stockbridge attorneys G. Vann Canada, Jr., Kevin O'Connell, and Tracy A. Borge.

Link Tactical Simulation Division

Aircraft Instructor Station.

The Link name has been synonymous with simulation for six decades, ever since Edwin A. Link created a new industry by inventing the first ground-based pilot training device.

In 1929, Mr. Link developed an airplane trainer to teach aviation skills to young pilots eager to learn how to fly. Link's small blue box became famous during World War II, when naval and army aviators took to the air after extensive training on the simulator.

The wartime success of the device encouraged the growth of competitors and by 1949, the Engineering and Research Corporation (ERCO) in Riverdale, Maryland, had developed an all-electric flight simulator. Widely recognized as the standard by the aviation and simulation communities, ERCO's advancement in electronic simulation for radar and sonar in anti-submarine warfare looked particularly appealing to the Link Company, which was later acquired by General Precision Equipment, Inc., in the early 1960s

In 1965, the two organizations merged their simulation activities under the Link name, and in 1967 new headquarters were established in the Montgomery Industrial Park in Silver Spring. About this same time, the Singer Company purchased General Precision, and split Link into two

divisions. The Link Flight Simulation Division dealt with movable instrumentation such as aircraft, spacecraft, and tanks while the Link Simulation Systems Division simulated naval tactical and operation systems, command and control systems for military land operations, maritime ships systems for industrial process and power generation systems.

In 1988, Link Simulation Systems was purchased from the Singer Company by the Canadian firm CAE Industries, Ltd. Today, Link Tactical Simulation's training expertise encompasses naval tactical and operation systems, command and control systems, and maintenance training. Tactics trainers realistically depict the entire naval tactical situation: the interactions of ships, submarines, and aircraft in a simulated gaming environment. Actual harbors and coastlines are depicted, as well as sensors, targets, weapons, communication, and countermeasures.

Link Tactical has produced numerous Submarine Combat System Team Trainers and Command and Control Trainers for U.S. and international navies. These highly sophisticated simulations of vehicle dynamics, ocean phenomena, and sensor performances help maintain and increase the combat effectiveness of crews for both attack and strategic submarines. Link command and control trainers for the U.S. Army provide interactive simulation of tactical operations, providing real-time practice in battle analysis and resource management decision-making.

Acoustic Student Operator Stations.

Schimel, Lieberman and Bender
Certified Public Accountants

Pictured left to right are Mel Lieberman, Barry Schimel (seated), and Bob Bender.

"Caring About Your Business Is Our Business" has been the motto of Schimel, Lieberman and Bender since the firm was started over twenty years ago.

As proof of their dedication to this philosophy, Schimel, Lieberman and Bender is committed to providing its clients with opportunities for dramatic financial and tax results.

"Schimel, Lieberman and Bender goes beyond the standard compliance work usually associated with accounting firms, therefore achieving more profitable financial results for its clients," says Barry R. Schimel, founder and managing director of the Rockville-based certified public accounting firm.

The type of respect that the firm has built resulted in Schimel, Lieberman and Bender being selected one of the top fifty small-to-medium sized "distinguished CPA firms in North America" by *CPA Digest.* Brian S. Peters, CPA, editorial director of the sponsoring group, said that he was

"impressed with the firm's innovative and unique credentials and its contribution to the accounting profession."

The firm's varied clientele includes service industries, retail companies and wholesale distribution businesses, construction and real estate firms, automobile dealers, automobile parts and accessory firms, trade associations, charitable and other non-profit organizations, and professionals.

Schimel, Lieberman and Bender provides profit maximization analysis, financial counseling, asset accumulation planning, business and executive tax planning, business valuations, business succession planning, real estate syndications, and mergers and acquisitions, as well as typical accounting, auditing, and tax services usually provided by CPA firms.

Sharing the important responsibilities of the firm with Barry R. Schimel, managing director, are two other shareholders, Melvyn L. Lieberman and Robert S. Bender.

Schimel, a recognized authority on real estate, accounting, insurance, tax, and financial planning has spoken and authored on these subjects nationwide.

Lieberman, who has written numerous national articles and appeared on many radio call-in shows, is director of the Schimel, Lieberman and Bender tax department, setting policies, procedures, and quality control.

Bender is the director of the firm's accounting and auditing department. Bender's devotion to community issues has involved the firm in major City of Rockville and Montgomery County committees. He has served on the City of Rockville's Economic Development Council, which had the responsibility of developing the first Rockville Business Forum. Additionally, he is vice president of the Rockville Chamber of Commerce and a member of the Montgomery County High Tech Council.

Sharing responsibilities with the community it serves has been a Schimel, Lieberman and Bender trademark over the years. For the last two years, the firm has provided support to the national "Call for Action" Consumer Network, providing answers to over seven hundred tax and business questions for residents in a three-state area. Schimel, Lieberman and Bender also serves on the District of Columbia Board of Trade, the Board of the Montgomery County Housing Opportunities Commission Resource Sharing Network, and as a member of the Montgomery County Chamber of Commerce. In fact, Schimel, Lieberman and Bender is represented in just about every chamber of commerce in Montgomery County and the Washington Metropolitan area.

Schimel, Lieberman & Bender, P.A.
Certified Public Accountants
Caring About Your Business is Our Business

KOH Systems, Inc.

Corporate headquarters in Rockville, Maryland.

KOH Systems, Inc., is a professional services firm that provides management and technical consulting support to government and industry. Founded in February 1980, the company was certified by the Small Business Administration in 1981 under the Section 8(a) program.

KOH Systems' first government contract was awarded in 1983 by the U.S. Department of Commerce to provide computer programming services to the U.S. Patent & Trademark Office. Since then, the company has maintained an outstanding record of corporate growth, increased capabilities, and financial success which have propelled the company's size from a staff of two working out of a garage in a Potomac neighborhood to more than 200 in sleek new headquarters in Rockville, and offices in Alexandria and Chesapeake, Virginia.

KOH Systems was founded for the purpose of providing the highest quality management and technical support services to federal, state, and local governments, and to private organizations. Offering expertise in all areas of management consulting and technical support, KOH Systems is grouped into five operating divisions: Management Services; Information Systems; Systems Technology; Litigation Support; and Engineering and Systems Support.

KOH Systems was originally founded by Kichul Koh, the husband of current president Yong-Soo Koh, who shortly thereafter was killed in a car accident. His widowed wife took over the company and built it from $300,000 in revenues to over $15 million. In recognition of her achievements, Mrs. Koh, now chairman, president, and sole owner of the company, received the Montgomery County 1989 Business Appreciation award and the *Washington Business Journal's* Professional Achievement award as one of the top twenty-five women business owners in the Greater Washington Metropolitan Area. KOH Systems has also for the past three years been named one of America's five hundred fastest growing private companies by *Inc.* magazine.

KOH's excellent performance record reflects the wealth of experience accumulated by members of its professional staff in many diversified areas of the professional services industry. This expertise has ensured effective solutions to clients' problems—solutions based on a thorough understanding of the requirements coupled with an intimate knowledge of the latest technological and organizational advances and the application of sound successful management practices.

Some of KOH's current clients include the Department of Commerce, Department of Energy, General Accounting Office, Department of Defense (Defense Logistics Agency, Navy) and Computer Data Systems, Inc.

Plans for the future are to strengthen KOH's competitive position to increase substantially its business with the private sector prior to the expiration of their 8(a) certification in 1992. The company will also work to expand their high tech product lines and to expand geographically outside of the Washington area, including overseas, and will strive to increase revenues to $20 million in the next three years.

Mrs. Yong-Soo Koh, president, (center) and corporate management staff.

273

Integrated Microcomputer Systems, Inc.

John T.C. Yeh, founder and president.

Integrated Microcomputer Systems, Inc., (IMS) is a computer software engineering and systems integration company providing corporate and government clients with optimum, long lasting, and total systems solutions.

IMS emphasizes sophisticated technologies in Local Area Network and Telecommunications, Workstation and Graphics, Open System Integration and Standards, Computer-Aided Software Engineering, Data Base and Fourth Generation Languages, Optical Technologies, Artificial Intelligence and Expert Systems, and Computer and Communications Security. IMS constantly assimilates new techniques and products in these areas.

IMS was founded by John T.C. Yeh, who was born deaf in Taiwan. After graduating from Gallaudet University and later earning a Masters degree in computer science from the University of Maryland, Yeh founded IMS with the aid of the Small Business Administration and his brothers. IMS was accepted in the SBA's 8(a) minority Business Program.

The path to IMS' present stability has been a staircase of success. In-

itially employing just three people, IMS got its start in a Rockville warehouse on January 15, 1979. Today, IMS employs more than 485 full-time computer professionals. Eight percent of the staff is disabled. With growth over the last ten years averaging an annual increase of more than 35 percent, the company looks forward to a strong future.

Early in IMS' history, the company began earning recognition for business growth and providing opportunity for minority and disabled employees and high quality services to customers. Displaying leadership in office automation, data base, and communications systems design and development, IMS' excellent performance won many awards that set the company apart from other 8(a) companies—among them the 1989 Large Employer of the Year award, given by the state of Maryland Governor's Committee on Employment of the Handicapped; the Peat Marwick KPMG High Tech Entrepreneur of the Year award; MCI's 1988 Supplier of the Year award; and the Arthur Young regional Entrepreneur of the Year award.

In 1990, the company won the

President's Commission on Employment of People with Disabilities Private Sector Employer of the Year award. These credentials for high quality performance in the demanding defense sector, which drives high tech innovation, have assured commercial customers that IMS is a reliable, low risk contracting partner.

IMS recently launched an Alliance program aimed at encouraging large and small companies to team together. The Alliance is an opportunity for IMS to share its knowledge gained during its growth, while developing beneficial business relationships for all concerned. As the company has grown, IMS has won a reputation in the county and the mid-Atlantic region for steady, stable growth. IMS' contributions to the local economy and growth of the computer services industry have been significant.

Years of preparation have positioned the company with a good reputation for sound corporate capabilities. With a professional staff that is qualified and dedicated, IMS has graduated from its 8(a) status, and has won contracts in open competitions. In the future, IMS will aggressively pursue

The senior management of IMS includes, left to right, Joseph Yeh, Dr. Jeffry Yeh, James Yeh, John Yeh, President, Dr. Howell Mei, William Rettig, and Vincent Lam.

IMS' 44,000 square foot headquarters facility in Rockville, is the nerve center of IMS national and international operations.

IMS invests in the latest computer technology to provide clients with centralized state-of-the-art service.

IMS has received many awards for technical excellence and business achievement from industry, government, and civic leaders.

marketing opportunities in the commercial sector.

IMS maintains its corporate headquarters in Rockville, Maryland, with branch offices in Dahlgren and Arlington, Virginia; Dayton, Ohio; Panama City, Florida; and Ridgecrest, California. IMS also owns an overseas subsidiary in Taipei, Taiwan, and maintains on site personnel at client locations in New York and throughout the Washington D.C. metropolitan area.

IMS is a success oriented company. Emphasizing quality, commitment, caring, and high productivity, IMS' goals are to engage employees in innovation and entrepreneurship and maintain the company as a recognized leader in the high tech information engineering industry.

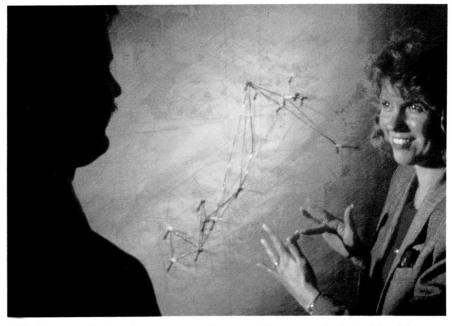

IMS clients benefit from the unique commitment and interpersonal relationship of the company workforce. Here, two highly-qualified hearing impaired IMS employees discuss a Local Area Network designed and implemented by IMS for a client.

Biomedical Research Institute

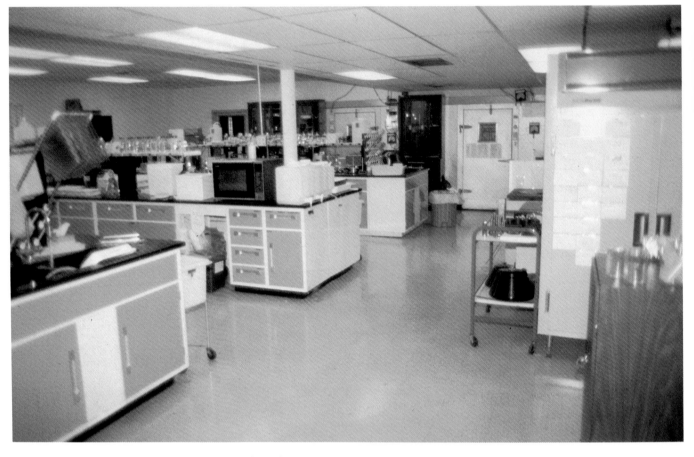

A typical laboratory setting at Biomedical Research Institute.

The American Foundation for Biological Research (AFBR), Biomedical Research Institute's (BRI), parent organization, was founded in 1948 in Illinois by J. Rockefeller Prentice. The original purpose of AFBR was to pursue Prentice's interest in Cryobiology (low temperature biology).

The first director of AFBR was B.J. Luyet, a Jesuit priest. Early work at AFBR led to techniques for freezing bull spermatozoa and using it in artificial insemination. The methods developed are still in use throughout the world in the dairy and beef industries.

BRI, a not-for-profit organization, was started in 1968, in its present location. BRinc, a wholly-owned for profit subsidiary of BRI, was incorporated in 1981. BRI currently occupies two buildings in Rockville and employs over sixty people. The institute conducts basic research and provides services to the scientific and business communities.

Research at BRI is primarily concerned with the development of vaccines for malaria and schistosomiasis, parasitic diseases that are the major health problems in many parts of the world.

BRI operates a large low-temperature repository, providing storage for biological, medical, and industrial materials under a wide range of temperatures and conditions. Repository clients include government agencies, universities, research institutes, and commercial organizations.

BRI has a long history of close cooperation with the U.S. Navy, the U.S. Army, the National Institutes of Health (NIH), the Red Cross, the U.S. Agency for International Development (USAID), and universities throughout the United States and abroad. The institute has also cooperated in the training of predoctoral and post-doctoral students from the United States and from several foreign

countries. Additionally, a fund has been established to finance travel by scholars to further their career development.

BRinc, the for-profit subsidiary, is a diversified operation with a strong product orientation. One of BRinc's current activities, Bovine Unlimited, offers a complete development package for the institution and operation of dairy and beef production facilities. The package is especially well suited to use in areas where there is no strong tradition of cattle production.

Biofluids, Inc.®

The National Institutes of Health, Biofluids leading customer.

Biofluids, Inc. is the supermarket that supplies biotechnology, pharmaceutical, and research facilities the products needed for their research and development both domestic and abroad.

Founded in December 1974 by former cancer researcher, Dr. Robert R. Rafajko, Biofluids, Inc. is located at 1146 Taft Street in Rockville. It is the oldest, continuous, privately-owned company of its field.

Dr. Rafajko was Vice-President of Research and Development for North American Biologicals located at the present location, but when a decision was made to close down the Rockville facility, he stayed behind to form his own company. Starting with just two employees and 2,000 square feet of space, and sales of less than $100,000

annually, the company now employs fourteen people and occupies 18,000 square feet and sales in excess of two million dollars.

Biofluids, Inc. started out with six products for use in cell research. Currently, Biofluids, Inc. has over 150 products used worldwide in the areas of cancer, immunology, neurology, genetics, and metabolic research. The company manufactures and quality controls solutions of vitamins, amino acids, minerals, complete growth media, buffers, antibiotics, reagents, and animal sera for *in vitro* cell research. It is one of the largest suppliers of sterile fetal calf serum, a component of almost all complete media used to propagate cells. Biofluids, Inc. supplies its products worldwide to such companies as Merrill Dow in France and

Nestle Services in Switzerland and such prestigious research institutions as the Children's Medical Research Foundation and the Walter and Eliza Hall Research Institute of Australia.

Biofluids, Inc. presently has a patent pending which allows growth of human lymphocytes without the addition of animal sera, leading the way to a serum-free production of lymphokines and other cellular products which will markedly reduce current production costs. In addition to the patent pending, Biofluids, Inc. now exclusively produces products being used by NIH researchers in lung cancer and bone cancer research and cystic fibrosis.

In the future, Biofluids, Inc. plans to remain on the cutting edge of developing new chemically defined media for growing all types of human, animal, and plant cells. Plans are to expand its market, both domestic and foreign. Finally, entrance into the equine veterinary field with new therapeutic and diagnostic products is in the planning stage.

A typical day unloading research materials at the NIH Clinical Center.

Bibliography

Boyd, T. H. S., *The History of Montgomery County, Maryland.* Clarksburg, 1879. Reprint Baltimore, Regional Publishing Company, 1972.

Brooks, D., and C. Federline, *A Worthy Innovation: A History of the Montgomery County Police.* Rockville, Maryland: Montgomery County Government, 1988.

Clarke, Nina H. and Lillian B. Brown, *History of the Black Public Schools of Montgomery County, Maryland 1872-1961*; New York: Vantage Press, 1978.

"Centennial Celebration of the Erection of Montgomery County, Maryland into a Separate Municipality Held at Rockville September 6, 1876." Baltimore: C. C. Saffell, 1877.

Clark, Wayne E., "The Origins of the Piscataway and Related Indian Cultures"; *Maryland Historical Magazine,* Spring, 1980; Vol. 75; No. 1. The Maryland Historical Society, Baltimore.

"Commission on the Future of Montgomery County," Rockville, Maryland; February, 1988.

Farquhar, Roger B. *Historic Montgomery County, Maryland, Old Homes and History.* Silver Spring, Maryland, 1952.

Gold Veins Near Great Falls, Maryland, Geological Survey Bulletin 1286. Governmental Printing Office, 1969.

Gutheim, Frederick, *The Potomac.* New York: Hold, Rinehart and Winston, 1974.

Hahn, Thomas F. *Chesapeake and Ohio Canal Old Picture Album.* Shepherdstown, West Virginia: The American Canal and Transportation Center, 1976.

Harper's New Monthly Magazine, September and October, 1866, Library of Congress.

Henson, Josiah. *The Life of Josiah Henson, Formerly a Slave, Now an Inhabitant of Canada, as Narrated by Himself.* Boston: A. D. Phelps, 1849.

Jewell, E. Guy, *From One Room to Open Space,* Rockville, Maryland: Montgomery County Public Schools, 1976.

Kelley, Robert, *The Shaping of the American Past to 1877.* Englewood Cliffs, N.J.: Prentice-Hall, Inc., 1975.

MacMaster, Richard K. and Ray Eldon Hiebert, *A Grateful Remembrance.* Rockville, Maryland: Montgomery County Government, 1976.

Maryland-National Capital Park and Planning Commission, Silver Spring, Maryland; printed materials concerning redevelopment in Silver Spring and Bethesda.

The Montgomery County Office of Economic Development, Rockville, Maryland; various publications.

Bazy Tankersley drives a Montgomery County-bred horse, Al-Marah Canadian Beau. Courtesy of Anne Tankersley Sturm

"Living in Montgomery County, Maryland. Picture Portfolio." Publication of Judd and Detweiler.

MacCord, Howard A.; Schmitt, Karl; Slattery, Richard G., "The Shepard Site Study." Baltimore: Archeological Society of Maryland, Maryland Academy of Sciences, July 1957.

McDaniel, George W. "Black Historical Resources in Upper Western Montgomery County, Maryland." Sugarloaf Regional Trails, July, 1979.

"Madonna of the Trails," *Washington Post,* 1982.

"Montgomery County Story." Montgomery County Historical Society quarterly publication, Rockville.

Office of Economic Development, Rockville. Numerous publications relating to the county.

Scharf, J. Thomas, *History of Western Maryland.* Philadelphia: 1882.

Sentinel. Rockville, 1855 to present.

Smith, Arthur Robert and J. V. Giles, *American Rape: A True Account of the Giles-Johnson Case.* New Republic, 1975.

Smith, Elbert B., *Francis Preston Blair.* New York: Macmilland Publishing Company, Inc. 1980.

Steers, Edward Jr., "The Escape and Capture of George A. Atzerodt." Unpublished manuscript.

The Suburban Record; Record Publishing Company, Silver Spring, Maryland.

Theodore Roosevelt's Letters to His Children. New York: Charles Scribner's Sons, 1919.

The Overtimes, Rockville: Montgomery County Government, April 1981.

The Washington Post, Washington D.C.

Index

Profiles in Leadership

About The Author

Margaret Coleman was born in Montana, grew up in Washington State, and moved east in 1969. She graduated from Hood College in Frederick with a degree in history, worked for Sugarloaf Regional Trails, wrote regular columns for county newspapers, and numerous magazine articles. She founded the Boyds/Clarksburg/Germantown Historical Society in 1979. A member and officer of the Montgomery County Committee of the Maryland Historical Trust for many years, she was elected president after the group reformed under the name Montgomery Preservation, Inc. She also founded and edited the "Montgomery County Preservationist" newsletter. When she's not writing, Margaret Coleman can usually be found tending her sheep, spinning their wool, or planting flowers in her very old garden.